# Nuclear Weapons and the American Churches

*"Not to promote war, but to preserve peace"*

PREPARED UNDER THE AUSPICES OF THE
STRATEGIC STUDIES INSTITUTE
U.S. ARMY WAR COLLEGE
CARLISLE BARRACKS, PENNSYLVANIA

# Nuclear Weapons and the American Churches
## *Ethical Positions on Modern Warfare*

Donald L. Davidson
CHAPLAIN (MAJOR), UNITED STATES ARMY

Westview Press
BOULDER, COLORADO

Copyright © 1983 by Westview Press, Inc.

Published in 1983 in the United States of America by
  Westview Press, Inc.
  5500 Central Avenue
  Boulder, Colorado 80301
  Frederick A. Praeger, President and Publisher

Library of Congress Catalog Card Number: 83-50552

ISBN 0-86531-706-2

Printed and bound in the United States of America

10   9   8   7   6   5   4   3   2

# Contents

# Acknowledgments

The preparation of this study has extended over three brief tours of duty at Harvard University, the Army Chaplain School, and the Army War College. Formal research for the project commenced in December 1981 when Kermit D. Johnson, then Chief of Chaplains, U.S. Army, requested that I prepare an indepth research paper objectively describing the just-war tradition and the current positions of American religious denominations on nuclear weapons and policies. When Patrick J. Hessian succeeded Chaplain Johnson as the Chief of Chaplains in 1982, he urged me to complete the study. Neither Chaplain Johnson nor Chaplain Hessian has sought to influence my opinion or the specific conclusions I have reached. They have, however, provided the encouragement and support essential for the completion of the document.

Originally I intended to describe the positions on nuclear weapons held by each major religious body in the United States. To assist in the research and to allow the denominations to speak for themselves, I sent a letter requesting information from sixty-six different groups (attached as Appendix A). This letter was addressed to all denominations with membership of at least 100,000, plus a few smaller groups like the historic peace churches. Included on the mailing list were Catholic, Protestant, Orthodox, Jewish, Morman, Christian Scientist, and other bodies less traditional in American culture. I am grateful to each of the forty-one denominations who responded to my request. The aggregate membership of the denominations discussed in the text is well over one-hundred million.

I have not, however, addressed the positions of all groups. None of the larger Eastern Orthodox churches or black denominations replied to my request for information. My investigation suggests that these groups have not commented extensively (if at all) on the moral issues of nuclear weapons. Jewish positions are covered only briefly because these bodies have published few official statements. Space and time limitations have also prevented discussion of some of the smaller groups who did send information. Though I attempted to be fair, I have occasionally criticized points in the positions I have discussed. This fact should not obscure my appreciation for the assistance given to this research and to the nation as we collectively reflect on the moral issues of war in the nuclear age.

Several persons have critically examined my work.
The text has been improved because of the observations of
Arthur J. Dyck, James T. Johnson, Ralph B. Potter, Paul
Ramsey, Michael Walzer, and Brother David Austin.  Others
who have contributed through advise and argument include
colleagues Reynold B. Connett, Richard Tupy, Donald E.
Lunday, Otto P. Chaney, John F. Scott, Albert P. Holmberg,
Robert G. Chaudrue, and Henry G. Gole.  As I have not
always accepted their criticism, however, I alone am
responsible for the deficiencies of the text.  I am
especially thankful to Connie Warner who prevailed over
many changes in preparing this manuscript.

Most of all I am indebted to my lovely wife, Joyce,
and my dear children, Karisa, Alatha and Creighton.  With
patience and love they have endured my absences and
intemperate moods during these months of research and
writing.

Donald L. Davidson
17 May 1983

# Introduction

Since the late 1970s a new debate on nuclear weapons
has emerged in the democracies on both sides of the
Atlantic.  Signs of a significant level of concern about
these weapons also exist in the Eastern bloc and Third
World nations.  The controversy challenges international
alignments, military strategy, economic policies, and
traditional moral views on war.  Leaders in the
anti-nuclear movement include politicians, scientists,
physicians, academicians, and religious officials.  In
the United States an elaborate network consisting of new
organizations and revived Vietnam War protest groups has
developed.  Perhaps the most visible element of the new
movement is the national freeze campaign.

There is little question, however, that concern
ranges far beyond the formal protest organizations; the
new controversy has become "politicized," or
"democratized."  Earlier disputes over nuclear policies
were confined largely to policymakers, "think tank"
strategists, and academic ethicists.  Currently, by
contrast, policy questions are being raised by broad
segments of the population.  The present debate has
prompted a large percentage of Americans, including
soldiers, to rethink their views on the development,
deployment, and use of nuclear weapons.  Fundamental
questions are being asked about the morality and
feasibility of war in the nuclear age.  The central issue
is how to protect and preserve values worth defending
while preventing nuclear war.

Of the various organizational proponents in the
contemporary nuclear debate, religious denominations have
by far the largest number of constituents.  Well over a
hundred million Americans are members of the Roman
Catholic Church and the major Protestant churches.
Therefore, positions advocated by ethicists,
denominational leaders, and policymaking bodies of the
prominent religious groups are significant.  Potentially,
at least, the collective positions of the churches
represent the most powerful influence on moral opinion in
the United States.  And, clearly, the churches view war
and nuclear weapons as moral issues.

Religious denominations in America and the West have
held diverse views on the morality of war.  The position
supported by the majority, however, has been that of the
just-war tradition.  Around 400 A.D. the African bishop

Augustine asked: Is it ever right for a Christian to participate in war? The three types of response to this question have been identified by Roland Bainton as pacifism, the holy war or crusader attitude, and the just-war position.[1] During the first three centuries after Jesus, the majority of Christians were pacifists, that is, they refused to participate in war. Pacifists have traditionally claimed that Jesus approved of only "passive" or nonviolent resistance to aggression. They frequently cite Jesus' teaching in the Sermon on the Mount where he affirmed: "Blessed are the peacemakers, for they will be called sons of God." "Love your enemies and pray for those who persecute you. . . ." "Do not resist an evil person. If someone strikes you on the right check, turn to him the other also."[2] Also remembered is Jesus' command at his arrest for Peter to put away his sword rather than forcefully resist (John 18:11).

The majority of pacifists do not deny that aggression and violence should be resisted. The means they approve, however, are nonviolent. The pacifist tradition is continued today in the historic peace churches--Quakers, Mennonites, Brethren and others. Since World War II an increasing number of Catholics and Protestants have also adopted the pacifist position.

The crusader or holy war position emerged following the medieval alliance between the church and state. The most striking examples of this ideological warfare are the Crusades (11th-13th centuries) and the Reformation Era religious wars (16th-17th centuries).[3] Holy wars have been extremely violent because the military engagement is seen as a fight to the death between forces of good and evil. The crusader is providing a religious service in protecting God's kingdom and stamping out the corruption of infidelity. Humanitarian considerations normally practiced in combat tend to be abrogated because the adversary is seen to be a wicked foe of righteousness. The enemy is outside the pale of God and must be defeated, no matter what the costs. Contemporary expressions of this position hold that moral and political limits and self-imposed restraints on force are unrealistic when confronted by the evils of aggression.

Augustine's answer to the question he posed in the fifth century has become known as the just-war position. He concluded that Christians should share in the responsibility of resisting aggression and maintaining social order, but with the recognition that all human life is sacred. In its historical development the just-war tradition rejected absolute pacifism as ineffectual against ruthless aggression. It justified some use of force for the protection of the innocent, but renounced unlimited force and the crusader goals of

punishing infidels and extending the[4]hegemony of
religious doctrine by violent means.

Through the contributions of philosophers,
theologians, lawyers, statesmen, and soldiers, a set of
criteria has emerged for evaluating whether or not
violent force is justified and to what extent it should
be applied. The _jus ad bellum_ (justice _of_ war) criteria
are used for judging when it is right to resort to war.
These permit legitimate national authorities to declare
war as a last resort if the nation's causes and
intentions are just and there is a reasonable possibility
of victory, without causing more harm than good. Because
of the devastation of war, war must always be justified.
Even then the just-war tradition only approves of war as
a lesser evil than aggression. The _jus in bello_ (justice
_in_ war) criteria are employed to moderate the
destructiveness of war by limiting its means and
protecting noncombatants.

Since the fifth century the just-war position has
been the dominant Western moral view on war.[5] It has
been the position advocated by the Roman Catholic Church
and, following the Reformation, most Protestant
denominations. Interest in this position waned in the
eighteenth and nineteenth centuries. The development of
modern weapons and the employment of large conscript
armies, however, have led in the twentieth century to
greater efforts to limit the legitimate causes and means
of war. This movement has been manifested in the
international law conventions and, among[6]Christians, a
renewed emphasis on just-war principles.

In the last few years, however, the nuclear weapons
debate has had the opposite effect. The continuing
buildup of nuclear arsenals and the recent talk of
fighting a limited nuclear war have prompted many to
question the capacity of the just-war tradition to
prevent nuclear war. James R. Crumley, Jr., for example,
affirms: "Lutherans are not pacifists, . . . But isn't
it true that the nuclear age has altered the way we are
to apply our theological and ethical presuppositions?"[7]
Some are more definite in their opinions: "A nuclear war
is so unimaginably destructive . . . as to make a
rationale of 'just war' a devilish joke."[8] As this
comment illustrates, in rejecting the use of nuclear
weapons some also eschew just-war theory on the
assumption that it justifies the use of these weapons.

Those who renounce nuclear weapons as unjust means
have created a fourth type of Christian response to
war--"nuclear pacifism."[9] Some in this group have
concluded that all war in the modern age is illicit
because of the possibility (at least among nuclear
powers) even in a conventional war of escalation to
nuclear weapons. This version is a new form of pacifism.
Others may be described as "just-war nuclear pacifists."

On the basis of just-war criteria, especially
discrimination (noncombatant immunity), due proportion,
and reasonable hope of success, these have rejected any
war using nuclear weapons. Wars without nuclear weapons
may still be justified if they meet the criteria of just
war. This is not a new position in principle. In the
past others have proscribed warfare that employs means
considered unjust, such as chemical and biological
weapons and indiscriminate bombardment.

Within the religious arena current discussions on
the morality of war in the nuclear age manifest all four
of the positions described above: pacifism, nuclear
pacifism, just war, and the crusader attitude. Among the
major denominations, however, the crusader position has
all but disappeared. In fact, it would be more accurate
to say that a crusade mentality now exists in opposition
to war. In documenting denominational positions,
research confronts a major problem: To what extent are
denominational pronouncements supported by members? I
know of no study that has resolved this question.

Perhaps the opinion poll conducted by The Christian
Science Monitor in the summer of 1982 is indicative of
the view from the pew concerning nuclear weapons. In
analyzing the results of this poll, the Monitor affirms
that to a majority of respondents: "Nuclear weapons are
morally repugnant--but the lesser of evils at this point,
so long as they are used only in non-use, to deter rather
than to fight."[10] The survey shows that 51 percent
approve of possessing nuclear weapons and threatening
their use, while 43 percent find such actions morally
unacceptable. Only 25 percent find the actual use of
nuclear weapons in a war morally acceptable; 68 percent
rejected this option. By a margin of 67 to 28 percent
the respondents rejected a threat of nuclear retaliation
in response to a non-nuclear attack on Western Europe.
Concerning "a unilateral American renunciation of nuclear
weapons," 58 percent said "no," while 36 percent said
"yes." Of those surveyed, 74 percent consider the arms
race immoral and 88 percent think it dangerous. A
majority sees the United States and the Soviet Union as
roughly equal in nuclear weapons and advocate a goal of
maintaining parity (60 percent). Concerning "overall
arms-control policy for the U.S.," 22 percent favored the
Kennedy-Hatfield nuclear freeze proposal; 7 percent
favored the Jackson-Warner freeze-after-building
proposal; and 46 percent supported George F. Kennan's
recommendation for "an across-the-board reduction of both
American and Soviet nuclear arsenals by 50 percent."

This study focuses on many of the questions
addressed in the Monitor poll. The moral positions
described, however, are those of ethicists and
denominational leaders. Also, extensive attention has
been given to the positions reflected in official

pronouncements of the major religious bodies. Because the issues of war and nuclear weapons are largely debated within the intellectual framework of the just-war tradition, the first two chapters describe the development and moral principles of this tradition. Chapter 3 considers the positions on nuclear issues held by contemporary just-war ethicists. The remaining chapters document the positions reflected in the pronouncements of religious leaders and the official statements of the larger denominations. Much attention has been given to the recent pastoral letter of the fifty million member Roman Catholic Church in America. It should also be recognized that churches representing an equal number of Protestants have issued pronouncements on these issues.

My approach to the issues of war and nuclear weapons is from the just-war perspective. Undoubtedly this has influenced my selection and interpretation of data. My objective in the following chapters, however, is to present an accurate description of the various positions. My brief evaluations are largely confined to the conclusion sections and the final chapter.

## NOTES

1. Roland H. Bainton, Christian Attitudes Toward War and Peace: A Historical Survey and Critical Re-evaluation (Nashville: Abingdon Press, 1960), p. 148.

2. These New Testament quotations are from "Matthew," Chapter 5 (New International Version).

3. The Thirty Years War, which ended in 1648, devastated much of Europe. The contemporary Iranian Revolution and Iran's war with Iraq are "holy wars" in Iran's perspective.

4. See William V. O'Brien, The Conduct of Just and Limited War (New York: Praeger, 1981), p. 22.

5. "Two Issues in Contemporary Defense: A Just War Critique," Military Chaplains' Review, DA Pamphlet 165-135, Fall, 1982; published by the U.S. Army Chaplain Board, Fort Monmouth, New Jersey, 07703. For more indepth discussion see Johnson's Just War Tradition and the Restraint of War: A Moral and Historical Inquiry (Princeton, New Jersey: Princeton University Press, 1981); and "What Guidance can Just War Tradition Provide for Contemporary Moral Thought About War?" New Catholic World 226 (March-April 1982): 81-84.

6.  These concerns led to the Kellogg-Briand Pact (1928), which proscribed wars of aggression, and the League of Nations, which was intended to serve as an arbiter in international conflicts. These steps proved insufficient, however, and in the depression torn Thirties, militarism again rampaged in the world. During World War II many jurists recognized that international law had not developed an adequate basis for punishing even the most heinous aggression. In just-war terminology, there was inadequate "jus ad bellum" provisions in international law. Again, following this war strong attempts were made to "outlaw" aggressive war in the United Nations Charter and the Charter of the Nuremberg Tribunal, both signed in 1945. For discussion on the laws of war, see Telford Taylor, <u>Nuremberg and Vietnam: An American Tragedy</u> (Chicago: Quadrangle Books, 1970). The epic work on international law, is L. Oppenheim, <u>International Law: A Treatise</u> (London: Longmans, Green and Co., 8th ed., 1955). James Johnson discusses the development of just-war doctrine in this period in "Just War Theory: What's the Use?", <u>Worldview</u> 19 (July-August 1976). Arthur J. Dyck, "Ethical Bases of the Military Profession," <u>Parameters</u> 10 (March 1980):44, alludes to the connection between the laws of war and just-war principles.

7.  Pastoral Letter addressed to members of the Lutheran Church in America, 9 November 1981.

8.  "What Monitor Readers Think About Nuclear Weapons," <u>The Christian Science Monitor</u>, 15 December 1982, p. 12.

9.  Thomas A. Shannon, <u>War or Peace? The Search for New Answers</u>, (Maryknoll, New York: Orbis Books, 1980), p. x.

10.  Elizabeth Pond, "Speaking Out on Nuclear Issues," <u>The Christian Science Monitor</u>, 15 December 1982, p. 1. This interpretative analysis accompanies the results of the readers poll which was also published in this edition of the <u>Monitor</u>.

# [ 1 ]
# The Development of the Just-War Tradition

## INTRODUCTION

The just-war tradition is an amalgamation of Western thought on war. Theologians, philosophers, statesmen, and soldiers have contributed to this tradition, which continues today in the teaching of many churches and in the codes of international law. In this chapter I highlight the development of this tradition by surveying the concepts of some of its more significant architects, including Cicero, Augustine, Aquinas, Bonet, Victoria, Suarez, Grotius, and Locke. When theologians look for the roots of Christian moral views on war, they most frequently turn to the works of Augustine. In many ways he could be considered the "father" of the Christian theory of just war. When Augustine sought to provide a rationale for Christian participation in war, however, he referred to an older tradition. So let us begin where he did, with the Roman tradition, as represented by the Stoic philosopher Cicero.[1]

## THE TRADITION BUILDERS

### Cicero (106-43 B.C.)

In the two centuries before Christ, Rome sought its "manifest destiny" by aggressively extending its control throughout the ancient world. Once the empire was essentially established, the role of the Army was to protect the <u>Pax Romana</u>, by defending the borders and maintaining internal security. Toward the end of this expansion period Cicero and others developed a legal concept of just war that was applied in conflict among peoples of the empire, but seldom in war with "pirates" or "barbarians."[2] A just war for Cicero was one waged "to recover lost goods, whether property or rights." His was a legal view that required prior guilt of an enemy. A primary concern of Cicero was to identify just causes for war, which he believed included punishment of an

1

enemy for its misdeeds and repulsion of an enemy attack
against one's own or an ally's territory or citizenry.[3]
Without a just cause, war was an act of piracy. Cicero's
principles for a just war can be summarized as
follows:[4]

> (1) Only the state (emperor) has the
> authority to initiate war (i.e., revolution
> is prohibited).
> (2) A formal declaration of hostilities
> followed by a thirty-day wait for response
> is required.
> (3) Oaths and commitments made in good faith
> to "legal" opponents should be honored.
> (4) Distinction should be made between the
> guilty and the innocent among the enemy.[5]
> (5) Once victory is assured, mercy should be
> shown to enemies, unless they have acted
> "cruelly" and "barbarously."
> (6) The general conduct of war should be
> guided by the principle of humanitas (or
> human nature, which for Cicero meant
> reasoned benevolence, magnanimity, and
> mercy).

These last two principles reflect Cicero's desire
for a "generous peace" following hostilities to
facilitate future harmony within the empire. He believed
that the firmest foundation for the empire could be
provided by cultivating support of Rome and a sense of
public duty among the peoples of the empire.[6]

## Augustine (354-430 A.D.)

A great deal of history occurred between the two
Romans, Cicero and Augustine. Cicero lived toward the
end of Rome's period of expansion, at the height of the
empire, whereas Augustine lived at its climax. In the
intervening period the early church was essentially
pacifistic. Christians were a persecuted minority who
generally refrained from participating in government
service, teaching in the university, practicing the craft
of woodworking, joining the Army, or doing anything which
might require emperor worship or idolatrous
activities.[7]

By Augustine's time, however, things were
substantially different. The emperor called himself a
"Christian" and the empire was considered a Christian
state. Idolatry was no longer required of government
servants. The end of Pax Romana was rapidly approaching
and the walls of the empire were crumbling. Indeed,
Augustine's home in Hippo, North Africa, was on the verge
of invasion by Vandals.

Within this context Augustine developed his Christian theory of just war, the first "fully elaborated theoretical defense of Christian participation in conflict."[8] Since by then Christians comprised a substantial proportion of the population, he believed that they should seek to increase justice by accepting positions of responsibility in administering and defending the empire. The basic question for Augustine was: How can Christians live responsibly in the world? His answer, though it contained many of the principles espoused by Cicero, was distinctively Christian in emphasis. Whereas Cicero stressed the Stoic virtues of wisdom, courage, and honor, Augustine emphasized Christian love and justice. He believed that ultimate happiness and peace came only from the Creator and could be fully attained only in eternal life. He also believed that each citizen of this world should responsibly seek harmony and peace in human society.[9] Caritas, or love, was Augustine's motivating principle for Christian participation in war. He rejected the use of violence by Christians for personal self-defense, for "public protection," or defense of one's neighbor, however, he affirmed that "no Christian ought to fail to resist evil by effective means which the state alone makes available to him."[10] Love of neighbor permits the use of force for defensive purposes, but love of enemy requires the limitation of force to only that necessary to protect the neighbor. All use of violence entails misery and even justifiable violence should be exercised with a "mournful" spirit. Roland Bainton provides the following mosaic of Augustine's thought on love and war:

> Love does not preclude a benevolent severity, nor that correction which compassion itself dictates. No one indeed is fit to inflict punishment save the one who has first overcome hate in his heart. The love of enemies admits of no dispensation, but love does not exclude wars of mercy waged by the good.[11]

Augustine was primarily concerned with the "jus ad bellum" question of the rightness of resorting to war. In his concept of justice, "it is the wrong-doing of the opposing party which compels the wise men to wage just war."[12] War was justified according to his theory, if the following criteria could be met:

(1) Just intentions: the restoration of peace.
(2) Just cause, to vindicate justice: those wars may be defined as just which avenge injuries, e.g., attacks on the state,

failure to make amends, and refusal to grant
passage.
(3) Just disposition: Christian love, to
protect victims of aggression.
(4) Just auspices: war waged only under
the authority of the ruler.
(5) Just conduct of war: the classical rules
of honoring oaths; no wanton destruction
or violence; no profanation of temples; no
looting or massacre; no vengeance,
reprisals or atrocities (though ambush
was permitted).

Like Cicero, Augustine was concerned to explicate
justifiable causes for war. As his criteria reflect,
however, his principal focus was on attitudes and
motives. Though war was at times a tragic necessity, the
destruction and brutality resulting from love of violence
and hatred of the enemy were not. War could be waged to
avenge injuries, but the final goal of conflict was to
establish a just peace. Through his emphasis on
attitudes and intentions, Augustine transformed Cicero's
formal, legal doctrine into a moral theory on war.[13]

In the combined works of Cicero and Augustine, we
have a broad outline of most of the "formal" elements of
the just-war doctrine. Much of the remaining development
is an adaptation of these principles for contemporary
contexts. At this early date, we begin to see legal and
moral concerns combined with customary practices.
Principles are justified on the bases of secular, natural
law, and religious appeals. Most modern criteria for a
just war are included, at least in skeletal form. Both
Cicero and Augustine discuss the following:

(1) Justifying causes: prior crimes or
injuries by the enemy.
(2) Proper authority: Cicero listed the
state or emperor; Augustine added God's
command.
(3) Just goals: to avenge injuries and
reestablish peace.
(4) Humanitarian conduct: distinguishing
innocent from guilty, showing mercy when
victory is assured, and maintaining fidelity
to oaths.

In addition to these four common criteria, Cicero
advocated a public declaration of war and Augustine
required a benevolent attitude. Not yet explicit in the
criteria are the principles of reasonable hope, last
resort, and due proportion (these last two are implicit
in some of Augustine's discussion). Also, there is no
clear distinction between offensive and defensive war,
though again, this demarcation is implicit in Augustine.

Noncombatant immunity, or the moral principle of
"discrimination", is present in the fourth century only
in rudimentary form. Noncombatants are not identified
and prisoners are customarily made slaves.

In the ensuing "darkness" of the early Middle Ages,
the influence of the just-war tradition paled, though it
was not extinguished. Despite the fall of Rome, Roman
law persisted in parts of Europe. In fact, it
experienced a revival in the twelfth century to again
exert influence on the development of just-war
theory.[14] Likewise, the influence of Augustine
subsided until the twelfth century when his work became
the principal source on war for Gratian's monumental
canon-law compendium, known as the Decretum. So
significant was the contribution of Gratian and his
canon-law successors, that James T. Johnson chooses to
locate the genesis of the "classic" medieval doctrine of
just war with him. According to Johnson, "only with
Gratian is a comprehensive and continuing inquiry
initiated into just moral and legal limits to war that
produced fruits that defined the just war doctrine of
Western Christendom in its classic form by the end of the
Middle Ages."[15] It is largely through the agency of
the canon lawyers that the just-war tradition became a
moral and legal doctrine regulating medieval society. It
is also quite possible that Thomas Aquinas became
acquainted with Augustine's views on war through
Gratian.[16]


## Thomas Aquinas (1225-1274 A.D.)

Aquinas is the name most frequently associated with
that theological movement known as Scholasticism. He was
the Church's theologian at the point in a united
Christendom (thirteenth century) when the Church was the
supreme institution in Europe. Still he is the foremost
systematic theologian of the Roman Catholic Church. His
unique achievement was a "synthesis of Aristotelian
philosophy and Christian theology."[17] Aquinas built
his system on reason and faith, natural law and
revelation. In just-war theory his primary contribution
was the systematic application of Augustine's thought on
war and Aristotle's concept of the "common good" to late
medieval society.

The ideological foundation upon which Thomas built
his theory was a natural law concept of justice.
"Justice," he said, "consists of those things that belong
to our intercourse with other men." Hence, an act of
justice is "rendering to each one his right. . . ."[18]
In order for a war to be just, the three jus ad bellum
criteria listed by Augustine were necessary: right
authority, just cause, and right intention. Concerning
right authority, Aquinas insisted that "it was not the

business of a private individual to declare war" because
he had a higher authority, the state, from which to seek
peaceful redress of rights.[19]  It was the business of
the sovereign, or ruling monarch, however, to provide for
the common good of those subject to his authority.  Thus,
it was licit for the sovereign authority--but only this
authority--"to have recourse to the sword" for defending
the "common weal" against "internal disturbances" and
"external enemies."[20]

Aquinas's discussion of just cause followed  closely
the thought of Augustine.  War was justified only against
those who deserved to be attacked; that is, the purpose
of war is to "avenge wrongs" or restore that which is
"seized unjustly."  Though he did not distinguish between
offensive and defensive war as modern theory and law do,
a just cause consisted in defense of community life,
property, and rights.  Defense of the common good by a
just war was a moral imperative and a licit prerogative
of every community.[21]

In defining right intentions, Aquinas again followed
Augustine.  It was necessary for belligerents to have
"rightful intention, so that they intend to advance good,
or the avoidance of evil."  He offers the following
quotation from Augustine as a description of rightful
intentions:

> True religion looks upon as peaceful those
> wars that are waged not for motives of
> aggrandizement, or cruelty, but with the
> object of security peace, of punishing
> evil doers, and of uplifting the good.[22]

It is noteworthy that Aquinas insisted on the
necessity of all three criteria in order for a war to be
just.  A war may be declared by a legitimate authority
for a just cause, "and yet be rendered unlawful through a
wicked intention."[23]

Before concluding our discussion on Aquinas's view
of intention, comment should also be made on the
principle of "double effect," which he devised for
resolving moral dilemmas.  The principle of double effect
seeks to answer the question:  Is it ever right to do
wrong to achieve a good end?  Applying this principle to
killing, the question could be phrased as follows:  Is it
right to kill (under normal circumstances killing is
wrong) an aggressive assailant to prevent him from
killing oneself or other innocent people (the good end)?
The principle of double effect, as traditionally employed
by Catholic theologicans, says "no," if killing the
assailant is a "direct effect" of one's intentions; but
"yes" if the killing is an "indirect effect" or side
effect of one's intentions.  Now let us return to
Aquinas.  He formulated the principle of double effect as
follows:

> Nothing hinders one act from having two
> effects, only one of which is intended while
> the other is beside the intention.
> . . . Accordingly, the act of self-defense
> may have two effects, one is the saving of
> one's life. The other is the slaying of the
> aggressor. Therefore, this act, since one's
> intention is to save one's own life, is
> not unlawful, seeing that it is natural
> to everything to keep itself in being as
> far as possible. And yet, though proceeding
> from a good intention, an act may be
> rendered unlawful, if it be out of
> proportion to the end. . . . it is lawful
> to repel force by force, provided one
> does not exceed the limits of a blameless
> defense.[24]

Aquinas is affirming that it is wrong to kill, but
right to defend oneself, even if in such defense, the
aggressor is unintentionally and unavoidable killed.
Simply stated, the principle of double effect says that
an unintended "side effect" may be "permitted" (1) if it
is unavoidable, (2) if the actor's intention is right,
(3) if the unintended effect is not a means to the
intended effect, and (4) if the unintended effect is not
disproportionate to the intended effect (i.e., more harm
resulting from the side effect than good from the
intended effect). Originally, the principle of double
effect was applied to the problem of killing an unjust
aggressor. After the seventeenth century, however, it
came to be applied mainly to the problem of killing the
innocent. Civilian or noncombatant casualties may be
"permitted" in war, but only as an unintended,
unavoidable, indirect effect that does not exceed of the
intended good effect against a legitimate military
target. Paul Ramsey and others have used the principle
of double effect in discussing the morality of aerial
bombardment and the use of nuclear weapons.[25]
 Thus far in our discussion we have focused on the
two principal religious sources in the development of the
just-war tradition: Christian Theology (Augustine and
Aquinas) and canon law (e.g., Gratian). The other two
primary sources in the tradition are secular, jus gentium
and chivalry. The jus gentium is that body of social
custom that emerged in the Middle Ages from the heritage
associated with Cicero and Roman law.[26] It was based
on a natural law view of the right of princes, distinct
from any emphasis on the prince as God's representative
(as in religious circles). The prince had authority to
wage war by virtue of his responsibility to establish
justice and order in his domain. Wars were costly,
however, so by mutual agreement princes developed
"customary" codes of warfare to limit destruction. The

chivalric code was based on the high ideals of
knighthood, that select class of warriors whose duty was
to defend the innocent and avenge injustice. Though the
chivalric code is reflected today in military customs,
wearing of distinctive uniforms, and in military
discipline, its peak was reached in the Hundred Years War
(1340-1453 A.D.) and in the writing of Honore Bonet.

As remains true today among theologians and
philosophers, the religious sources in the just-war
tradition were more concerned with the <u>jus ad bellum</u>
issues of the rightness in resorting to war. The secular
sources, warriors and heads of state, were more attentive
to the ways and weapons of war to reduce manpower and
material costs. For example, religious sources
frequently mentioned the need to avoid harm to
noncombatants. The most complete list of noncombatants,
however, comes from the chivalric tradition. This was
recorded by Bonet in <u>L' Arbre des battailes</u> (<u>Tree of
Battles</u>, 1387 A.D.) and included clergymen, pilgrims,
travelers, merchants, peasants, farmers, wives, widows,
orphans, "the poor," and the property of the
innocent.[27]

By the fourteenth century these four sources,
theology, canon law, the right of princes (<u>jus gentium</u>)
and chivalry, had been synthesized to form the "classic"
just-war doctrine, which recognized both secular and
religious justifications for war. The religious wars
following the Reformation, however, convinced many that
wars for religious causes or differences were not
justifiable. Increasingly, theories of just war were
based on natural law. This movement, which began in the
sixteenth century, eventually emerged as the modern moral
doctrine of just war and contemporary international law
of war. At the dawn of the modern era, the three most
significant proponents of the just war were Franciscus de
Victoria, Franciscus Suarez, and Hugo Grotius.[28] Each
of these three, and most theorists since them, founded
their precepts on secular grounds such as natural law,
the social contract, human rights, or
humanitarianism.[29]

## Victoria (1492-1546 A.D.) and Suarez (1548-1617 A.D.)

Victoria wrote in the post-Christendom era at the
height of the Spanish "conquest" of the New World. He
appealed to natural law or reasoned concepts which he
believed both the Spanish and New World Indians could
recognize as valid restraints.[30] Because of
differences in religion and culture, Victoria sought a
common understanding through reason. The significance of
Victoria's contribution at this point should not be
missed. In recognizing the Indian's capacity to reason,
he was affirming that they were full human beings, not

simply "savages," or aliens, or "enemies." These are
germinal thoughts in a universal view of humanity.
Concerning just cause for war, he specifically rejected
the old crusade idea of conquest for the purpose of
converting the Indians to the Christian faith. He also
spurned extension of the empire as justification for
war. He concluded that " 'there is a single and only
just cause for commencing a war, namely, wrong
received.' "[31] Victoria advocated a concept closely
approximating the contemporary view that the only
justifiable war is a defensive war. Another significant
contribution was made by Victoria and his successor
Suarez in their consideration of how the justice of one's
cause was determined. Both emphasized that only the
sovereign had the responsibility and the authority to
make this judgment, but this responsibility should not be
taken lightly or manipulated by ulterior considerations.
Suarez affirmed: " 'I hold, first, that the sovereign
ruler is bound to make a diligent examination of the
cause and its justice, and that after making this
examination, he ought to act in accordance with the
knowledge thus obtained.' "[32] The ruler was not
"required" to consult others in making this examination,
but he "ought" to. Victoria explained: " 'The prince is
but a man and is not by himself capable of examining into
the causes of a war and the possibility of a mistake on
his part is not unlikely. . . . Therefore war ought not
to be made on the sole judgment of the king, nor indeed,
on the judgment of a few, but on that of many, and they
wise and upright men.' "[33] Both Victoria and Suarez
agreed that the determination of justice was the
responsibility of the ruler and not his subjects. The
citizen may "in good conscience" rest on the judgment of
his prince and the latter's counselors, unless the war is
"manifestly unjust." In such cases, citizens should
refuse to serve in an unjust war. The Spaniards' points
are clear: (1) The ruler ought to be certain of the
justice of cause before resorting to war; (2) this
determination should be advised by the best counselors
available; and (3) citizens should refuse to serve in war
only if they are certain that the war is unjust. If the
justice of one's cause cannot be determined or if the
cause of both sides is unjust, the issue should be
submitted to arbitration. Victoria and Suarez also
raised the possibility of justice on both sides, or at
least the perception of each side that its cause was
just. In such cases, if the issue could not be settled
by arbitration both sides should seek to limit the
destructiveness of the war by scrupulously following the
jus in bello rules of combat and by seeking an amicable
peace following the war.[34]
    In our own age of ideological disputes, the claim of
justice by both sides is certainly prevalent; and the
problem of determining justice among competing claims has

contributed in the modern era to an elevation of <u>jus in bello</u> concerns and a neglect of <u>jus ad bellum</u> issues.[35] Perhaps this is unavoidable, but neglecting these issues surely begs the question. Until an international arbiter with sufficient authority is established, nations must still make judgments on the justice of war. The essential question is: Which criteria guide these judgments?

## Hugo Grotius (1583-1645 A.D.)

Grotius was greatly influenced by his theological predecessors, Aquinas, Victoria, and Calvin; but he was by profession a secular jurist, and one who profoundly affected the development of international law. Grotius sought to specify rules for international conduct based on natural law, which he considered to be the foundation of civilization. He believed that if nations could agree on the rules, these could become enforceable international laws. Of the medieval criteria for justifying war, right authority, just cause, and rightful intentions, Grotius primarily addressed just cause. In his opinion, "the justifiable causes generally assigned for war are three: defense, indemnity, and punishment." His chief concern was with defense, which he considered a legal right devolving from the natural right of self-defense. Though all actions "necessary" for the defense of life and property were legal, retaliation should not be "excessive" or "disproportionate." Thus, a just or "solemn" war was a defensive war.[36] Prior to the commencement of hostilities, Grotius advocated dialogue in the form of negotiation or arbitration by a neutral party. The causes of war should be made public so that everyone may decide as to their justice. If possible, conflict should be resolved through peaceful agreement. When this is not possible, war could be waged as a last resort in accord with mutually acceptable rules of engagement (<u>jus gentium</u> or "customary laws"). Preemptive strikes were discouraged, and permitted by "expedience" only if there was absolute certainty of the enemy's aggressive intentions. Grotius's discussion of the rules of warfare is complex. By natural law reckoning, the entire population of a belligerent nation is subject to attack, salvery, death, and spoliation. Definite "moderations," however, have been imposed on natural law principles governing the conduct of battle by Christian charity, custom, and the dictates of "purest equity." These moderations require the following: (1) War should be prosecuted only until satisfaction for the harm actually done is secured; (2) women, children, priests, students, farmers, merchants, and captives are to be considered innocent (noncombatants); (3) authors of an unjust war are to be held more liable than their

subjects who fight; and (4) only the amount of force
necessary to achieve victory should be used. Grotius
affirmed that if a war is justified, then the means to
gain victory are also just. His "moderations," however,
were absolute limits on means, not subject to overriding
by arguments from "military necessity."[37]

## John Locke (1632-1704 A.D.)

The last person we will consider in the development
of the tradition is the Englishman, John Locke. Like
Grotius, his Dutch predecessor, Locke was concerned about
political theory and issues of state. To understand his
views on war, we need to have some grasp of his political
theory, not an insignificant objective in its own merit,
as Locke's theory has been quite instrumental in the
development of American political doctrine. Locke's
theory of state belongs to that natural law tradition
known as the "social contract," a concept of government
perhaps first clearly articulated by Aquinas.[38] Locke
sought to specify the nature of the relationship between
governments and citizens. In a context where no
government existed the people are said by Locke to be
living in a "state of nature." In this condition
individuals are free by natural right to seek their own
goals and provide their own defense. If the people
conclude, however, that it is to their mutual advantage,
they could form a government by establishing a community
"contract." The responsibility of government in this
social contract is to use the collective resources of the
people to provide for the common good, including internal
and external security, and other functions deemed
necessary or desirable by the people. In this contract
arrangement, government is by the people for the benefit
of the people. Citizens voluntarily surrender to the
government their individual right to make war in
self-defense.[39] Therefore, "private" war is not an
individual right as long as government exercises its
power to judge and enforce justice. If government is
incapable, defaults, or abuses its responsibility, the
trust of the people is forfeited and power devolves "into
the hands of those who gave it." If necessary the people
can assert their supreme power by force (i.e.,
revolution).[40] The authority of the government is
limited to only those rights which have been reposed in
government by the people. Therefore, government has the
authority to exercise force necessary for public defense,
but not aggression, because this was not a right of
individuals in the "state of nature." Locke states this
point forthrightly:

> Nor, to take the matter from the other
> side, has any government the right

> arbitrarily to attack its neighbors'
> lives, liberties, and possessions:
> Individual men in the state of nature
> have no power arbitrarily to commit
> rapine, or attack the life, liberty,
> health, and possessions of others, and
> they cannot be understood to have trans-
> ferred any such powers to the government.
> Therefore, rulers can never legitimately
> use the public force in war against the
> people of another society for the purpose
> of subjugating them.[41]

As a part of the contract among themselves and with
government, citizens should participate in the just and
lawful exercise of force by government; likewise, they
have the right to oppose the use of unjust and unlawful
force by government against themselves, their society, or
an external society. The right to resort to war,
according to Locke, grows out of the individual's and
society's right for self-defense. Therefore, defensive
wars are just, aggressive wars are unjust. In addition
to self-defense, a nation has the right to reparations
for damage from enemy actions. In waging justifiable war
and exacting reparations, however, clear distinctions
should be made between the guilty and the innocent. The
premise that renders a war just in the law of nature is
the right of innocent people to defend their lives and
property against aggressors. Therefore, a nation
justifiably returning the attack does not have the right
to harm the person or property of innocent people on the
other side. Thus, enemy forces can be attacked and
guilty parties can be killed and punished, but harm to
noncombatants should be avoided. Likewise, destruction
of houses, barns, crops, and other natural products
should be minimized because these provide for the needs
of noncombatants. Land conquered by a just side cannot
be ruled in perpetuity, nor can reparations be demanded
to the point that starvation results. Both of these acts
violate the rights of the innocent (those not responsible
for the war). Johnson affirms that this emphasis by
Locke is an original contribution to just-war tradition;
that is, in the dictates of the "fundamental law of
nature," the rights of the innocent populous of an
aggressor nation are as inviolable as the rights of the
innocent of a defender nation.[43] Locke's contribution
to the tradition may be outlined as follows:

Jus ad bellum principles
(1) Governments have the responsibility of
providing national security.
(2) Citizens have the responsibility of
supporting wars of national defense; that
is, resisting aggression by foreign states.

(3) Citizens have the right to resist domestic or international aggression by their own government.

### Jus in bello principles
(1) Means necessary for defense against aggression are permissible.
(2) Reparations and punishment of aggressors are permissible.
(3) Rights (including property) of nonaggressors on both sides should be protected.
(4) Destruction of resources necessary for sustaining life should be minimized.
(5) Annexation or perpetual rule of conquered territory is forbidden (though interim governments may be established if there are no qualified officials among the nonaggressor population of the enemy).

## CONCLUSION

From this overview of the development of the just-war tradition, several points are clear. The tradition simultaneously consists of principles ancient and modern, secular and religious, legal and moral. There is no one, absolute theory; there are many theories with common themes. The tradition is a mosaic of thought fashioned by theologians, philosophers, jurists, statesmen, and soldiers. The just-war tradition has been forged from the exigencies of battle. For example: Augustine wrote at a time when external invasion ravaged the empire; Aquinas sought to build a united Europe by limiting petty wars; knights fought for the preservation of life and property through codes of chivalry; Victoria sought to minimize loss of life in the Spanish conquest; and Locke wrote during the seventeenth century struggle between monarchists and republicans. Clearly, the tradition was developed by the application of critical thought in effort to address issues of justice and human needs in times of crisis. The following quotation by Ralph Potter underscores the practical and reflective aspects of the just-war tradition:

> . . . The just war doctrine is the precipitate of moral reflection upon political experience in the West. Its criteria provide an index to the moral economy underlying the use of force; they specify the types of actions that will eventually entail a high political and moral cost. Of all forms of thinking about the limits of justifiable use of

force, the just war doctrine comes
closest to providing relevant principles
that are intelligible, generalizable, and
capable of consistent application.[44]

NOTES

1.   The Roman (and Greek) influences on Augustine's
thought should not be isolated from Biblical and
Christian influences.  Indeed much of his language comes
from the Christian, rather than Roman Tradition.  See
below.

2.   The principle of just war generally applied in
wars with peoples with whom Rome had legal or contractual
relations.  See Frederick H. Russell, The Just-War in The
Middle Ages (New York:  Cambridge University Press,
1975), pp. 5-8.  Contemporary ethicists are sometimes
reluctant to retrace just-war concepts as far back as
Rome because the Roman doctrine "primarily benefited Rome
to the detriment of other peoples" (Russell, ibid. p. 7).
It was a legal concept that fit well with Rome's ambition
to extend its sovereignty, or at least maintain the
status quo.  In this regard the Roman theory serves as a
reminder that a person or nation can invoke concepts of
justice for self-advantage, the antithesis of genuine
justice.  Despite its shortcomings, Cicero's work merits
our attention because his principles directly influenced
later just-war advocates.

3.   Ibid., p. 5.  "Defending" its allies was one of
the ways Rome extended its sovereignty over Europe and
the Middle East.

4.   For a discussion of Cicero's views, see Russell,
The Just-War in the Middle Ages, pp. 4-8, and Roland H.
Bainton, Christian Attitudes Toward War and Peace:  A
Historical Survey and Critical Re-evaluation (Nashville:
Abingdon Press, 1960), pp. 41-42.  Hereafter cited as
Christian Attitudes Toward War.

5.   Cicero did not formally identify noncombatants.
According to Russell, he did specify that "only those
guilty of resisting Rome were to be punished."  Ibid., p.
7.

6.   See Abbott A. Brayton and Stephana J. Landwear,
The Politics of War and Peace:  A Survey of Thought
(Washington, D.C.:  University Press of America, 1981),
pp. 145-47, an anthology containing a brief document
written by Cicero.

7.   See <u>On Idolatry</u> written by Tertullian about 200 A.D., or Johnson, <u>Just War Tradition</u>, pp. xxvii-xxx. There were Christians serving in the Army prior to Augustine and a few of his predecessors, notably Ambrose in <u>De Fide Christiana</u> (ca.378 A.D.), encouraged Christian participation in defending the empire against barbarians and heretics. It is Augustine's work, however, that set the tone for later Christian views on war.

8.   Paul Ramsey, <u>Basic Christian Ethics</u> (Chicago: University of Chicago Press, 1950), p. 172.

9.   See Book XIX of Augustine, <u>The City of God</u>, trans. Marcos Dods (New York:   The Modern Library, 1950), pp. 669-709.

10.   Ramsey, <u>Basic Christian Ethics</u>, p. 172.

11.   Bainton, <u>Christian Attitudes Toward War</u>, p. 97.

12.   Augustine, <u>The City of God</u>, p. 683.

13.   Russell, <u>The Just-War in the Middle Ages</u>, pp. 25-26.

14.   Russell indicated that Roman law continued to hold strong influence in Italy, southern France, and part of Spain (<u>The Just-War in the Middle Ages</u>, p. 40).   After the fall of Rome, the eastern part of the Roman Empire continued to exist until the fifteenth century as the Byzantine Empire, centered in Constantinople (Byzantium). The zenith of the Eastern empire was reached during the reign of Emperor Justinian (537-565 A.D.).   Perhaps the principal legacy of Justinian was a collection of literature on law including the <u>Codex</u>, the <u>Digesta</u> (of legal opinions), and the <u>Institutiones</u>.   The Justinian Code was a continuation of classical Roman law and was a chief source for Western civil lawyers in the Middle Ages.   In the Twelfth Century the Italian city of Bologna was the center for a revival of Roman jurispurdence. This movement became the conduit through which much of the customary codes known collectively as <u>jus gentium</u> have been transmitted in history.   Not coincidentally, Bologna was also the birth place of the medieval science of canon law.   Around 1140, a monk named Gratian completed a massive compilation of canon law known as the <u>Decretum</u> ("Concordia Discordantium Canonum").   Through the watershed influence of the <u>Decretum</u>, natural law, Roman law and Augustine's theories on war were revived.

15.   Johnson, <u>Just War Tradition</u>, p. 121.

16.   Ibid., p. 122.

17. Waldo Beach and H. Richard Niebuhr, Christian Ethics: Sources of the Living Tradition, 2 ed. (New York: John Wiley and Sons, 1973), p. 203.

18. From Summa Theologica, cited from Brayton and Landwehr, The Politics of War and Peace, p. 68.

19. Ibid., p. 69. Pursuing this line of argument Aquinas implicitly denied that the petty conflicts of the Middle Ages were just wars. Also he rejected sedition as rebellion against the common good. See Russell, The Just-War in the Middle Ages, p. 270.

20. Brayton and Landwehr, ibid., p. 69. Aquinas affirmed that private persons lacked the authority to kill malefactors, and thus, to declare war. Princes on the other hand, were entrusted with public authority to care for the common good of the community, and thus, had the authority to kill malefactors and declare war. Aquinas's theory provided no basis for justifiable revolution (see above note). He did affirm, however, that princes should be just, promoters of the common good, and obedient to the law. And the purpose of the law was to provide for the common good. This emphasis on the precedence of the common good (which is basic to American political theory due largely to the influence of Locke and Rousseau) reflects the influence on Aquinas by Aristotle.

21. Russell, The Just-War in the Middle Ages, p. 262.

22. Brayton and Landwehr, The Politics of War and Peace, pp. 69-70. The section of Summa Theologica from which this quotation comes is also reprinted in George W. Forell, Christian Social Teaching: A Reader in Christian Social Teachings from the Bible to the Present (Minneapolis: Augsburg Publishing House, 1971), pp. 137f.

23. Brayton and Landwehr, ibid., p. 70.

24. Summa Theologica, II-II, Question 64, Art. 7; cited from Paul Ramsey, War and The Christian Conscience: How Shall Modern War Be Conducted Justly? (Durham, NC.: Duke University Press, 1961), pp. 39-40.

25. Paul Ramsey has used the principle of double effect extensively in his modern development of just-war theory; See War and the Christian Conscience. He has also been extensively criticized for doing so by many. For example, see Robert W. Tucker, Just War and Vatican Council II: A Critique (New York: The Council on Religion and International Affairs, 1966), pp. 28-29,

passim., and Ramsey's reply in this same volume. For an excellent contemporary discussion on the Catholic dialogue, see Richard A. McCormick, S.J., *Ambiguity in Moral Choice* (Milwaukee: Marquette University Press, 1973).

26. In classical times, *jus gentium*, which means "law of the nations," was law that applied to aliens and to relations with other states. Thus in the Middle Ages, through the continuing influence of Roman law, *jus gentium* came to be applied to relations between sovereigns.

27. See James Turner Johnson, *Ideology, Reason, and The Limitation of War: Religious and Secular Concepts, 1200-1740* (Princeton: Princeton University Press, 1975), pp. 66-72.

28. Actually each of these men died before the date frequently identified as the beginning of the modern era, 1648. Of course, history does not turn corners so sharply that one year could be established as an absolute demarcation between eras. We consider them in the modern era because their thought has certainly influenced modern views. Indeed, Grotius is frequently cited as the "father" of modern international law.

29. Victoria, whose name is variously spelled "Vitoria" and "Vittoria," and Grotius used natural law language. The international law conventions speak of "humanitarianism," "laws of humanity," "dictates of public conscience," "customary or unwritten laws." Locke and, today, John Rawls use the concept of the social contract. Michael Walzer bases his theory on human rights. Even theological arguments today are often couched in secular terms. In *Pacem in Terris*, for example, Pope John XXIII spoke of human rights and the "common good of the entire human family." All of these efforts can be seen as seeking to find a common foundation for principles of war. Since the Reformation and especially in the pluralistic modern world, religion has failed to provide a common base. Natural law may generally be understood to refer to those "laws" recognizable through "reason" as common to the nature of human society and the world. The concern of modern theories is clear and admirable: In a pluralistic world and in cross-cultural conflicts, how can we agree on a common set of principles by which to limit warfare? It is yet to be demonstrated that secular bases are significantly more effective in providing this common ground than was religion. Amidst the Iranian hostage crisis, for example, Khomeini rejected appeals to international law with the question: "Whose international law? It wasn't written by Muslems!"

30.  See Johnson, _Just War Tradition_, pp. 75-77.

31.  Johnson, _Ideology, Reason, and The Limitation of War_, p. 154.

32.  _On War_, section VI, I:  cited from Johnson, _Ideology, Reason and The Limitation of War_, p. 179.

33.  _De Indis et De Jure Belli Relectiones_, Section 24, cited from Johnson, _Ideology, Reason, and The Limitation of War_, p. 181.

34.  Johnson, ibid., p. 194-95.

35.  See _INTRODUCTION_, note 6, above.  During the recovery of just-war principles and the development of international law in the twentieth century, most focus has been on ways to protect noncombatants and limit the destructiveness of war (_in bello_ issues).

36.  These quotations are from Grotius's seminal work, _De Jure Belli ac Pacis_ ("Rights of War and Peace"); cited from Brayton and Landwehr, _The Politics of War and Peace_, pp. 101-5.

37.  Johnson, _Ideology, Reason, and The Limitation of War_, p. 231.

38.  _Social Contract:  Essays by Locke, Hume, and Rousseau_, with an Introduction by Sir Ernest Barker (New York:  Oxford University Press, 1962), p. viii.  Other great thinkers of the "social contract" tradition include Hobbes, Spinoza, Rousseau, Grotius and Kant.

39.  Locke, "An Essay Concerning the True Original, Extent and End of Civil Government" (known as the "Second Treatise") Paragraph 88; reprinted in Barker, _Social Contract,,_ p. 51.

40.  Ibid., Paragraphs 155, 211-41 (Barker, ibid., pp. 122-43).

41.  Cited from Johnson, _Ideology, Reason, and The Limitation of War_, p. 233.

42.  Locke, "An Essay," Paragraphs 203-10 (Barker, _Social Contract_, pp. 118-22).

43.  Johnson, _Ideology, Reason, and the Limitation of War_, p. 240.

44.  Ralph B. Potter, Jr., _War and Moral Discourse_ (Richmond, VA:  John Knox Press, 1969), p. 62.

# [ 2 ]
## The Just-War Criteria:
## A Contemporary Description

INTRODUCTION

When Augustine discussed just-war principles, he sought to establish criteria to determine whether or not Christians could morally participate in a war. Though Christians still use the criteria for this reason, the doctrine today is generally applied to evaluate the justification of the war itself. An analogy may be made between the criteria and those moral principles applicable to the use of violence in domestic society.[1] The dictates of conscience, moral reasoning, and common sense agree that indiscriminate killing of persons is wrong and cannot be tolerated. No society can long survive without restraints on criminal acts! Any taking of human life without moral justification is murder; it is intrinsically wrong. The only conditions that justify killing are those necessary for the protection of human life, that is, defense of self and others. Even when justified, however, killing is still subject to moral restrictions and should be avoided if possible. Only the amount of force necessary to restrain aggression is legitimate; and while exercising force, caution must be taken to protect innocent bystanders. These moral principles are reflected in the criminal law codes that regulate civil society.

Similarly, the just-war criteria seek to determine under what conditions and by what means war is morally justifiable. The doctrine begins with the assumption that the taking of human life even in war is wrong, that it is murder, unless it conforms to the principles of justice. Essentially, war is justifiable only if conducted for defensive purposes. Disproportionate use of force or indiscriminate killing in war is morally wrong. If we return to the thought of Augustine for a moment, we see that just-war doctrine attempts to hold together two claims for those with national responsibility: the moral responsibility to protect the

lives of citizens through national security, and the
responsibility to use national security forces morally.

The just-war criteria discussed in the following
paragraphs include the jus ad bellum principles which
identify requisite conditions for resorting to war.
These are just cause, right authority, right intention,
public declaration, last resort, reasonable hope, and
proportionality. Also considered are the jus in bello
principles of proportionality and discrimination
(noncombatant immunity), the criteria for determining
just means. Before turning to them, however, it is
helpful to distinguish between "formal" and "substantive"
views of the criteria.

Some who discuss just-war theory consider the
principles "formal" criteria; others see them as
"substantive" proscriptions. A formal view is one that
presents a broad outline, or the general form of an idea.
A substantive position seeks to specify the content or
substance within an idea. According to James Childress
the "formal" function of just-war theory is to provide a
"framework," or a procedure for analyzing disputes or
issues. In this function, the just-war criteria are to
be distinguished from policy. They "constitute a formal
framework within which different substantive
interpretations of justice and morality as applied to war
can be debated."[2] A formal theory requires, for
example, a just cause before resorting to war; but it
does not define what constitutes a just cause. This
definition requires a substantive theory of justice.

In contemporary discussions among just-war
advocates, there is little debate around which criteria
to include; that is, there is general agreement on the
formal aspects of the theory. Disagreement does exist,
however, over substantive issues such as what constitutes
justifiable cause, or who is a noncombatant. As we turn
now to a discussion of the criteria, their adequacy as a
formal framework for debating policy should be assessed;
that is, do they identify considerations essential for
evaluating war and its means? Also, contemporary views
of the criteria should be studied for their contribution
toward substantive policies for regulating war.


THE JUST-WAR CRITERIA


Just Cause

What is justice? Though Americans find it hard to
agree on specific definitions, we have a general sense of
what constitutes justice. It is the impartial
distribution of rewards and punishments; justice is
"equal opportunity" and "fair treatment." It is, as
Aquinas affirmed, "rendering to each one his right."

Like "life" and "liberty," justice is a fundamental
principle of the nation.  The Preamble to the
Constitution states:

> WE THE PEOPLE of the United States, in Order
> to form a more perfect Union, establish
> Justice, insure domestic Tranquility,
> provide for the common defense, promote
> the general Welfare, and secure the
> Blessings of Liberty to ourselves and
> our Posterity, do ordain and establish
> this Constitution for the United States
> of America.[3]  (Underline added.)

Assuming that justice is a regulatory moral
principle for domestic and foreign policy, we must then
ask, what constitutes a just cause for war?  Walzer and
Potter affirm that violation of human (and national)
rights provide the moral basis for just cause.
International law labels such violations crimes of
"aggression."  Walzer states the case most forcefully:
"Nothing but aggression can justify war."[4]  With
Victoria, he concludes that there "is a single and only
just cause for commencing a war, namely, a wrong
received."[5]  The relation between rights and aggression
is clear in Walzer's description of aggression:

> Aggression is the name we give to the
> crime of war.  We know the crime because
> of our knowledge of the peace it
> interrupts--not the mere absence of
> fighting, but the peace-with-rights, a
> condition of liberty and security that
> can exist only in the absence of
> aggression itself.  The wrong the
> aggressor commits is to force men and
> women to risk their lives for the sake
> of their rights.  It is to confront them
> with the choice:  your rights or (some
> of) your lives!  Groups of citizens
> respond in different ways to that
> choice. . . .  But they are always
> justified in fighting; and in most
> cases, given that harsh choice, fighting
> is the morally preferred response. . . .
> . . . Aggression is a singular and
> undifferentiated crime because, in all
> its forms, it challenges rights that
> are worth dying for.[6]

Walzer reveals the connection between his views and
just-war tradition when affirming the importance of
resisting aggression; he writes:

> Resistance is important so that rights can
> be maintained and future aggressors
> deterred. The theory of aggression restates
> the old doctrine of the just war: it
> explains when fighting is a crime and when
> it is permissible, perhaps even morally
> desirable. The victim of aggression
> fights in self-defense, but he isn't only
> defending himself, for aggression is a
> crime against society as a whole.[7]

Like Walzer (and Augustine, Aquinas, Victoria, and
Grotius), Potter states that "a just cause for war can
only arise out of the necessity to restrain and correct a
wrongdoing of others on behalf of the public good."[8]
He specifies three causes which justify war. The first
is "to protect the innocent from unjust attack." The
nation victimized by unjust aggression has the right to
defend itself; that is, "to repel force by force," and to
seek alliances with other nations for the purposes of
improving its defensive capability. The second cause
justifying war, according to Potter, is "to restore
rights wrongfully denied." This cause permits a war of
"intervention," including crossing another nation's
borders "to correct a flagrant and persistent denial of
justice--as a defense of the innocent." He cites as an
example of justifiable intervention coming to the defense
of the black community in South Africa should the racist
regime governing that country launch an indiscriminate
assault on the black population. Walzer also recognizes
the justification of intervention in very limited
circumstances. He described the Indian invasion of East
Pakistan (Bangladesh) in 1971 to stop the aggression of
the Bengali people by Pakistani government troops as
justifiable intervention.[9] Other examples might
include resisting a siege of Berlin or the oppression of
Amin in Uganda. The third just cause listed by Potter is
"to reestablish an order necessary for decent human
existence." This cause admits the possibility of
"justifiable revolution."[10] Though revolution was not
recognized as a right of a people in the Middle Ages, it
has been an accepted principle since John Calvin and
Locke. Indeed, revolution is the birthright of our own
nation, a right documented in the Declaration of
Independence:

> . . . Governments are instituted among Men,
> deriving their just powers from the consent
> of the governed.

> . . . But when a long train of abuses and
> usurpations, pursuing invariably the same
> Object evinces a design to reduce them

under absolute Despotism, it is their
right, it is their duty, to throw off
such Government, and to provide new Guards
for their future security.[11]

Policy makers today face crucial and complex issues
concerning intervention and revolution. The modern
context is exacerbated by the ideological conflict
between democracy and communism. A just war according to
Marx-Leninist definition is any war that supports the
spread of international communism. A just cause within
this ideology is "any class struggle leading to war,"
especially "liberation war."[12] "Wars of National
Liberation" constitute a primary category of communist
just wars. Thus, the challenge for American policy
makers is to distinguish between wars of revolution,
justified because of governmental oppression, and wars of
national liberation instigated by external interference.
Just-war theorists disagree when discussing specific
cases. The following principles from the just-war
tradition can, however, be identified as guidelines
relevant to this issue:

(1) Differences in religious or political
ideology are not in themselves justification
for war or intervention.
(2) Nations should hold strong presumptions
against intervening in the internal affairs
of other nations or taking sides in a civil
war.
(3) Nations are justified in coming to the
aid of another nation when that nation is
unjustly attacked by a third nation.
(4) Intervention is justified on the request
of the government to balance support given
by a third nation to an insurrection or
insurgency movement.
(5) Intervention is justified in behalf of
a revolutionary force seeking to overthrow
an extremely opporessive regime, provided
that this force has general popular support
and has requested intervention.
(6) Intervention is justified to stop massive
abuse of human rights.
(7) Intervention is not justified if definitive determination can not be made as to
whether or not the unrest in another nation
is justifiable revolution with broad popular
support or unjustified intervention by a
third nation with little popular support.

These principles for intervention, though
necessarily somewhat vague and imprecise, seek to hold

together the two poles of the right of national
self-determination and the justifiable defense of victims
of aggression. Crucial in deciding the justification of
intervention is the will of the people in the nation
experiencing violent conflict.[13]

Two extremely serious problems are associated with
the criterion of just cause. The complexity of
international relations and, as Walzer says, the lies
that governments tell often make it difficult, if not
impossible, to determine which side's cause is just.[14]
Victoria recognized this dilemma and concluded in such
cases that each belligerent should scrupulously adhere to
the rules of fighting and seek mutuality satisfying terms
for peace. Dyck and Potter more closely follow Locke's
admonition to seek negotiated or arbitrated settlement.

The second problem with just cause is associated
with the first. Wars do not just happen; someone starts
them. But determining who is the aggressor is not always
easy when international law simply defines the aggressor
as the one who "shoots first." Yet, nations sometimes
aggress or threaten another nation's security without
initiating physical violence, prompting a preemptive
strike from the nation challenged. According to
international law, preemptive strikes are illegal.
Johnson and Walzer object, however, claiming that in
certain circumstances they are morally justifiable.
Walzer cites the Israeli first strike against Egypt on 5
June 1967 in the Six Day War as a clear example. Egypt
had announced a policy of extermination toward Israel.
On 14 May the Egyptian government put its military forces
on "maximum alert." Four days later Egypt expelled the
United Nations Emergency Force from the Sinai and
strengthened its forces on the Israeli border. By the
end of May, Nasser had announced that he was closing the
Straits of Tiran to Israeli shipping and he formed
mutual-support treaties with Jordan, Syria and Iraq. The
day after the treaty with Iraq was announced the Israelis
struck the Egyptian air force on the ground. Walzer
concluded that the Israeli strike was justified because
it met his criteria for a preemptive strike: (1) a
manifest intent to injure, (2) active preparation that
makes the intent a positive danger, and (3) a general
situation in which the risk of defeat is greatly
magnified by the delaying of the fight.[15]

Just cause is the premier criterion of _jus ad
bellum_; however, it does not stand alone. A nation's
cause may be just, but still resorting to war may not be
moral or prudent. The remaining criteria are necessary
for making this determination.

## Right Authority

This criterion determines who is to decide whether
or not resorting to war is justified. In war between
nations, the right authority is the sovereign government
of the nation by virtue of its responsibility to provide
for the common defense. Certainly a lower authority does
not have the right to declare war on another nation. In
war within a nation, a rightful authority is one that has
substantial popular support before resorting to
revolution or civil war. Though just-war theorists
commonly advocate this theme, which originated during the
Reformation, I have found no one who satisfactorily
delineates what constitutes "substantial popular
support."[16]

The other side of this question of authority is
whether or not citizens ought to support a war declared
by the established authority. In the sixteenth century
Victoria suggested that the prince ought to seek
consultation and be certain that war is justified before
turning to hostile action; and the citizen should trust
the judgment of the government and support the war effort
unless he is certain that the war is unjustified.
Childress, for example, affirms that unless a war is
"manifestly unjust" the citizen ought to presume "that
the authorities, if they are legitimate and have followed
proper procedures, have decided correctly."[17] In a
democracy like ours, however, where the citizen is both
subject and ruler, he concludes that decisions concerning
war should have general popular support. Johnson
suggests that public consensus on this issue should be
forged through a public debate in which the government is
responsible for publicizing facts and each citizen is
responsible for forming a judgment. Normal political
processes should then be followed in which the
government's decision on war reflects the will of the
people.[18]

Military personnel frequently express the opinion
that _jus ad bellum_ issues are not the concern of the
soldier. The President and Congress have the authority
to make decisions concerning war, and the responsibility
of the military in this area is to follow orders, not
make policy. Arthur Dyck concludes that this view is not
fully correct. Officers are policy implementators, not
makers. It is the responsibility of military leaders to
advise and make policy recommendations, however, and this
can be done only if officers are informed on both
military and moral issues. Therefore, Dyck affirms that
military officers should have competent knowledge in
just-war doctrine as well as military capabilities and
strategy.[19] It seems reasonable to conclude from the
just-war perspective that officers should assume that
government decisions are correct, at least until they are

firmly convinced otherwise.  At this point, however, they
should recall that their oath of office compels them to
support the Constitution, not a government acting
contrary to constitutional principles, and to obey
"lawful" orders (or those that comply with the
Constitution).


## Right Intention

     This criterion focuses on attitudes and goals in
war.  Augustine suggested that the right attitude was
love of neighbors and enemies.  Among contemporary
writers, Paul Ramsey has continued this theme, at least
when addressing other Christians.  "It is the work of
love and mercy," he says, "to deliver as many as possible
of God's children from tyranny, and to protect [them]
from oppression. . . ."[20]  Jesus taught his disciples
to turn their own cheek, but he did not instruct them to
lift up the face of another oppressed man to be struck on
both cheeks.  When commenting on the work of Aquinas,
Ramsey affirmed:  "Profoundly at work in his line of
reasoning is what justice transformed by love requires to
be extended even to him who wrongfully attacks."[21]
According to Ramsey, the principle of "double effect"
emphasizes that the right intention in war is to defend
life.  Taking the life of even an unjust person (i.e.,
aggressor) should be avoided if possible.[22]
     Most of the contemporary discussion around intention
concentrates on the attitudes with which war is fought.
Ramsey's work lies primarily within the context of jus in
bello.  Similar observations, however, can be made in
reference to the attitudes prevailing when deciding
whether or not to resort to war.[23]  The jus ad bellum
consideration of intentions strongly influenced the
rejection of wars for religion, the crusade idea.
Contemporary commentaries also tend not to equate love
and right intention, unless addressed specifically to
religious audiences.  The focus is more on the
impropriety of the motives of vengeance, cruelty, and
hatred.  A generalized hatred toward the enemy leads too
quickly to events like those at Beirut or My Lai.  Once
the enemy is viewed as something less than human,
atrocities are more likely to occur.
     The other major idea discussed under the criterion
of right intention is the goals for which war is waged.
If aggression constitutes a just cause for war, then a
justifiable goal for war is stopping aggression; that is,
a restoration of a just peace.  During the Korean War a
heated debate emerged between limited war advocates and
those who claimed that there is no substitute for
victory.  Walzer's conclusion on this issue is that "in a
just war, its goals properly limited, there is indeed

nothing like winning."[24]   He recognizes the tension
between the importance of winning and justifiable goals.
Certainly justice would not be served if a manifestly
unjust aggressor achieved victory over a nation
justifiably defending itself.   From the moral point of
view, aggression ought to be defeated!   But the other
side of this issue is how far you may go in winning.   Do
you simply stop aggression?   Do you also punish the
aggressor leaders for their actions?   Would you go a step
further and dictate a regime to govern the defeated
aggressor nation?   Is it right to go even further,
annexing the defeated nation and establishing a permanent
government?   In other words, what are justifiable goals
in waging war?   In responding to this question, Walzer
concludes:

> The theory of ends in war is shaped by the
> same rights that justify the fighting in
> the first place--most importantly, by the
> right of nations, even of enemy nations, to
> continue national existence and, except in
> extreme circumstances, to the political
> prerogatives of nationality.[25]

He agrees with Locke that establishing a perpetual
rule over the defeated nation is not a justifiable goal
for war.   He does recognize the propriety of punishing
the leaders of the aggressor nation and insists that "it
is vitally important that they not be allowed to benefit"
from their "crimes."[26]   The goals of stopping
aggression, punishing the leaders of aggression to deter
future aggression, and establishing temporary (though not
permanent) occupational forces were validated by
Nurenberg and appear consistent with just-war tradition.
A related issue is how and when to terminate
hostilities?   This question involves a jus in bello
consideration of goals.   John Rawls expresses a view that
has wide currency among contemporary writers:

> The aim of war is a just peace, and therefore
> the means employed must not destroy the
> possibility of peace or encourage a
> contempt for human life that puts the
> safety of ourselves and of mankind in
> jeopardy.[27]

Generally, the just-war tradition argues against
total destruction of the enemy and unconditional
surrender.   Just-war writers also warn against rushing so
quickly toward a cessation of combat that an "unjust"
peace is established.   Walzer concurs with the American
negotiators in the Korean War who refused to accede to
North Korean demands for forcible repatriation of

prisoners as a condition for ceasefire. Although their
decision prolonged the fighting, the American negotiators
"insisted on the principle of free choice, lest the peace
be as coercive as war itself."[28] A just peace, the
proper goal of war, is one that lays the foundation for
future harmonious relations between belligerents, rather
than leaving conditions and attitudes that abet future
wars.[29]

## Formal Declaration

This criterion states that the legitimate authority
of a nation should formally declare its intentions before
resorting to war. American law also requires a formal
declaration to invoke a "legal" status between
belligerent nations. "The Law of Land Warfare" (U.S.
Army Manual, FM 27-10) records: "The Contracting Powers
recognize that hostilities between themselves must not
commence without previous and explicit warning, in the
form either of a reasoned declaration of war or of an
ultimatum with conditional declaration of war." The
manual then adds the interpretive comment that surprise
is still possible because "nothing in the foregoing rule
requires that any particular length of time shall lapse
between a declaration of war and the commencement of
hostilities."[30] This interpretation seems to nullify
what Potter sees as the purposes of this criterion:
(1) to indicate to a potential enemy how war can be
avoided; (2) to give notice to other nations so that they
may assess the justice of the cause and conduct
themselves accordingly; and (3) to establish with
certainty that war is being waged on the initiative of
the will of the people rather than a small clique.[31]
Potter's views are consistent with the just-war
tradition; however, there is not a clear consensus on
this criterion among contemporary writers. Childress
indicates that a formal declaration may not always be
appropriate; and Johnson considers this criterion
unimportant today because of the movement to apply the
laws of war in all armed conflict, not just in conditions
of officially declared war.[32] The Egyptian-Israeli Six
Day War, discussed above under the principle of just
cause, appears to be a legitimate example of when an
advanced formal declaration would be inappropriate. The
objective of this criterion is sound, however, and if
publication in advance is not practical, still there is a
need to declare intentions and to state the conditions
acceptable for ending hostilities.

## Last Resort

When one reflects on the vast destruction, death, and injury that accompany modern war, there is a compulsion to recoil from any use of violence. Yet, heinous atrocities (e.g., Dachau, Bataan, Warsaw), marshal driving impulses to rescue sufferers and punish aggressors. The just-war doctrine attempts to hold both of these poles in tension rather than siding completely with either one. In discussing this tension Potter concludes:

> Moral power belongs to those who affirm both the obligation to contend for justice and the ideal not to harm. The two claims must be held together. . . . There is a constant temptation to relieve the tension by scanting one claim or the other and thus by simplifying the moral situation.[33]

The criterion of just cause admits the propriety of defending human rights, by force if necessary. The principle of last resort emphasizes that recourse to force is moral only when truly necessary, and when other viable alternatives are not available. Last resort reminds us of our moral duty not to harm, that resorting to war must be done reluctantly. Just cause is not license and should lead to war only as a last resort. When possible, conflict between and within nations should be resolved by means other than war, such as negotiation, arbitration, appeal to international institutions, and economic sanctions. The Catholic moralist Francis J. Connell states the thesis of last resort as follows:

> . . . rulers of nations may not declare war against another nation unless they are sure they are in the right, and have first tried all peaceful measures that might contribute toward righting the wrong inflicted by this other nation.[34]

The principle of last resort does not insist that every conceivable alternative to war be attempted. The nature of some aggressive acts may preclude some alternatives. It does require, however, that all realistic options be considered before deciding on the alternative of war.

## Proportionality

The principle of proportionality evaluates the effects or ends of war. It does this by calculating the

value of expected results. In this regard,
proportionality is "counting the costs," or cost-benefit
analysis. In ethical decisionmaking there is frequently
a tension between "ends" and "means," between the "good"
result desired and conceptions of what is "right" action.
Those who consider results the only valid criterion for
selecting a course of action are in effect saying that
"the ends justify the means." The just-war tradition
attempts to incorporate both elements, good results and
right action, in making decisions about war. In the jus
ad bellum sense this principle insists that there be "due
proportion, that is, less evil following from acting
rather than not acting in the manner contemplated."[35]
War is not justifiable if it will produce more
destruction than it prevents. In the language of the
limited-war idea, proportionality means that "the costs
of the war must not outweigh the benefits.[36]
Understood this way, proportion has the potential for
overriding just cause. In just-war doctrine, a nation
may have just cause, right intentions, justifiable goals,
and may consider war as a last resort, and still may not
be morally justified in going to war if the results on
balance, are negative. Ramsey writes:

> It can never be right to resort to war, no
> matter how just the cause, unless a
> proportionality can be established between
> military/political objectives and their
> price, or unless one has reason to believe
> that in the end more good will be done than
> undone or a greater measure of evil
> prevented.[37]

The principle of proportionality is related to
another concept which at times is discussed as a separate
criterion. This concept resolves that under most
conditions nations should not go to war unless there is a
reasonable hope of success. Political leaders "are
stewards of the welfare of the nation and the life of
each citizen."[38] Lives and goods are to be defended,
but not squandered. If there is not reasonable
expectation of success, or a balance of good to be
achieved in war, then resort to war squanders the lives
and resources of the nation. Therefore, it is possible
for war to be a moral option only if there is due
proportion and a reasonable hope of success.

The principle of proportionality also has been
applied to jus in bello issues in the modern era. In
this context the principle states that the means of
fighting, including tactics and weapons, should be
proportionate to the provocation and the mission; namely,
one does not use a sledge hammer to kill a fly! It is
not right to cause unnecessary suffering.

Proportionality in the conduct of combat is related to
the principle of war called "economy of force."[39] Both
suggest that assets be judiciously employed to achieve
victory with minimum loss of lives and resources.
Economy of force, however, is primarily concerned with
the efficient use of resources, whereas proportionality
seeks to determine how much force is justified in
response to particular cases of aggression. Even if
resources were ample and sufficient means were available,
still it would be morally wrong to destroy a village by
airstrikes and artillery because of fire from a single
sniper. Critics frequently cited such cases in Vietnam
as illustrations of disproportionate means. Some
antagonists moved from the combat context to jus ad
bellum conclusions. In effect, they were saying that
disproportionate means overrode the justice of the cause,
that "overkill" destroyed more values than the war was
preserving.
     The essence of the principle of due proportion is to
proscribe unnecessary suffering. This principle is
reflected in the international laws of war in the
prohibitions against such acts as attacks on undefended
buildings or towns, use of poisons, torture, and
unnecessary destruction of food, property, and other[40]
domestic resources.


Discrimination

     One distinction between just-war theory and the
limited-war idea is that in the latter proportionality,
in the terms of "cost-benefit analysis," has more
prominence. Just-war theory places greater emphasis on
protecting the innocent, or "discriminating" between
warriors and noncombatants. Many just-war theorists tend
to view noncombatant immunity as an "absolute" principle,
whereas limited-war advocates more frequently consider
the principle a "relative" concept. Ramsey insists on
the priority of immunity over proportionality.[41]
Johnson, however, considers Ramsey's emphasis on the
absoluteness and priority of discrimination an "extreme"[42]
position within the just-war tradition.
     Of all the just-war criteria, the principle of
noncombatant immunity is most frequently represented in
the international laws of war. Walzer observes:

          The war convention rests first on a certain
          view of combatants, which stipulates their
          battlefield equality. But it rests more
          deeply on a certain view of noncombatants,
          which holds that they are men and women
          with rights and that they cannot be used
          for some military purpose, even if it is a[43]
          legitimate purpose.

Virtually every moral commentary on war since World
War II, whether focused on the air battle or ground
combat, has discussed the problem of noncombatant
immunity. The issue is not whether noncombatants should
be immune to attack; there has been general agreement on
this point since classical times. Rather, the problem is
deciding "who" is a noncombatant; that is, the problem of
discrimination. The difficulty of differentiating
between combatants and noncombatants has escalated with
each stage in the development of modern warfare:  the
advent of conscript armies and large standing armies in
Napoleon's era, new weaponry developed in the industrial
revolution, the mobilization of whole societies in major
wars, the large scale employment of guerrilla or
insurgency war and terrorism, and the invention of
weapons of mass destruction.

Traditionally, noncombatants have been distinguished
either in terms of their "function" during war or their
"class." This last method identifies noncombatants as
those persons belonging to certain classes or
professions, such as medical personnel, the clergy,
farmers, merchants, and others designated as "protected
persons." The functional method of discrimination
classifies as noncombatants those who do not "contribute
directly" to fighting the war. Writers vary, however, in
specifying what constitutes direct participation. The
elderly, infirmed, and infants are normally considered
noncombatants. Soldiers in uniform are combatants,
unless they wear certain distinctive symbols which
identify them as noncombatants, or they have been
rendered incapable of hostile acts. For example, medical
personnel and chaplains wear distinctive symbols;
prisoners of war and soldiers with incapacitating wounds
are incapable of hostile action, and, thus, are
noncombatants. Persons who violate their noncombatant
status are subject to attack.[44]  Among civilians, those
who make war decisions or produce war materials are
generally considered as direct contributors to the war
effort and, thus, are combatants. Those who perform
services or produce goods necessary for living are
noncombatants, even though their services or goods may be
used by military personnel. This line of reasoning, for
example, allows bombardment of munitions factories, but
not canneries. In describing whom a combatant could
attack, Anscombe stated:

> But people whose mere existence and activity
> supporting existence by growing crops, making
> clothes, etc., constitutes an impediment to
> him--such people are innocent and it is
> murderous to attack them, or make them a
> target for an attack which he judges will
> help him towards victory. For murder is

the deliberate killing of the innocent,
whether for its own sake or as a means
to some further end.[45]

Anscombe maintains that noncombatants can be
distinguished, at least a large portion of them, for
"even in war, a very large number of the enemy population
are just engaged in maintaining the life of the country,
or are sick, or aged, or children."[46] Our experience
in Vietnam, however, demonstrates how complex identifying
noncombatants can be. Is a child carrying live
munitions, for example, a combatant or noncombatant?
Nevertheless, in insurgency warfare, where a principal
goal is winning the allegiance of the populace,
noncombatant immunity is even more crucial. Also it
should be remembered that unconventional war, as its name
implies, is not a paradigm for all warfare.

Another serious dilemma associated with the
principle of noncombatant immunity is the issue of
"military necessity." This asks if moral rules (and
legal statutes) can be set aside for the sake of
accomplishing a legitimate military objective. Is it
right for a defending nation to employ proscribed means
if these are necessary to avoid defeat by an aggressor?

Answers to this question vary, depending on one's
concept of moral principles and the rule of military
necessity. Those who view moral principles as absolutes
oppose overriding the principle of immunity in cases of
military necessity. Those who conceive of principles as
general guides are more inclined to set aside norms when
they conflict with objectives. The latter suggest that
the laws of war and just-war principles do not impede
military effectiveness, because they do not preclude any
action militarily necessary in war.[47]

A third position[48] falls between these two. It
describes ethical principles as "ideal" (or prima-facie)
duties. They are always "actual" duties except in
contexts where one ideal duty conflicts with another. In
such cases both can not be honored, and the context
strongly influences which duty one should fulfill. When
an ideal duty is set aside, it still retains its
importance and should be restored as soon as possible.
In the question of military necessity, the duty not to
harm noncombatants conflicts with the duty to protect
human life by defeating aggression. For an action to
qualify as a military necessity, however, the context
must be one in which defeat is truly an issue. In
circumstances where these two duties actually conflict,
ethicists who hold this view of moral principles
generally accept the validity of military necessity.

Military necessity, however, has often been invoked
in the past to justify violations of immunity which were
not essential to victory, as the German doctrine of

Kriegsraison illustrates. In summary, this doctrine
stated that military necessity "overrides and renders
inoperative the ordinary laws and customs of war."[49]
With this doctrine in World War II, Germans claimed as
"military necessity" the extermination of millions of
Poles, Russians, Gypsies, and Jews; medical experiments
on prisoners; and the deportation of citizens of occupied
territories to slave labor.[50] Many ethicists also
criticize the allied fire bombing of Dresden and Tokyo
and the atomic bombing of Nagasaki and Hiroshima as
violations of the principle of immunity and abuse of the
concept of military necessity.

The international lawyers McDougal and Feliciano
suggest that in the view reflected in the doctrine of
Kriegsraison, military necessity has come to mean
"relative expediency and comparative convenience and
advantageousness."[51]

Walzer rejects this thinking in even stronger
language:

> The doctrine justifies not only whatever is
> necessary to win the war, but also whatever
> is necessary to reduce the risks of losing,
> or simply to reduce losses in the course of
> the war. In fact, it is not about necessity
> at all; it is a way of speaking in code, or
> a hyperbolic way of speaking, about
> probability and risk.

Walzer rejects some applications of military
necessity but not the basic concept.

How then shall we evaluate claims of military
necessity? A good starting point is Potter's general
affirmation that "the principles governing the right and
wrong use of force cannot be broken with [moral]
immunity. There is a high cost to defying each and every
one."[52] Therefore, our predisposition must favor
adhering to the principle of noncombatant immunity. That
a proposed action really is a military necessity always
requires substantiation. Next, the principle of immunity
should shape our policies for fighting, and especially
target selection. Ramsey insists at this point that
warfare ought to be "counter-force," that is, directed at
combatants. Noncombatants, he says, are never legitimate
targets in themselves for direct attack.[53] Actual
military necessity may permit the harming of
noncombatants, according to Johnson, but only at the
point where the jus in bello principle of immunity has
become a jus ad bellum emergency; that is, when necessary
to enable a nation with just cause to avoid defeat at the
hands of an unjust aggressor.[54] Walzer states this
position clearly. Kant insisted that we do no injustice
"though the heavens fall."[55] Walzer rephrases Kant in

his maxim: "do justice unless the heavens are (really) about to fall."[56] He explains:

> These, then are the limits of the realism of necessity. Utilitarian calculation can force us to violate the rules of war only when we are face-to-face not merely with defeat but with a defeat likely to bring disaster to a political community. But these calculations have no similar effects when what is at stake is only the speed or the scope of victory. They are relevant only to the conflict between winning and fighting well, not to the internal problems of combat itself.[57]

Walzer thus admits that immunity can be overridden in cases of "supreme emergency," or when a nation's political survival is at stake. He allows military necessity in its extreme form, only when there are _jus ad bellum_ consequences.

The question in the case of military necessity is where to draw the line. It is certainly reasonable to draw this line well short of the _Kriegsraison_ doctrine. However, this does not mean that the principles are absolute, and the rules should never be overridden. Troop commanders are rightly concerned for the welfare of their personnel in combat. Indeed, they are morally and legally responsible for their safety. Therefore, I would draw the line as follows: Combat commanders can take actions necessary to avoid the destruction of their personnel, even if it may mean indirectly harming civilians as long as due proportion is not exceeded. This premise runs great risk of abuse, and must, therefore, be applied with exacting moral discipline. An example of the circumstances I have in mind is that a commander could call in close-air support to avoid being overrun by the enemy, even though he knew that civilians would be killed in the process. Such action is allowed under the principle of "double effect" (cf. Aquinas, above) in that intended targets of the air attack would be enemy troops. The innocent civilians would be unintended victims. This kind of action remains subject to the restraints of due proportion and noncombatant immunity continues in principle. Combat decisions such as this must also consider the fact that soldiers are legitimate targets of attack, noncombatants are not.

CONCLUSION

We have now concluded our description of the just-war criteria. One final word is in order before we consider more directly the issues associated with nuclear weapons. Walzer stated: "War is always judged twice, first with reference to the reasons states have for fighting, secondly with reference to the means they adopt."[58] He is affirming that both _jus ad bellum_ and _jus in bello_ criteria are essential for a complete moral doctrine of just-war. The position of Dyck, Potter, Johnson, Childress, and Walzer is that each of the just-war criteria are necessary.[59] They have evolved over the centuries because theologians and philosophers have recognized their moral rightness, but also because statesmen and soldiers have acknowledged their practical value. It is not to the commander's advantage if civilians turn to underground subversion or "fifth column" terrorism because of abusive treatment. War is even more violent when enemy troops "fight to the death" because they are more afraid of becoming prisoners of war. And certainly, in the age of modern weaponry, opting for war is prudent only for a justifiable cause and as a last resort when there is a reasonable hope of defeating aggression and restoring a just peace.


NOTES

1.  Analogies similar to the one which follows are presented by Childress in "Just-War Theories: The Bases, Interrelations, Priorities, and Functions of Their Criteria," _Theological Studies_ 39 (September 1978): 428-31; Potter, "The Moral Logic of War," _McCormick Quarterly_ 23 (May 1970): 203f; Walzer, _Just and Unjust Wars: A Moral Argument with Historical Illustrations_ (New York: Basic Books, Inc., 1977), pp. 53-62.

2.  James F. Childress, "Just-War Criteria," in _War or Peace? The Search for New Answers_, ed. Thomas A. Shannon (Maryknoll, New York: Orbis Books, 1980), p. 51. James T. Johnson, interview, Rutgers University, 5 January 1982.

3.  Henry Steele Commager, ed., _Documents of American History_, 5th ed. (New York: Appleton-Century-Crafts, Inc., 1949), p. 139.

4.  Walzer, _Just and Unjust Wars_, p. 62.

5.  Ibid.

6.  Ibid., pp. 51 and 53.

7.  Ibid., p. 59.

8.  Potter, "The Moral Logic of War," p. 207.

9. Walzer, Just and Unjust Wars, p. 108.

10. The three causes for war are discussed by Potter in "The Moral Logic of War," pp. 207-16.

11. Commager, Documents of American History, pp. 100-101.

12. For further discussion see "The Poverty of Philosophy" and "The Communist Manifesto" by Marx, reprinted in Karl Marx: Selected Writings, edited by David McLellan, especially pp. 215 and 246. Paul Ramsey provides an extended discussion of revolution in War and the Christian Conscience, Chapter 6, "Justifiable Revolution," and in The Just War, p. 189, from which the quotation in the text is cited. Here Ramsey is quoting from Y.A. Korovin, et. al., Academy of Sciences of the U.S.S.R., International Law (Moscow: Foreign Languages Publishing House), p. 402. Support of liberation movements is fundamental to the "Brezhnev Doctrine."

13. See Walzer, Just and Unjust Wars, Chapter 6, "Interventions."

14. Ibid., p. 74.

15. Ibid., p. 81.

16. See for example James Turner Johnson, "What Guidance can Just-War Tradition Provide for Contemporary Moral Thought About War," New Catholic World 226 (March-April 1982):83.

17. Childress, "Just-War Theories," p. 436. Ramsey and Johnson generally concur with Childress.

18. James T. Johnson, personal interview, Fort Monmouth, New Jersey, 9 April 1982. See also "Just War Theory: What's the Use?," Worldview 19 (July-August 1976).

19. Personal interview, Cambridge, Massachusetts, 7 February 1981.

20. Ramsey, The Just War, p. 143.

21. Ramsey, War and the Christian Conscience, pp. 43-44.

22. Ibid., p. 43.

23. See Johnson, "Just War Theory: What's the Use?", p. 43.

24. Walzer, Just and Unjust Wars, p. 122.

25. Ibid., p. 123.

26. Ibid.

27. Rawls, A Theory of Justice (Cambridge, Massachusetts: The Belknap Press of Harvard University Press, 1971), p. 379.

28. Walzer, Just and Unjust Wars, p. 123.

29. See Childress, "Just-War Theories," pp. 438-39.

30. See U.S. Army Field Manual 27-10: The Law of Land Warfare, 15 July 1956, p. 15. This law is a Hague Convention protocol.

31. Potter, "The Moral Logic of War," p. 219.

32. Johnson, "Toward Reconstructing The Jus Ad Bellum," The Monist 57 (October 1973):487, note 46.

33. Potter, War and Moral Discourse, p. 53.

34. Connell, "Is the H-Bomb Right or Wrong," The Sign (March 1950): 11-13; quoted from Ramsey, War and The Christian Conscience, p. 78.

35. Dyck, "Ethical Bases of the Military Profession," p. 44.

36. See Johnson, Just War Tradition, pp. 204f. Johnson also discusses here the often noted difficulty in proportionality and utilarian theory in general of accurate calculation of effects, or end results.

37. Ramsey, The Just War, p. 195.

38. Potter, "The Moral Logic of War," p. 219.

39. See U.S. Army Field Manual 100-1: The Army, 14 August 1981, p. 15.

40. See U.S. Army Field Manual 27-10: The Law of Land Warfare, passim.

41. Ramsey believes that questions of justice take precedence. Therefore, he emphasizes that the principle of protecting the innocent, which is manifested in the criteria of just cause and discrimination, should be considered prior to discussions of effects. That is, a nation should determine if it is "right" to resort to war

or use certain weapons in the protection of the innocent
from aggression before asking if these actions are
proportionate responses. This does not mean for Ramsey
that proportionality may not rule out these proposed
actions. See Ramsey, War and The Christian Conscience,
Chapter One, and pp. 143-45, 154, 351, passim; Ramsey,
The Just War, p. 155.

42. See Johnson, Just War Tradition, Chapter Seven.
Johnson points out that noncombatant immunity was an idea
emphasized more by chivalry than theology in the Middle
Ages. He views Walzer's position which allows
discrimination to be overriden, but only in "supreme
emergencies," as more characteristic of the tradition
than Ramsey's absolutist position. It is worth noting,
however, that many contemporary theological and
philosophical writers also consider this principle
absolute, or at least nearly so; cf. Richard Wasserstrom,
Thomas Nagel, Jeffrie Murphy, Alan Donagan, and others.
See discussion below.

43. Walzer, Just and Unjust Wars, p. 137.

44. For example, persons in civilian clothing
carrying weapons, chaplains carrying weapons, prisoners
who seek to escape or commit hostile acts, and wounded
soldiers who attempt hostile acts are combatants.

45. Elizabeth Anscombe, "War and Murder", originally
published in 1961, cited from Wakin, War, Morality, and
the Military Profession (Boulder: Westview Press, 1979),
p. 289.

46. Ibid., p. 297.

47. This view is congruent with the limited-war
concept and with utilitarian ethical theory, even the
"rule" kind.

48. This position has been developed from the theory
of the British philosopher Sir David Ross. This view
considers ethical principles to be prima-facie duties,
rather than absolute or relative guidelines. They are
intrinsically right, but not always fitting. This view
is a modification of the traditional deontic theory of
ethics and should not be confused with "situation
ethics." For further discussion, see Childress,
"Just-War Theories," and William K. Frankena, Ethics, 2nd
edition (Englewood Cliffs, New Jersey: Prentice-Hall,
Inc., 1973), pp. 55-56.

49. Myres S. McDougal and Florentino P. Feliciano,
Law and Minimum World Public Order: The Legal

Regulations of International Coercion (New Haven:   Yale
University Press, 1961), p. 672.

50.   These ruthless acts were claimed as acts of
"military necessity" by various Germans in the war crimes
trials following World War II; cf. McDougal and
Feliciano, pp. 676-677.

51.   Ibid., p. 672.

52.   Potter, "The Moral Logic of War," p. 225.

53.   Ramsey, War and The Christian Conscience, pp.
68, 70n, 148-49, 228-29, 320-23, passim.   Ramsey's
"counter-force" strategy rejects "Counter-Value
Strategy," which advocated the targeting of nuclear
weapons on enemy cities.   Ramsey insists that only enemy
forces (including war industries) are legitimate targets.

54.   For Walzer and Brandt, Hitler's Germany is the
paradigmatic example of an aggressor against whom a
nation could morally override the principle of immunity,
if necessary, to avoid defeat.

55.   Cited from Murphy in Wakin, War, Morality, and
the Military Profession, p. 354.

56.   Walzer, Just and Unjust Wars, p. 231.

57.   Ibid., p. 268.

58.   Ibid., p. 21.

59.   As noted earlier, Johnson, who has taken on the
task of restoring to international recognition the jus ad
bellum criteria, does not emphasize "public declaration;"
this omission, however, results from his position that
all military conflict is subject to these moral
principles, not legally declared wars only.

# [ 3 ]
# Nuclear Weapons: Prospectives from Just-War Ethicists

INTRODUCTION

In the first two chapters we surveyed the development and criteria of the just-war tradition. The objective of this chapter is to investigate how advocates of this tradition treat the issues raised in the contemporary debate over nuclear weapons. One issue in the debate, however, is the validity of the just-war tradition in the nuclear age. In this regard, the present discussion is a return to the polemics of the early 1960s. In the summer of 1960, an editorial in Worldview claimed that nuclear weapons make the norms of just war obsolete; the criteria are "anachronisms."[1] The following year Walter Stein edited a book of essays by British Roman Catholic scholars which described nuclear war as "not merely a catastrophic menace, but a wickedness."[2]

Some twenty years later, Bishop John J. O'Connor published a book in which he recorded the following statement by an American Roman Catholic priest, Richard McSorley: "It's a sin to build a nuclear weapon." Bishop O'Connor also quotes a Catholic sociologist as saying: "[T]he weaponry of modern war--that classified as 'conventional' no less than nuclear--is of such a nature as to render the criteria of the 'Just War' meaningless . . . ."[3] (These statements do not represent O'Connor's view.)

In 1982 the Peace and Social Concerns Coordinator of the Friends United Meeting (Quaker) wrote: "The 'just-war' theory is out of date. It makes nonsense when one is talking about nuclear weapons and nuclear war."[4]

These quotations suggest that the just-war tradition is no longer useful. The tradition is accused of being too permissive. The term "debate" which we have been using, however, implies that there is more than one view on this issue. Ironically, it was the debate in the sixties that stimulated the work by Ramsey, the theologian most frequently credited with restoring the

credibility (at least for many) of the just-war
tradition. In response to the editorial in Worldview
(1960), Ramsey wrote:

> The just-war theory cannot be repealed; it
> can only be violated. It states the limits
> beyond which war as such becomes in itself
> a wholly non-human and non-political activity,
> and the point beyond which military force
> becomes senseless violence, and our weapons
> no longer weapons of "war". This is not
> because war has an "essence" or "nature" but
> because man has; and because political
> society has a nature to which military means
> must be kept subordinate.[5]

Ramsey concludes that the just-war principles
compose the most valid doctrine for judging the morality
of war, even in the nuclear age.

Before we examine the various positions on nuclear
weapons in this and subsequent chapters, it is important
to recognize that the nuclear weapons issue is extremely
complex. If one concludes that the use of nuclear
weapons is morally permissible under certain conditions,
these conditions require careful definition. What moral
principles, if not those of just war, will be used to
determine these limits? If one concludes that the use of
these weapons cannot be morally justified, the question
of how to prevent their use remains. If the
determination is made that nuclear weapons are morally
unusable, does this decision also proscribe the
manufacture and possession of such weapons for the
purpose of deterring their use by others? Is a negative
answer to this question a call for unilateral or
multilateral nuclear disarmament? Presently, the Soviet
Union has substantially greater "conventional" forces
than the United States. If nuclear weapons were
considered immoral means of defense, should the United
States enlarge its conventional forces to achieve parity
with the Soviet Union? Should the nation effect these
increases even if they require a larger defense budget
and a compulsory draft?

The whole discussion of nuclear weapons is clouded
by an imprecise use of terms. Are debaters referring to
"all" nuclear weapons or specific classes of weapons?
When one advocates "banning the bomb" is one rejecting
the use of multimegaton strategic weapons or fractional
kiloton tactical weapons, or both? When Army strategists
say that deterrence policy "does not preclude the first
use of nuclear weapons," does this refer only to tactical
weapons or to all nuclear weapons?[6]

When the "nuclear pacifist" declares that nuclear
warfare, or all warfare because of the potential

escalation to nuclear weapons, is morally illicit, what
policy or principles does he or she advocate for
delimiting conventional and sub-conventional warfare?
This list of questions is not exhaustive, but it does
suggest the complexity of the issues surrounding nuclear
weapons and that simple answers are inadequate. The
questions also delineate the kinds of data we are looking
for as we explore and differentiate various contemporary
positions in the nuclear debate. We begin the
examination of the just-war positions with Reinhold
Niebuhr, the dominant Protestant ethicist at the
beginning of the nuclear age.[7]


THE FIRST REACTION:   REINHOLD NIEBUHR

The mushroom cloud that marked the successful
completion of the Manhattan Project was received with
excitement and joy.  It meant that America had won the
race with Hitler to create the first atomic bomb.
Perhaps it is characteristic of the tragic irony of
nuclear weapons that such a devastating power could be
called a "miracle of deliverance."[8]
Reinhold Niebuhr's response following the use of the
bomb in Japan appears to us today to be an
understatement:  "Everybody recognizes that the atomic
bomb has introduced a new dimension into the already
complex realities of a technological society."[9]
Niebuhr argued that when considering the alternative
of allowing the Germans to first perfect the weapon, "it
was not possible to refuse to develop it."[10]  His
forecast of the ultimate effect of the bomb on
international relations, however, was ominous:

> Ultimately, of course, the bomb may make
> for peace, because it proves that we must
> achieve an organized society in global
> terms or perish.  But the prospect for
> the next decades, or indeed for the next
> century, is not reassuring.[11]

Niebuhr again addressed the issue of nuclear weapons
five years later, following the development of the
hydrogen bomb.  In 1950 he wrote:  "The Age of atomic
bombs, suddenly developing into a thousand times more
lethal hydrogen bombs, is very different from the age of
scythe and plowshare.  It confronts us with the
possibility of mutual mass annihilation."  He continued:

> Thus we have come into the tragic position
> of developing a form of destruction which,
> if used by our enemies against us, would
> mean our physical annihilation; and if

used by us against our enemies, would mean our moral annihilation. What shall we do?[12]

Niebuhr clearly perceived the moral dilemma which this new weaponry had introduced: how do we defend against aggression and yet prevent nuclear war? Despite the destructive capacity of hydrogen weapons, he was not ready to return to the pacifist position. The pacifists have an easy answer, he said, which was simply to renounce the use of such weapons, unilaterally, if necessary. Niebuhr concluded that because we do not have "moral access to the Russian will," the United States could not risk annihilation or subjugation by rejecting the new bomb. He posed the question as follows:

Could we risk letting the Russians have the bomb while we are without it? The answer is that no responsible statesman will risk putting his nation in that position of defenselessness. Individuals may, but nations do not, thus risk their very existence.

Niebuhr stressed the necessity of a strong defense against the Soviet Union, but he also cautioned against undue reliance on military strength and questioned if the use of nuclear weapons did not exceed the morally legitimate price a nation can pay for self-defense. "If we had to use this kind of destruction in order to save our lives," he asked, "would we find life worth living?"[13]

Concerning the hydrogen bomb, Niebuhr made two proposals. The first was that the United States seek an agreement with the Soviet leaders not to produce the hydrogen weapon for military use. He was pessimistic about the possibility of negotiation and rejected "general disarmament" as a price too high to pay for agreement because this would leave Europe defenseless against Communism. He favored his second proposal, which was to "produce the H-Bomb but make a solemn covenant never to use it first."[14] He concluded:

A nation does not have the power to say that it would rather be annihilated than to produce a certain weapon. For, as the scientists have asserted, the production of that weapon may serve to guarantee that it will never be used. But to use such a weapon first represents a quite different moral hazard. It ought not to be impossible for nations to meet that hazard successfully.[15]

In 1955 Niebuhr's position remained the same. He
responded to pacifist proposals for foreign policy by
affirming that military force should be retained as an
instrument of politics for the defense of inalienable
human rights. Military weakness, he said, invites
aggression. Statesmen should be careful about the risk
of war, especially in the atomic age. "But no nation
will choose present submission as the alternative for a
future risk. That is why pacifism remains an irrelevance
even in an atomic age."[16]
    Niebuhr did not use just-war terminology, but his
position falls clearly within this tradition. He
preceeded the development of tactical nuclear weapons
and, thus, addressed only the strategic issue. On this
he concluded that nuclear weapons should not be used
first, and, possibly, not at all. He did not favor
unilateral nuclear disarmament, though he would have
supported a bilateral agreement not to produce hydrogen
weapons. In the absence of such agreement, he advocated
the retention of strategic weapons for the purpose of
deterrence.
    In assessing Niebuhr's position, the following
influences are noteworthy. First, his long held belief
that power must be opposed by power if justice is to
prevail is clearly evidenced. He believed that Western
Europe and America too easily acquiesced to Hitler's
early aggression and did not wish to see this repeated
with the Soviets. Secondly, Niebuhr wrote during the
"hot" days of the "cold war." He distrusted Soviet
intentions; rather, he believed they were serious in
their stated ambition to establish a universal communist
world. Niebuhr may be considered the first just-war
spokesman in the nuclear age. He framed the moral issues
which we presently debate. His ideas were further
developed by the major spokesman for just war in the
sixties, Paul Ramsey.


THE SEARCH FOR A MORAL STRATEGY:   PAUL RAMSEY

    The work of Paul Ramsey continues a theme
characteristic of Niebuhr. Because of his view of
individual and collective human nature, he too concluded
that power must be opposed by power. Ramsey believed
that force sufficient to restrain aggression should be
maintained at the national level or developed at the
international level. His assessment of the current
status of the United Nations led him to conclude that
nations must be responsible for their own defense.[17]
    The 1960s in which Ramsey wrote were years of
strategic controversy similar to the 1980s. In this
debate, Ramsey waged "war" on two fronts. Against
pacifists he argued that Christian love and justice

demand defense against aggression, even in the nuclear
age.  "Pacifism," he claimed, "has corrupted enormous
numbers of people."  It has no way of avoiding wickedness
or setting limits to it.  Pacifists believe that there is
no moral difference between murder and killing in war.
Thus, they believe that "soldiers are only 'licensed
murderers' and that murderers are only unlicensed
soldiers."[18]
     Against total-war enthusists (whom he called
"bellicists") and the nuclear strategists of his day,
Ramsey marshalled the just-war principles of
discrimination and proportionality.  One of the
particular targets of his attack was the selection of
"counter-society" or "counter-population" targets in
nuclear strategies.  Stated simply, Ramsey opposed aiming
nuclear weapons at non-military targets!  Indiscriminate
bombing or counter-people warfare, he said, is
"intrinsically wrong."  In this sense, multimegaton
weapons in his day were "morally unshootable" because
they could not be used discriminately and were targeted
on population centers.[19]  This kind of warfare is
morally unjustifiable even as a "second strike," or a
counter attack.

>        If it is unjust for an enemy to destroy our
>        society, the fact that he does or tries to
>        do so first cannot make it any less of an
>        injustice for us to destroy his. . . .
>        This kind of reprisal can only be justified
>        by a very immoral "moral" system, or by a
>        positivism that seeks to "make" right in
>        the second place what was ruled to be wrong
>        in the first.[20]

     Ramsey clearly rejects "all-out" or total nuclear
war as a morally possible option.  He affirms, however,
that it is not the nature of the weapon (including
multimegaton weapons), but the nature of the target and
the user's intentions that are the morally relevant
elements.  That is, if an appropriate target can be
identified, and the right conditions exist, it is not
intrinsically wrong to use nuclear weapons.  In The
Limits of Nuclear War, published in 1965, Ramsey stated
that, "counter-force nuclear war is the upper limit of
rational, politically purposive military action."[21]
Thus, he does not reject the use of tactical nuclear
weapons, or even strategic weapons in clearly defined
circumstances.  Ramsey appears reluctant to make
statements such as this, however, and he is quick to
delineate the targets and conditions which he believes
possibly justify the use of these weapons.
     Ramsey is not advocating the use of nuclear weapons;
rather, he is seeking to establish "firebreaks" or

"boundaries" in the use of force. At most, he would see
any use of nuclear weapons as a last resort in a supreme
emergency; but even a supreme emergency would not justify
the indiscriminate or disproportionate use of nuclear
weapons.

In discussing nuclear weapons, Ramsey's primary
endeavor was to modify deterrent strategies advocated in
the 1950s and 1960s. These included the now familiar
strategies of "massive retaliation," "optimum max,"
"counter-value," and "assured destruction," each of which
viewed large population centers as prime targets for
nuclear attack.[22]

In contravention to these, Ramsey offered his own
policy proposals for a strategy of deterrence and for the
"just conduct" of war in the nuclear age. These may be
outlined as follows: (1) To avoid excessive dependence
on nuclear weapons for defense and to counter non-nuclear
aggression this nation and other Western nations should
enlarge their subconventional and conventional forces.
(2) This nation should announce that "as a matter of
policy," we will never be the first to use strategic
nuclear weapons, or tactical ones against an enemy's
"heartland"; we will use tactical weapons, but only
against forces to stop an invasion across a clearly
defined boundary, "our own or one we are pledged by
treaty to defend." (3) This nation should maintain
nuclear capability for counter-forces retaliatory strikes
over an enemy's territory to dissuade his offensive use
of tactical nuclear weapons over the territory of another
nation. (4) We ought not _say_ to the enemy that we
possess tactical nuclear weapons only for deterrence and
that we do not _actually_ _intend_ to use them over his
territory. (5) Likewise, we should not announce that our
counter-forces nuclear strategy is "nothing but
deterrence." The capstone of this policy is the
deterrence of city destruction by the bluff of city
destruction. The enemy should expect to be counter
attacked in kind if he uses nuclear weapons.[23]

Ramsey qualifies these policy proposals by
differentiating between a "declared" deter-the-war policy
and an "actual" fight-the-war policy. Along with these
policy recommendations, he would pass a note under the
table to policy makers suggesting that they "declare"
their intentions to use these weapons, but not "actually"
intend to use them. Later, Ramsey modified his position
concerning an explicit "threat" or "bluff" to use nuclear
weapons against enemy cities. He concluded that such
threats were immoral because it is wrong to threaten what
is wrong to do. He did affirm, however:

> . . . it is moral to mount a deterrent whose
> effects flow from shared fear of the
> "collateral" (unintended civil) damage

unavoidably connected with targeting modern
weapons of war, especially nuclear weapons
upon legitimate military objectives. If the
letter defines justice in the actual conduct
of war, the former is a just form of
deterrence. The one is just war; the
other is the just use of the non-use of
weapons.[24]

Ramsey appears to suggest in these comments that
strategic weapons should be maintained primarily for the
sake of deterrence, and actually used only as a limited,
defensive response against legitimate military targets
(e.g., enemy nuclear force), not population targets
(i.e., noncombatants). We should not hold cities
"hostage" with nuclear weapons. We should not tell the
enemy that we are going to target his civilian
population; but the enemy will recognize that unintended
civil damage is an inevitable by-product of fusion
weapons, an effect that enhances deterrence. We should
not say to the enemy that we will not use nuclear weapons
for defense; and we should say to the enemy that his
nuclear force has deterred us from first use of strategic
weapons.

Ramsey's response to our basic questions may be
summarized as follows: He sees just-war doctrine as the
only viable moral position in the nuclear age, as in
previous ages. Strategic nuclear weapons should never be
used, first or in retaliation, directly against
noncombatant targets. Possibly they can be used in
counter attack against a military target if they do not
exceed the limits of proportionality. For Ramsey,
"all-out" nuclear war, or counter-society war, violates
the moral principles of noncombatant immunity,
proportionality and reasonable hope of success (all-out
nuclear war is "unwinable"). Tactical nuclear weapons
may be used in defense over "friendly" or border
territory against an invading force and within the
constraints of discrimination and proportion. Ramsey
considers the neutron bomb a more discriminating weapon
than current tactical weapons if it is true that its
radiation effect is shorter lasting.[25] In the sixties,
when Ramsey wrote his major works on war, he saw
maintaining a balance of nuclear force as the only
feasible deterrence to nuclear war. Therefore, he
advocated a defensive deterrent policy, supplemented by
efforts to negotiate arms reductions.

THE "OUTER LIMITS" OF JUST WAR--DETERRENCE:
MICHAEL WALZER

In the final analysis, it may well be that Hitler's
most menacing effect was his attempt to develop the

atomic bomb. Michael Walzer seems to agree with Niebuhr
that America had no moral choice but to win this arms
race. However, he sees no morally justifiable case for
the use of nuclear weapons! He criticizes their use at
Hiroshima and Nagasaki. Walzer insists that had our
policy toward Japan not wrongly been one of
"unconditional surrender," Truman's utilitarian argument
of fewer casualties (or lesser evil) would have been
inapplicable. He concludes that the atomic bombing of
Japan's cities was not a case of military necessity
resulting from a "supreme emergency."[26]

Walzer's invoking of military necessity at this
point in his argument seems to imply that a supreme
emergency may justify some use of nuclear weapons. The
remainder of his argument, however, largely refutes this
interpretation. On the following page in _Just and Unjust
Wars_ he states:

> Truman used the atomic bomb to end a war that
> seemed to him limitless in its horrors. And
> then, for a few minutes or hours in August
> 1945, the people of Hiroshima endured a war
> that actually was limitless in its
> horrors. . . . Atomic war was death indeed,
> indiscriminate and total, and after
> Hiroshima, the first task of political
> leaders everywhere was to prevent its
> recurrence.
>
> The means they adopted is the promise of
> reprisal in kind. Against the threat of
> an immoral attack, they have put the threat
> of an immoral response. This is the basic
> form of nuclear deterrence.[27]

As the last paragraph of this quotation implies,
Walzer, too, is more interested in discussing deterrence.
We will pursue his argument on this subject after we
detail his view on the use of strategic and tactical
weapons. Walzer clearly rejects "all-out" nuclear war
with strategic weapons. He agrees with Ramsey that
initiating a large-scale attack, or responding in kind,
is morally unthinkable. In his words:

> It is a feature of massive retaliation that
> while there is or may be some rational
> purpose in threatening it, there could be
> none in carrying it out. Were our "bluff"
> ever to be called and our population centers
> suddenly attacked, the resulting war could
> not (in any usual sense of the word) be
> "won". We could only drag our enemies
> after us into the abyss. The use of our

deterrent capacity would be an act of pure
destructiveness. For this reason, massive
retaliation, if not literally unthinkable[28]
has always seemed undo-able.

Walzer goes beyond Ramsey, however, in rejecting
attempts to fit nuclear war within the limits of
just-war. Though "tactical and counter-force warfare
meets the formal requirements of jus in bello," it is
unacceptable because it violates proportionality limits.
Even if legitimate military targets were attacked, the
cost in human life would exceed the value of the target.
In an exchange of strategic missiles the number of people
killed, even as "collateral damage," could not be
justified by the goals of the war--"particularly since
the dead would include many if not most of the people for
whose defense the war was being fought. . . ."[29]
Walzer also rejects limited nuclear war, or the use
of tactical weapons, because of the probability of
escalation. He affirms: "It is not necessarily the case
that every war would become a total war, but the danger
of escalation is so great as to preclude the first use of
nuclear weapons--except by someone willing to face their
final use."[30]
For Walzer, then, the use of strategic weapons is
unthinkable because of their disproportionate damage; and
the use of tactical weapons is also unthinkable because
this could lead to the use of strategic weapons.
If, in Walzer's view, it is wrong to use nuclear
weapons, is it also immoral to possess them for the sake
of deterrence? In short his answer is "yes," but for the
moment such possession is necessary. It is wrong to
threaten the use of these weapons, but not as wrong as
the actual use; and if possessing them prevents the
actual use, it is necessary to keep a "balance of terror"
until a better way can be found. "Against an enemy
actually willing to use the bomb, self-defense is
impossible, and it makes sense to say that the only
compensating step is the (immoral) threat to respond in
kind. No country capable of making such a threat is
likely to refuse to make it."[31]
"Mutual disarmament" is a clearly preferable
alternative for Walzer, but he recognizes that it is an
alternative available only to countries willing to work
closely together. Deterrence is the "likely choice" of
any nation working alone. Thus, he concludes:

Supreme emergency has become a permanent
condition. Deterrence is a way of coping
with that condition, and though it is a
bad way there may well be no other that
is practical in a world of sovereign and
suspicious states. We threaten evil in

order not to do it, and the doing of it
would be so terrible that the threat
seems in comparison to be morally
defensible.[32]

The temporary possession of nuclear weapons,
according to Walzer, is necessary in the present context
to prevent the use of nuclear weapons. He supports a
policy of deterrence and urges steps to increase its
stability. Nevertheless, deterrence is an immoral threat
to use immoral weapons; and "our familiar notions about
jus in bello require us to condemn even the threat to use
them." He adds, however, that other, also familiar,
notions having to do with aggression and the right of
self-defense, "seem to require exactly that threat. So
we move uneasily beyond the limits of justice for the
sake of justice (and of peace)."[33]

Walzer's answers to our questions are summarized as
follows: The doctrine of just-war defines the moral
limits of war in the nuclear age. Nuclear war is
prohibited because it goes beyond the limits of moral
criteria. "Nuclear deterrence marks their outer
limits. . . . Nuclear war is and will remain morally
unacceptable, and there is no case for its
rehabilitation." Though deterrence for the moment falls
"under the standard of necessity," it is a "bad way" of
preventing nuclear war, and "other ways" must be
sought.[34]

DESIGNING A MORALLY USABLE DEFENSE: JAMES T. JOHNSON

In our discussion of nuclear weapons and strategy,
our approach has been sequential. Niebuhr and Ramsey
were leading Protestant spokesmen of the fifties and
sixties. Walzer, a political philosopher of Jewish
heritage has been a dominate voice in the late seventies
and in the current discussion. James Johnson, whose
historical work in reconstructing just-war tradition has
been treated above, has in recent writings turned to
consider the normative implications of this tradition for
contemporary war. As Walzer urged, Johnson is seeking
"other ways" of answering the nuclear dilemma. Johnson
states his thesis as follows: "If the potential or
actual use of military force is to be envisioned as a
moral possibility, then it behooves us to design that
force so that it can be used morally."[35]

Johnson believes that there are national and human
values worth defending, even if this requires military
force. The upper levels of our means of defense, that
is, the strategic and possibly the tactical nuclear
weapons presently deployed, may not be morally usable.
Therefore, if we are to defend our values without

sacrificing them, we have "a moral imperative to develop
effective means of war" that may be used morally. This
requires the production of weapons that can deter or
defend against nuclear weapons and yet not themselves
exceed the limits of proportionality and noncombatant
immunity. With Niebuhr, Ramsey, and Walzer, Johnson
insists that deterrence is essential. The principle
moral problem is that, since the inception of nuclear
weapons, deterrent strategy has targeted population
centers. This was true of "massive retaliation" in the
fifties, and it remains true (though to a lesser degree)
of the current "countervailing strategy."[36]

In opposition to this feature of deterrence, Johnson
agrees with Ramsey that as a first step, "counter-force"
targeting of strategic and tactical weapons is morally
required. He doubts, however, that targets can be
identified against which the largest existing weapons
could be morally used. As the nature of the targets is
not likely to change substantially, the weapons must. He
concludes that just-war reasoning implies that:

> Nuclear weapons of the strategic type, and
> probably also relatively low-yield but
> "dirty" weapons of the tactical type,
> could probably not justifiably be employed
> in war.

> This line of reasoning does not lead to an
> absolute ban on nuclear weaponry, though
> it does impose some rather strict moral
> ceilings on their use. . . ."nuclear-war
> pacifism". . . . may be correct in the
> context of contemporary nuclear weapons
> and counter population deterrent strategy.[37]

There is a great deal of talk these days about the
"risk" of nuclear war. The reaction to President
Reagan's comments in October/November 1981 about the
possibility of using nuclear weapons in Europe,
demonstrates the level of this concern. Any mention of
the "use" of nuclear weapons ignites fervent discussion
about the risk of nuclear war. Johnson is also acutely
aware of the risk associated with deterrence. After
acknowledging the claim that deterrent strategy has
worked thus far, that is, there has been no nuclear war,
Johnson remarks:

> Nonetheless, so far as the nuclear deterrent
> element of United States defense policy is
> concerned, an enormous risk clearly exists
> that some event, whether accidental or
> designed, will produce a massive nuclear
> interchange between the West and East.

Should this occur, it will be little
comfort indeed for critics to note that
the deterrent proved to be ineffective,
that the fact that these strategic arsenals
were used shows the whole policy to have
been a grand mistake.[38]

His conclusion that the weapons currently deployed
are probably morally unusable, combined with his
recognition of the "risk" involved in possessing these
weapons, leads Johnson to propose an alternative set of
propositions for guiding the development of a "morally
legitimate defense" strategy. He summarizes these
propositions as follows:

(1) Noncombatants should be protected from
the ravages of war, and a defense policy
specifically oriented around harm or a
threat to harm noncombatants is morally
wanting.
(2) Armaments should be judged morally not
in terms of whether they are nuclear or not
but rather in terms of their intended use
in war.
(3) A moral defense strategy should aim at
the development of weapons of defense and
offense that may be morally employed if need
arise.
(4) A defense strategy should be flexible and
thus should incorporate potential responses to
aggression at every conceivable level from a
simple military presence up to and including
all-out war. This implies a much heavier
reliance on conventional forces than we now
have.
(5) A moral defense strategy for the United
States should involve resumption of the
military draft.[39]

Johnson's first two proposals come directly out of
the just-war criteria. For him, as well as for Ramsey,
the immunity of noncombatants is the central principle of
the just-war tradition. It is the moral driving force
behind arguments for "counter-force" targeting and
discriminating weapons. His emphasis on intentions
recognizes that conventional weapons can be used as
indiscriminately as nuclear weapons; and both kind have
the capacity for very immoral employment. Thus, drawing
the line between conventional and nuclear weapons is
inadequate. Focusing on the weapons rather than on the
people who use them is also inadequate. People, not
things (or weapons), are moral or immoral. The argument
that weapons dictate the end of war is utterly rejected

by Johnson. This is the kind of thinking that leads to warfare limited only by the technical capacity of weapons. He affirms: "Weapons are but tools of human intentions, and the reason we now live in a world where entire populations are threatened by nuclear missiles is that we have come to regard such threats as appropriate."[40]

It is not the weapons, but the assumptions about war of those who produce them and the intentions in war of those who use them that are morally questionable. If war is to be a moral possibility in the nuclear age, according to Johnson, we must begin with the recognition that people, not the weapons they use, are in control and that the people who control are themselves guided by moral principles.

This leads him to this third point. People developing strategy for a morally legitimate defense should develop morally usable weapons which can replace strategic nuclear weapons. "This, I believe, is the real key to nuclear disarmament."[41] After briefly surveying the history of arms control efforts, he concludes that "an effective ban on nuclear weapons is likely to be possible only after replacements have been found that limit their utility and/or surpass them in the effects desired." To be both effective and morally usable, these new weapons must adequately deter war and protect our highest values, and they must be discriminating and proportionate counter-force weapons.

What kind of weapons does he see qualifying under this criteria? He considers the land-based MX missile and anti-ballistic missile system as basically "more of the same," without significant military or moral advantages. He advocates movement toward a line of defense located in lower space. This would include developing military applications for the space shuttle and laser technology. Johnson is not certain about the technical possibilities or the effect of a "space war" on the atmosphere. Morally, however, he sees such development as a definite improvement. Such a means of defense "amounts to removing the theater of potential war away from populated areas . . ."[42] and thus represents an attempt to guarantee the protection of noncombatants.

He also sees the deployment of the "neutron bomb" and the cruise missile as progress toward more morally acceptable means of defense, as the following quotation indicates:

> Insofar, then, as tactical neutron warheads may be used in the counter-force mode intended, and insofar as the claim is true that they are relatively less destructive of property and produce shorter-lived radiation effects than equivalent fission weapons (whose major

power lies in their blast effect, like
conventional explosives), the deployment of
tactical fusion (or "neutron") warheads
represents a step toward achieving the
twin moral goals of limited, proportionate
warfare with as low as possible an effect
on the lives of noncombatants.

As far as the cruise missile is concerned,
suffice it here to say that the accuracy
of such missiles under real conditions as
compared with ballistic missiles is claimed
to be significantly improved, making
possible the use of small warheads, and
holding open the possibility of substituting
conventional for nuclear warheads in a
significant number of instances. I do not,
I hasten to say, know whether this potential
for restraint has been realized, but to
do so would be a morally appropriate step.[43]

In discussing new types of weapons, Johnson is not
so much interested in identifying specific items of
military hardware as he is in outlining morally
sufficient characteristics and pointing in the right
direction. He sees his weapons recommendations as
incremental steps toward nuclear-arms reductions and
eventually an elimination òf the need to rely on such
weapons for deterrence. This intention is associated
with his fourth proposal, that we should be capable of
"flexible response." His position is basically
consistent with countervailing strategy, that we should
be prepared to respond to aggression at all possible
levels. Though Johnson recognizes the moral
justification of preemptive strikes under certain
conditions, he counsels extreme caution on use of these
weapons and urges a "no all-out response" policy for
nuclear weapons. But, fundamentally, an ethical response
today requires finding new weapons and reducing our
thirty-year reliance on nuclear weapons by increasing
conventional forces. To expand our conventional
capability, however, involves other considerations, not
the least of which is economic. Conventional forces are
expensive. This, in part, is what led to our
over-reliance on nuclear weapons. To solve the economic
burden of personnel costs, Johnson advocates a resumption
of the military draft. His reasons for resuming
conscription, however, are more than economic. Like
Rousseau, he believes that the "burdens of citizenship"
should be equally shared.[44] Therefore a fair
selective-service system that produces a military force
"more closely representative of the nation's citizenry"
is preferable to the all-volunteer force of today, "which

is disproportionately composed of the poor, the poorly
educated, and the nonwhite."[45]

TOWARD A JUST DEFENSE WITHOUT NUCLEAR WEAPONS?:
THE ROMAN CATHOLIC DISCUSSION

A strange anomaly characterizes religious
perspectives in the contemporary world, and especially in
American Christianity.  There are frequently greater
differences in belief within denominations than between
denominations.  I mean by this statement that positions
held on many issues cannot be differentiated along
denominational lines.  This is particularly true
concerning the positions held by Roman Catholics on the
issues associated with war and nuclear weapons.
Positions advocated by various clergy today range from
traditional pacifism to armed revolution.  The debate
within the Church is a microcosm of the larger debate.
Indeed, many Catholics are leaders in the anti-nuclear[46]
movement and leaders in the national defense program.
Indicative of the direction of the Catholic
discussion is Bishop Terence Cardinal Cooke's recent
letter to Catholic military chaplains, in which he
considered it necessary to address two principal
questions:  "(1) Has the Church changed its position on
military service?  (2) Must a Catholic refuse to have[47]
anything at all to do with nuclear weapons?"
Cardinal Cooke's answer to these questions, essentially,
is "no".
Several factors have contributed to the current
diversity among Roman Catholics, including official
acknowledgement by the Church of pacifism as a legitimate
moral position; a renewed emphasis on human rights; a
recognition of the destructive capacity of nuclear
arsenals; the development of new weapons and the lack of
significant progress in arms-limitation negotiations;
rhetoric about "fighting" and "winning" a nuclear war;
and the often quoted call by Vatican Council II for "an[48]
evaluation of war with an entirely new attitude."
These factors have led Catholics to a fundamental
reevaluation of the use of military force.  Writing in
1980, Thomas A. Shannon offered the following description
of Catholic positions in regard to nuclear issues:

> Nuclear warfare, together with deterrence
> policies based on the possession of these
> weapons, has challenged the way many think
> about war.  For some, the implications of
> nuclear warfare are so overwhelming and
> morally unacceptable that a new kind of
> pacifist has been born, the nuclear pacifist,
> one who could justify and participate in

a conventional or traditional just-war, but
who could do neither if nuclear weapons were
used. For others, the use of nuclear weapons
was the <u>coup de grace</u> for the just-war theory,
for they showed its total inadequacy for
analyzing contemporary warfare. The framework and theory of statecraft assumed by the
just-war theory no longer addressed the
modern world, it was argued, and new models
for analysis would have to be found. Still
others thought the categories of the just-
war theory were adequate to handle nuclear
warfare, especially when the primary issue
was deterrence rather than the actual use
of such weapons. The legitimacy of this
position was further enhanced by the development of strategic nuclear weapons. Such
varieties of positions have stimulated a
new debate on the just-war theory, both
formally and substantively.[49]

It is my observation that among Catholics there has
been a general edging from the traditional just-war view
toward the position identified by Shannon as "nuclear
pacifism."[50] This observation is based on three
recurring themes in papal statements in this period.
These themes include recognition of the right of states
for legitimate defense, condemnation of aggressive
warfare, and rejection of the use of weapons of "mass
destruction" (i.e., strategic nuclear weapons). As not
all Catholic thinkers have reached similar conclusions on
papal statements, these themes require closer analysis.
Unquestionably there is a growing prejudice in Catholic
thought against modern warfare as a means for resolving
international conflict.
Just-war doctrine has been the central moral
position on war held by the Catholic Church since the
fifth century. However, in the eighteenth and nineteenth
centuries the doctrine was ignored by Catholic
theologians. Revulsion at the massive destruction and
death in World War I led Alfred Vanderpol and others to
again think in just-war terms about limiting the causes
of war. Pope Pius XII, who presided over the Church
during and after World War II, "both affirmed the
just-war ethic and modified its content."[51] He
affirmed the right of states to legitimate defense; but
he reduced the legitimate causes of war from three
(defense, avenging evil, and restoring violated rights)
to one: the "defense of one's nation or of others being
unjustly attacked."[52] He rejected aggressive war, but
not defensive war, and he did not proscribe absolutely
nuclear weapons.

The mood of the Catholic Church began to change during the pontificate of John XXIII (1958-1963). His last encyclical <u>Pacem in Terris</u> (1963) has been classified by some as a "pacifist" document. Others, including Bryan Hehir, Paul Ramsey, and Bishop O'Connor, believe that John XXIII remained in the just-war tradition as formulated by Pius XII. Hehir characterizes Pope John's position as a "toleration of the use of force" for defensive purposes, "not a moral endorsement."[53] The most controversial passage in <u>Pacem in Terris</u> is one which reads: "Thus, in the age which boasts of its atomic power, it no longer makes sense to maintain that war is a fit instrument with which to repair the violation of justice."[54] Ramsey and others argue that this is not a rejection of defensive war to stop aggression still in progress. <u>Pacem in Terris</u> is an urgent plea for the recognition of human rights, stable national and international order, and peaceful methods for resolving conflict.

Explicit endorsement of the pacifist position was given, not by John XXIII, but by the ecumenical council which he called, Vatican Council II (1962-1965). Though he died shortly after the council opened, his pastoral spirit dominated the tone of deliberations. It is also important to note that Vatican Council II occurred during the years of sharpest controversy in the earlier nuclear debate. Simultaneously with the meeting of the council, Ramsey developed his "graduated deterrence" strategy for "counter-force" warfare, based largely on the just-war criteria of discrimination, or noncombatant immunity. The Vatican II document which directly addresses the issues of war and modern weapons is entitled "Pastoral Constitution on the Church in the Modern World."[55]

Like <u>Pacem in Terris</u>, this document is also frequently cited by Catholic pacifists. Certainly the central theme of this document is a plea for peace.[56] But, in my estimate, the position espoused is firmly within the modern concept of just-war doctrine. The section on war begins with a critique of the savagery of modern war, including scientific weapons (e.g., nuclear), the practices of terrorism and extermination (e.g., Nazi holocaust), and attempts to subjugate other nations. The document then urges support for international agreements and conventions on war. Moreover, it calls for legal provisions for "those who for reasons of conscience refuse to bear arms, provided however, that they accept some other form of service to the human community."[57]

The document also affirms that Catholic members serving the armed forces of their countries "should regard themselves as agents of security and freedom on behalf of their people. As long as they fulfill this role properly, they are making a genuine contribution to the establishment of peace."[58] The following statement, which is cited from this same section, is a concise summary of the just-war position:

> Certainly, war has not been rooted out of human affairs. As long as the danger of war remains and there is not competent and sufficiently powerful authority at the international level, governments cannot be denied the right to legitimate defense once every means of peaceful settlement has been exhausted.[59]

With this prelude, the council then turns to the question of "total war." Because "scientific weapons" can inflict "massive and indiscriminate destruction far exceeding the bounds of legitimate defense," the council called for "an evaluation of war with an entirely new attitude."[60] The council then condemns "total war" with the following declaration: "Any act of war aimed indiscriminately at the destruction of entire cities or of extensive areas along with their population is a crime against God and man himself. It merits unequivocal and unhesitating condemnation."[61]

On the question of the arms race, the document recognizes that at the present time scientific weapons "may" be the most effective way to "deter" possible enemy attack. Yet, the arms race is not a "safe" way to preserve peace and it is "an utterly treacherous trap for humanity, and one which injures the poor to an intolerable degree." Thus, the council again advocates "new approaches initiated by reformed attitudes" to remove this trap and restore genuine peace "by emancipating the world from crushing anxiety."[62]

The council goes on to call for all to work for the day when, by international consent, "all war can be completely outlawed." The attainment of this goal, the council recognizes, requires the establishment of "some universal public authority acknowledged as such by all, and endowed with effective power to safeguard, on behalf of all, security, regard for justice, and respect for rights." Until this universal authority is set up, the council calls on international centers to seek vigorously better means for obtaining common security.

> Hence, everyone must labor to put an end at last to the arms race, and to make a true beginning of disarmament, not indeed a unilateral disarmament, but one proceeded at an equal pace according to agreement, and backed up by authentic and workable safeguards. (Underline added.)[63]

While this is not a pacifist document, as some claim, it is a call for peace and mutual nuclear disarmament, accompanied by a recognition of the right of national defense, with arms sufficient to deter aggression. Until such time when nuclear weapons are eliminated, the council, like Ramsey, using the principle of discrimination, rejects all strategy for their use that involves "counter-population" or "counter-city" attacks. Pacem in Terris and "The Pastoral Constitution on the Church in the Modern World" (Vatican II) are seminal documents in the contemporary Catholic discussion. They contain the seeds from which current positions have developed.

Probably all parties in the contemporary debate would see themselves as seeking ways to prevent war and as laboring to put an end to the arms race. All would condemn wars of aggression and war as a means for settling international dispute, though probably a majority would recognize the right of national defense. The differences in current positions lie primarily in the means deemed appropriate for achieving these ends. Some advocate a strategy permitting limited, counter-forces warfare using tactical nuclear weapons as a last resort for defensive purposes, but reject any use of strategic nuclear weapons. Some within this position permit the retention of nuclear weapons for purposes of deterrence. Still others condemn even the possession of nuclear weapons, because the "threat" (inherent in deterrence) of using them is immoral. Many contemporary thinkers follow the Vatican II theme of urging the development of a stronger international authority as the structure for common defense. A significant number also support the "freezing" of nuclear arms production combined with negotiated arms reductions leading to mutual nuclear disarmament. A smaller number of Catholics advocate nuclear disarmament, initiated unilaterally if necessary. Perhaps a similar number reject recourse to war for any cause, even defensive, by the superpowers, because of the potential for escalation to nuclear weapons. And some claim that no war is possible in the modern age because of the destructiveness of both conventional and nuclear weapons.[64]

As I indicated earlier, it is impossible to identify "the position" held by Catholics on these issues today. Bishop O'Connor, however, does offer the following conclusions, which he suggests constitute the current position of the Church, though he cautions that the "official" position is still evolving.

> (1) The Church condemns war of aggression, unlimited war, acts of war "directed to the indiscriminate destruction of whole cities or vast areas with their inhabitants," the use

of weapons of mass destruction.
(2) The Church does not condemn defensive war,
limited war, acts of war directed to the
destruction of military targets, the manufacture or possession of nuclear weapons,
the use of weapons of limited destruction.
(3) The Church seriously questions the
strategy of nuclear deterrence, abhors the
arms race, considering it a treacherous
trap for humanity, potentially destructive
of all life, and draining resources
critically needed to feed the hungry and
generally advance civilization.
(4) The Church calls for the eventual goal
of banning nuclear weapons, urging that in
the meanwhile, there be continuing, balanced,
mutual, progressive reductions in nuclear
weapons "backed up by authentic and workable
safeguards," and urging negotiations and
treaties that will help reduce risks of
nuclear war.[65]

CONCLUSION

In this chapter I have attempted to establish a
bridge between the discussion of the just-war tradition
and the contemporary public debate on nuclear weapons. I
have surveyed what leading just-war ethicists have said
about nuclear weapons and deterrence in the last thirty
years to provide a context for understanding the current
debate. The Roman Catholic discussion was introduced in
this chapter for two reasons. First, the Catholic Church
has traditionally advocated the just-war position and,
therefore, it is included as a part of what just-war
ethicists are saying about nuclear war. Secondly, the
Catholic dialogue serves as an overview to the larger
debate on nuclear weapons. The varying positions among
Catholics comprise a catalogue of the major positions
held by other religious groups.
What can be said in conclusion about the positions
held by Ramsey, Walzer, and Johnson concerning the basic
questions we are discussing? Each has affirmed that the
just-war doctrine is essential for evaluating the
morality of non-nuclear warfare. Each believes that this
doctrine provides at least a set of "formal" criteria by
which to judge the weapons and strategies of nuclear
warfare and deterrence. These three ethicists have also
concluded that deterrence is "risky" and undesirable, but
for the moment justified for preventing nuclear war. As
long as the Soviet Union (or another potential adversary)
possesses nuclear weapons, so should the United States as
a means to prevent the use of these weapons. Concerning

the use of nuclear weapons, positions vary. Each rejects the "all-out" use of strategic weapons for any cause, including response or retaliation. For Ramsey any use of strategic or tactical weapons must be limited, a last reasonable resort, and directed only at "counter-force" targets. Even then, many military targets may be disqualified because of unintended, disproportionate, and indiscriminate collateral damage. In discussing the use of nuclear weapons, Ramsey is primarily seeking to establish "firebreaks" for deterring the use of these weapons.

Johnson concludes that, in general, strategic and some tactical nuclear weapons are probably morally unusable in their present form. But he advocates dealing with the moral dilemma thus posed by developing a credible non-nuclear military force, both for deterrence and, if necessary, for use. With Ramsey, he considers the development of "counter-force" strategy and weapons such as the cruise missile and neutron bomb as steps in the right direction. Walzer's conclusion is brief: nuclear weapons are morally unusable! Strategic weapons are indiscriminate and disproportionate. Tactical weapons cannot be used because, even if determined not to be indiscriminate and disproportionate (which is questionable for him), their use, in all probability, will result in escalation to strategic weapons. The Catholic discussion includes all of these positions, plus the further conclusion by some that nuclear weapons have eliminated the possibility of a just (justifiable?) war in the present age.

Thus, just-war ethicists continue to use the doctrine of just war; some to conclude that war involving nuclear weapons is "barely possible," under extreme conditions; others to conclude that war involving nuclear weapons is morally unjustifiable.


NOTES

1. Editorial, Worldview (Jul-Aug 1960), cited from Ramsey, The Just War, p. 150.

2. Stein, ed., Nuclear Weapons and Christian Conscience (London: Merlin Press, 1961), published in the United States as Nuclear Weapons: A Catholic Response (New York: Sheed and Ward, 1962), p. 142. Cited from Potter, War and Moral Discourse, p. 120.

3. O'Connor, In Defense of Life (Boston: Daughters of St. Paul, 1981), pp. 17 and 18. Bishop O'Connor is presenting these statements as examples of the thought of some contemporary Roman Catholics in America.

4. Frank C. Massey, personal letter to Donald L. Davidson, 23 February 1982.

5. This statement was originally published in an article entitled "The Case for Making 'Just War' Possible" in 1960, which was reprinted in The Just War (1968), p. 164.

6. U.S. Army Field Manual 100-1: The Army, p. 21.

7. Niebuhr did not specifically advocate the just-war tradition. His "ethical realism," however, contains the basic insights of this tradition.

8. This was Churchill's reaction after the bombing of Hiroshima and Nagasahi. See Walzer, Just and Unjust Wars, p. 267.

9. Niebuhr, "The Atomic Bomb," Christianity and Society (Fall 1945), reprinted in Love and Justice: Selections from the Shorter Writings of Reinhold Neibuhr, ed. D. B. Robertson (Glaucester, MA: Peter Smith, 1976), p. 232.

10. Ibid., p. 233.

11. Ibid., pp. 234-35.

12. Niebuhr, "The Hydrogen Bomb," Love and Justice, p. 235.

13. Ibid., p. 237.

14. Ibid., p. 237.

15. Ibid., p. 237.

16. Niebuhr, "Is There Another Way," Love and Justice, p. 301.

17. Ramsey, The Just War, pp. 198-200.

18. Ibid., p. 154.

19. Ibid., p. 154.

20. Ibid., pp. 245, 247-48.

21. Cited from The Just War, p. 214.

22. For further information on these strategies, see The Just War, Chapter 11; and Strategic Thought in the

<u>Nuclear Age</u>, Lawrence Martin, ed. (Baltimore: Johns
Hopkins Press, 1980), Chapter 5, "The Evolution of
Strategic Nuclear Doctrine," by Henry S. Rowen.

23. Ramsey, <u>The Just War</u>, pp. 235-45.

24. Ibid., p. 315.

25. See "Consider the Morning Glory" by Ramsey in
<u>Worldview</u> 20 (December 1977).

26. Walzer, <u>Just and Unjust Wars</u>, p. 268.

27. Ibid., p. 269.

28. Ibid., pp. 274-75.

29. Ibid., pp. 276-77.

30. Ibid.

31. Ibid., p. 274.

32. Ibid.

33. Ibid., p. 282. Also personal interview,
26 April 1982, Institute of Advanced Studies, Princeton,
New Jersey.

34. Ibid., p. 283.

35. Johnson, "Morally Legitimate Defense," <u>Warfare
in the 1990's</u>, proceedings of a conference sponsored by
the Institute for Theological Encounter with Science and
Technology, 9-11 October 1981, p. 44.

36. See Presidential Directive 59.

37. Johnson, <u>Just War Tradition</u>, p. 364.

38. Johnson, "Morally Legitimate Defense," p. 30.
Ironically, Johnson's work may be criticized by those who
do not distinguish "types" of nuclear weapons or who
believe that the use of any type may escalate to unusable
weapons. This is because he too, though in different
way, talks about the "use" of nuclear weapons. His
position would appear to conflict with Walzer's statement
that "nuclear war is and will remain morally
unacceptable, and there is no case for its
rehabilitation" (<u>Just and Unjust Wars</u>, p. 283). Johnson,
himself, points out that efforts to move deterrent
strategies toward "counter-force" warfare have been
opposed on the grounds that they reduce the fear

associated with nuclear weapons and, thus, increase the possibility of their use. Protests of this nature occurred after McNamara's announcement of a shift to "counter-force" targeting in 1962, the introduction of the neutron bomb, and President Carter's publicizing of "countervailing strategy" in 1979. I understand Johnson's position, however, to be one of "incremental steps" in arms reductions, which could lead to the elimination of indiscriminate and disproportionate weapons, and thus avoid escalation to unusable weapons.

39. Johnson, "Morally Legitimate Defense," pp. 31-32.

40. Ibid., p. 44.

41. Ibid., p. 37.

42. Ibid., p. 39.

43. Ibid., pp. 40-41. For a longer discussion by Johnson on the cruise and neutron weapons, see "The Cruise Missile and the Neutron Bomb: Some Moral Reflections," Worldview 20 (December 1977): 20-26.

44. Ibid., pp. 42-43.

45. Ibid. In 1977 Johnson admitted that increasing the size of the conventional force, reducing reliance on nuclear forces, (i.e., trading technology for manpower), and reinstating the draft, though logically related and morally preferable solutions, were politically difficult issues with much public opposition. See "On 'No First Use' of Nuclear Weapons," Worldview 20 (March 1977): 43-44.

46. This observation is not intended to imply that all Catholics support the anti-nuclear movement or that Catholics are the exclusive or even principal leaders of this movement. This is not the case. In a recent demonstration at the gates of Fort Monmouth, NJ, the protesters included at least Catholics, Quakers, Presbyterians, and representatives from anti-nuclear groups which are independent from official ecclesiastical structures. See "Anti-Nuclear Protesters Warn of Possibility of Annihilation," Asbury Park Press, 14 March 1982, p. A16; and "Catholics Reassess Beliefs on War in Nuclear Age," The New York Times, 23 December 1981, p. A16.

47. Military Vicariate, 1011 First Avenue, New York, NY 10022, letter dated 7 December 1981. Cardinal Cooke

is the Military Vicar for Catholics serving in the United
States military services.

48. "Pastoral Constitution on the Church in the
Modern World," The Documents of Vatican II, ed. Walter M.
Abbott, S.J. (New York: The American Press, 1966),
p. 293.

49. Shannon, War or Peace? The Search for New
Answers (Maryknoll, NY: Orbis Books, 1980), p. x.
Hereafter cited as War or Peace?

50. I would argue, however, that Shannon's
description of "nuclear pacifism" is still well within
the limits of the just-war tradition (see sections on
Michael Walzer and James Johnson above). I am suggesting
that the first and third positions he identifies are both
nuances within the just-war doctrine. This concept seems
consistent with the thought of J. Bryan Hehir (see War or
Peace?, pp. 22-25), a leading Catholic spokesman.

51. J. Bryan Hehir, "The Just-War Ethic and Catholic
Theology: Dynamics of Change and Continuity," in War or
Peace?, p. 17.

52. Ibid.

53. Ibid., p. 20.

54. Cited from O'Connor, In Defense of Life, p. 39.
Understanding of this passage is complicated by varying
translations, see O'Connor, In Defense of Life, p. 42 and
Ramsey, The Just War, pp. 192f, 204f.

55. Frequently, this document is identified by its
Latin title, Gaudium et Spes.

56. The discussion of war is included in the section
entitled "The Avoidance of War," which together with
another section, "Building Up the International
Community," comprise the chapter entitled "The Fostering
of Peace and the Promotion of a Community of Nations."

57. The Documents of Vatican II, p. 292.

58. Ibid., p. 293.

59. Ibid., pp. 292-93.

60. Ibid., p. 293.

61. Ibid., p. 294.

62.   Ibid., p. 295.

63.   Ibid., p. 296.

64.   It is ironic that in some parts of the world,
other ordained members of the Catholic Church advocate
wars of revolution and intervention for the preservation
or recovery of human rights.  This fact identifies a
crucial, ethical problem in the modern world.  Frequently
our ethical conclusions are formed in a limited context
(e.g., the nuclear arms race).  These then conflict with
conclusions reached in another context (e.g., a Third
World country).  I am not saying that conclusions cannot
vary with the context; I am suggesting that we should
strive for consistency in basic principles.  If the basic
premise that using force to defend life is morally wrong
(or right) in one context, this should hold in other
contexts.  The positions held on this basic premise is
the distinction between pacifism and the just-war
position.  In the preceeding paragraph in the text
quantitative adjectives (e.g., "some," "many") were used
to indicate the relative strengths of various positions.
I make no claim for specific numerical accuracy in these
general comments.  Hopefully, this can be clarified in
subsequent chapters (but I have no great expectation that
this is possible).

65.   O'Connor, _In Defense of Life_, p. 83.

# [ 4 ]
# The Roman Catholic Discussion:
# A Closer Look

INTRODUCTION

The fifty million Roman Catholics in America equal
23 percent of the national population. The Catholic
Church is four times larger than any other religious body
in the United States. It has more members than all of
the churches affiliated with the National Council of
Churches, an organization of Protestant and Orthodox
bodies. Therefore, a closer look at the positions
advocated by this powerful moral force in American
society is warranted.

In the previous chapter we sketched an overview of
various views within the Church, and then concluded with
Bishop O'Connor's description of the Church's "official"
position. O'Connor is viewed by many Catholics as a
conservative voice representing traditional thought in
the Church. These critics also point out that the
Church's official position changes slowly and one must
look at the nuances within official documents to detect
the emerging trends. These nuances, they claim, when
combined with the general nature of official statements,
suggest that the Church is slowly moving from the
just-war position identified by O'Connor toward "nuclear
pacifism" and the historic position of "pacifism."

Indications of this movement can be seen in the
shifting positions of many American bishops in recent
years. The number of bishops affiliated with Pax
Christi, an unofficial organization that primarily
advocates the pacifist position, has increased from three
to approximately sixty.[1] Brother Austin David, FSC, of
the Pope John Paul II Center for Prayer and Study for
Peace (founded December 1981), estimates that possibly
one-third of the approximately 280 active American
Bishops have identified themselves with the Catholic
Peace movement.[2] These figures show movement among
Catholics, but they also suggest that Hehir is correct
when he observes that the "pacifist response has found a
growing receptivity among Catholics in our own day," but

the "dominant" position "still reflected in the teaching
of the Church today" is the just-war tradition.[3]
    In this chapter we review the early development of
the American Catholic peace movement, and then focus on
Pax Christi U.S.A., which represents the position
supported by some 20 percent of the active American
bishops.  Also we analyze statements by four bishops who
are influential advocates within the current peace
movement.  Finally, we conclude with an assessment of the
pastoral letter issued by the National Conference of
Catholic Bishops in May 1983.


ROOTS OF THE CATHOLIC PEACE MOVEMENT

    Thomas C. Cornell identifies Dorothy Day and the
Catholic Worker movement which she co-founded in 1933 as
the principle antecedents of the present Catholic
pacifist movement.[4]  Catholic Worker is the name of the
organization and periodical established by Day.  Like the
early Reinhold Niebuhr, Day associated with the communist
movement in America and adopted an "uncompromising
pacifist stance."[5]  The Catholic Worker vigorously
opposed World War II and the Korean War.  Through a front
organization called the Association of Catholic
Conscientious Objectors, the Catholic Worker established
a camp in New Hampshire for training conscientious
objectors.  In the 1950s Day and the Catholic Worker
became increasingly active in civil disobedience by
demonstrating against nuclear weapons and the National
Civil Defense program.  The next decade Dorothy Day,
Thomas Merton, Gordon C. Zahn, Eileen Egan, Daniel and
Philip Berrigan, and James H. Forrest were instrumental
in founding the Catholic Peace Fellowship as an affiliate
unit within the Fellowship of Reconciliation, an
international, interreligious pacifist organization.
    Cornell indicates that in 1963 the Catholic Worker
led the first protest in America against U.S. involvement
in the Vietnam War and against "Diem Tyranny."[6]  Within
two years the means of protest had escalated from quiet
vigils to burning draft cards, draft resistance and other
forms of civil disobedience.  Then on 8 November 1965 a
Catholic Worker staff volunteer named Roger LaPorte set
himself ablaze before the United Nations building to
protest the war in Vietnam.  Before his death LaPorte
declared:  "I am a Catholic.  I am against all war."[7]
    In 1967 Philip and Daniel Berrigan and others raided
the Selective Service office in Cantonsville, Maryland,
and seized draft records, which they promptly burned with
homemade napalm.  This action was followed by similar
raids across the country by protesters often recruited
from local Catholic Worker organizations.  But, the
excesses of LaPorte and of Berrigan-type raids soon

persuaded Dorothy Day, the Catholic Worker organizations
and the Catholic Peace Fellowship to turn primarily to
mass demonstrations, draft counseling and other
nonviolent forms of protest.

PAX CHRISTI U.S.A.

Gordon Zahn, one of the early supporters of the
Catholic Peace Fellowship, was also a principal organizer
of Pax Christi U.S.A. This organization is an affiliate
of Pax Christi International, established in 1945 in
France. Though not an official organ of the Catholic
Church, Joseph Fahey affirms that Pax Christi received
the "blessing" and "approval" of the Pope in 1947 and
again in 1948.[8]

Pax Christi U.S.A. was founded in 1973 from an
antecedent organization named "Pax," in existence from
1962-1972. The membership of this movement is open to
non-pacifists; however, the organization's goal is to
strive for peace through nonviolence, as its Statement of
Purpose indicates:

> Pax Christi U.S.A. intends to contribute to
> the building of peace and justice by exploring
> and articulating the ideal of Christian
> nonviolence and by striving to apply it to
> personal life and to the structures of
> society. Pax Christi U.S.A. invites
> concerned Catholics to respond to the
> Church's call to evaluate war with an
> entirely new attitude and to take an active
> role in making secure a peace based on
> justice and love.

> As a section of Pax Christi International,
> Pax Christi U.S.A. seeks with the help of
> its episcopal members to establish peace-
> making as a priority for the American
> Catholic Church. To accomplish this, Pax
> Christi U.S.A. will work with various
> Catholic communities and agencies, and
> will also collaborate with other groups
> committed to nonviolent peacemaking.

> Pax Christi U.S.A. will find its strength
> in the efforts of committed individuals to
> follow the Gospel imperative of peacemaking
> --an imperative repeated throughout the
> Christian tradition, most recently by Pope
> Paul VI: "If peace is truly desired, then
> it is possible, and if it is possible, then
> it is a duty."[9]

In further defining its purpose, the organization cites five priorities which it supports. The first of these is "to foster both nuclear and general disarmament." Pax Christi believes that "the construction and possession of nuclear weapons represents a profound immorality in the contemporary world." Secondly, the organization promotes a strong global authority as an agency for meeting human needs justly and nonviolently. In pursuit of this goal, Pax Christi International supports the United Nations and is represented at this body as a non-governmental organization. Thirdly, Pax Christi supports "all who, for reasons of conscience, refuse to bear arms" and who conscientiously object to particular wars. It endorses the establishment of a "World Peace Tax Fund" with the provision that individuals could designate part of their taxes to be used by the fund in support of peace groups, peace education, and human needs. The fourth priority is to "examine" militarism in the nation's schools and to replace ROTC programs with "courses of study in peace and justice." The last priority cited by Pax Christi is to "pursue the Gospel mandate of nonviolent living . . . and nonviolent civilian and social defense."[10]

According to Joseph Fahey, Pax Christi has come to question the "relevancy of just-war principles in contemporary times" because of the development of "indiscriminate weaponry" (i.e., nuclear weapons), the continuing arms race, and because Vatican Council II implicitly held that "there is no such thing as a 'just' nuclear war."[11] After analyzing recent trends in Catholic thought, Fahey observes:

> By further implication (and this must be placed in the full context of other papal and conciliar statements) it is clear that the very concept of a "just war" in this latter half of the twentieth century is not only questioned but challenged. Is the Catholic Church moving away from its centuries-old tradition of the "just war" and toward a positive philosophy of international relations that would outlaw war itself? The answer is patently "yes." But this does not, of course, mean that many Catholics are ready to embrace the position of their leadership. That is why Pax Christi's mission of education for peace is so vitally important in our time. . . .
>
> In summary, then, it is fair to say that Pax Christi does not believe that the just-war principles are relevant in a nuclear age and

thus it proposes a positive path of disarmament, development, and justice.  However,
Pax Christi does not hold the just-war
principles to be totally irrelevant since
it permits them to be followed in the case
of an individual conscience.[12]

Fahey is equally critical of the doctrine of
deterrence.  He argues, in behalf of Pax Christi, that
deterrence assumes a perpetual state of "constant
hostility" between nations, without the possibility of
trust or reconciliation.  He claims that deterrence is
based on the assumptions that "armed strength will
guarantee security," and that the "only ultimate way" of
resolving international differences is through violence
or the threat of violence.  He asserts that the doctrine
of deterrence is based on the unethical principles of
"might makes right," "two wrongs make a right," and "the
ends justify the means."  Fahey concludes:  "Deterrence
is, in short, a morally bankrupt philosophy whose
continued development will not prevent war but in fact
will cause it."[13]  Based on this assessment, Pax
Christi U.S.A. adopted a position of "non-support of the
ratification of the SALT II treaty" because it believed
that the treaty perpetuated the arms race and endorsed
the doctrines of deterrence and mutually assured
destruction (MAD).

Early in the existence of the Ad Hoc Committee
established to draft the new pastoral letter on war and
peace for the National Conference of Catholic Bishops
(NCCB), seventeen bishops endorsed a letter sent to
Archbishop Joseph L. Bernardin, the committee chairman.
These bishops, all members of Pax Christi U.S.A., sought
to offer a counterpoint to the argument presented by
Bishop O'Connor in his book, In Defense of Life.  The Pax
Christi bishops wanted the committee to consider several
questions, including the following:

> (1) Can continued or increased expenditures
> on the arms race be justified in the
> light of urgent human needs in a world
> of poverty?
> (2) Can the nuclear arms race between the
> superpowers be continued without greatly
> increasing the risks of war?
> (3) If the indiscriminate use of weapons of
> mass destruction is morally wrong (as
> Catholic teaching clearly holds), how can
> the threat to use them (which is essential
> to our strategy of deterrence) be morally
> justifiable?
> (4) Is it right, then, for our country to
> possess nuclear weapons?  Is it right for

> our citizens and corporations to engage in
> the manufacture and development of such
> weapons?
> (5) What moral limits should be set on the
> targeting policies governing American
> weapons systems?
> (6) Is it realistic to expect that nuclear
> war can be fought on a limited basis?
> (7) Is it morally responsible for policy
> makers to suggest that nuclear wars can
> be won?
> (8) How are members of the military to
> form their consciences in a command
> structure in a way that respects non-
> combatant life, particularly if they are
> likely to be involved in the targeting
> and use of nuclear weapons?[14]

Buttressing their position with citations from
Scripture and Pope John Paul II, the bishops urged the Ad
Hoc Committee to renounce the arms race and to propose
nonviolent methods of civil defense.  The Pax Christi
letter concludes by advocating "unilateral initiatives"
as a means for setting in motion a disarmament process.
The bishops affirm:  "Granted, unilateral initiatives
involve serious risks, but in our view these risks are
called for in the light of the far greater risks of an
arms race which the Vatican has called 'a machine gone
mad'."[15]

Even a casual reading of the various drafts will
reveal that Pax Christi ideas pervasively influenced the
development of the NCCB pastoral letter (see below).
Also, we will encounter many of the Pax Christi themes in
the positions analyzed in the next section.  There can be
no doubt that this organization exerts an increasing and
substantial influence among American bishops.  Presently,
some forty dioceses use Pax Christi materials in their
peace education programs.


SELECTED PEACE ADVOCATES

Some contemporary Catholic peace advocates approach
the nuclear issue from the pacifist position, others from
the just-war tradition.  Fahey, Zahn, and others
discussed in the previous section are pacifists.  The
four bishops considered in this section are nuclear
pacifists.  There is a thin line between the positions of
Archbishop Hunthausen and Bishop Matthiesen and pacifism.
Archbishop Quinn and Bishop Mahony, however, clearly base
their positions on the just-war tradition.  These four
bishops are discussed in this section because their views
have received wide publicity in the current debate; also

they advocate actions that represent distinctive aspects of the anti-nuclear movement.

## Archbishop Raymond Hunthausen: Seattle, Washington

When the editors of Christianity and Crisis sought to illustrate the dimensions of the nuclear debate, they juxtaposed speeches by Alexander M. Haig, Jr., and Archbishop Raymond Hunthausen.[16] James V. Schall, a Jesuit professor at Georgetown University, described Hunthausen as "the most extreme of the American bishops."[17] Hunthausen's position is not a new version of "better red than dead." In fact, he practically ignores the effects of the Soviet threat and weapons. His concern is focused on the weapons and policies of the United States. He believes that the arms race and continued nuclear preparation will lead inevitably to nuclear war.

In an address delivered to the Pacific Northwest Synod of the Lutheran Church in American on 12 June 1981, Hunthausen outlined his position.[18] Though "deeply shocked" by the atomic bombing of Japan, he indicated that it was an article published by the Jesuit Father Richard McSorley in 1976 that finally prompted him to address the nuclear issue. In "It's a Sin to Build a Nuclear Weapon," printed in the U.S. Catholic, McSorley wrote: "The taproot of violence is our society today is our intention to use nuclear weapons. Once we have agreed to that, all other evil is minor in comparison."

Hunthausen agreed. "Our willingness to destroy life everywhere on this earth, for the sake of our security as Americans," he claimed, "is at the root of many other terrible events in our country."[19] He added that the United States maintained nuclear weapons to protect its privileged place and to exploit the world economically.

Hunthausen was also challenged by the article to speak out against what he considered to be a "first-strike" nuclear doctrine and new, highly accurate weapons being developed to implement this doctrine. These weapons include the MX and cruise missiles, and especially the Trident submarine, which was to be based near Seattle. He exclaimed that "Trident is the Auschwitz of Puget Sound" because one submarine had the capacity to destroy 408 separate areas, with a destructive power equivalent of 2,040 Hiroshima bombs.[20] Hunthausen concluded that following Christ and bearing one's cross in the nuclear age demanded "unilateral disarmament." Real security rested not in "demonic" nuclear weapons, but in a loving, caring God.

The following winter on 10 February 1982, Hunthausen presented a lecture at Gonzaga University entitled "The

Church, The Gospel and the Arms Race." In this lecture
he continued to advocate unilateral disarmament and
declared that, in placing security in nuclear weapons,
Americans were guilty of "nuclear idolatry."[21]
Hunthausen then turned his attention to the "alleged"
threat of the Russians, whom amazingly he compared with
the Samaritans of Jesus' day.[22] He observed:

> I don't believe we would fear the Russians
> nearly so much if we could decide to get
> rid of our own nuclear weapons. The
> rational basis of our fear today is the
> fear which the Russians in turn have on us,
> because of our weapons. We fear because
> our own trigger finger can provoke a
> nuclear war. If we were to lay down our
> weapons and put our faith in God instead,
> I believe we would be able to see the
> Russians once again as people. In any
> event, I do not understand the logic of
> inflicting nuclear war on a repressed
> people in the name of preserving anybody's
> freedom.

Hunthausen's analysis in this statement is
questionable. Though he does not acknowledge the
credibility of Soviet aggression or the contribution of
Soviet nuclear weapons to the world's fear of holocaust,
he does recognize that the Soviet regime is repressive.
Yet, he fails to differentiate between repression and
freedom. Indeed, in these two addresses, Hunthausen
refers to the Soviets as "people," and Americans as
"imperialists," "exploiters," and "idolaters." American
nuclear weapons are "diabolic," but Soviet weapons are
ignored.

Hunthausen resolved that action is demanded--some
form of nonviolent resistance--to initiate the process of
disarmament and, thus, avoid the "extermination of the
human family."[23] This action could include writing
elected officials or protesting through marches or
demonstrations. The action he chose was to withhold
fifty percent of his federal income tax to demonstrate
his opposition to using fifty cents of each tax dollar
for national defense buildup. This symbolic gesture
amounted to withholding $125, which he deposited in a
fund supporting peaceful purposes.[24]

Hunthausen indicates that he recognizes the need for
nations to protect their citizens. He says that he is
primarily protesting the nuclear means adopted by this
nation. His call for "unilateral disarmament" and
nonviolent means makes his claim appear questionable, or
at least inconsistent.

Hunthausen would probably describe himself as a "nuclear pacifist," as opposed to "pacifist." He has been criticized for ignoring Soviet actions and weapons, and isolating US actions and weapons from the world context. He has also been accused of distorting recent papal statements in supporting his position by selective quotations.

## Bishop Leroy T. Matthiesen: Amarillo, Texas

In general articles discussing contemporary American bishops, a name frequently linked with Hunthausen is Bishop Leroy T. Matthiesen of Amarillo, Texas.[25] In the spring of 1981, a man in his late fifties sought moral counseling from Bishop Matthiesen. This man was one of 2,400 employees at Pantex, a final assembly plant for nuclear weapons in Amarillo. He was worried that working at Pantex might be morally wrong. As the man was near retirement and had many persons dependent upon him, Matthiesen advised him to continue his employment with the armament plant. But this encounter, the bishop later said, opened his eyes to the dangers posed by the nuclear arms race.[26]

The announcement by the Reagan Administration in August 1981 of the decision to produce and stockpile the radiation enhanced (neutron) warhead was strongly criticized by Matthiesen. He claimed that this decision was of "immediate concern" to those living next door to Pantex, "the nation's final assembly point for nuclear weapons, including the neutron bombs."[27] Matthiesen rejected the arms race as "madness," and then offered a different message to the employees of Pantex:

> We beg our administration to stop accelerating the arms race. We beg our military to use common sense and moderation in our defense posture. We urge individuals involved in the production and stockpiling of nuclear bombs to consider what they are doing, to resign from such activities and to seek employment in peaceful pursuits.[28]

Matthiesen's public statement drew immediate criticism from Amarillo citizens. The opposition grew much more intense in February 1982 when Matthiesen received a grant of $10,000 to help develop a "Solidarity Peace Fund." These funds, donated by the Oblates of Mary Immaculate, headquartered in St. Paul, Minnesota, were intended to provide counseling services and interim financial support for employees who chose to leave their jobs at Pantex.[29]

Matthiesen turned the money over to the Catholic Family Service agency in his diocese which was to provide the counseling and dispense financial assistance. Popular reaction was immediate and acrimonious. Several employees at Pantex threatened to withdraw their contributions from the United Way because of its financial support to Catholic Family Service. Within a month the United Way cut off its $61,000 grant to the social service agency rather than confront the potential lose of over $200,000 in donations from Pantex employees.

Matthiesen has been accused of being a traitor and an agent of the Soviet Union. He has been offered one-way tickets to Moscow by some. Others, however, have praised him as a man of conscience. The twelve Catholic bishops of Texas have endorsed his stand against the neutron bomb. The statement of support for Matthiesen was drafted by the secretary of the Texas bishops, Bishop Joseph A. Fiortenza of San Angelo, who, like Matthiesen, is a member of Pax Christi.

In an interview with a Washington Post writer in November 1981, Bishop Matthiesen indicated that he was not questioning the defense of America or our free way of life. He was challenging the arms race and the nuclear means employed in defense policies. He, like Hunthausen, could be considered a "nuclear pacifist." Also, like his Seattle colleague, Matthiesen has been accused of making his critique in a vacuum. He does not address the international military context or offer alternatives to nuclear deterrence.[30]

Several basic questions remain unanswered in Matthiesen's statement. In advocating a non-nuclear defense policy, would he support an increased conventional means of defense to compensate for the loss of nuclear weapons? Does he propose unilateral or multilateral nuclear disarmament? Is he, in fact, rejecting nuclear deterrence, or is he rejecting only the development of new, destabilizing weapons like the neutron bomb?

Archbishop John R. Quinn:  San Francisco, California

The positions advocated by Archbishop John R. Quinn in the last five years chronicle the emerging attitudes of many American bishops toward nuclear weapons. He has opposed both the development of new counterforce weapons and preparations for civil defense on the grounds that these steps make the "unthinkable" (nuclear warfare) more "do-able," and, thus, more likely.

In 1978, while president of the National Conference of Catholic Bishops (NCCB), Quinn applauded President Carter's decision to defer production of neutron warheads. Like James Johnson, he recognized that this

weapon was morally a step in the right direction when
compared with existing tactical nuclear weapons. The
neutron warhead, in the context of U.S. deterrence
policy, is essentially a defensive weapon that would
cause less loss of life and property in the target area
than would existing weapons. In the broader picture,
however, he believed that developing this new weapon
would "intensify the nuclear arms spiral." Also, he
argued that:

> The introduction of this new and more
> "manageable" weapon tends to narrow the gap
> politically and psychologically between
> conventional war and nuclear war. In
> other words, it could render more probable
> the escalation of any war in Europe to the
> level of nuclear warfare.[31]

Bryan Hehir agreed with Quinn's logic. He concurred
that deployment of the neutron warhead and the cruise
missile would destabilize deterrence by weakening the
"firebreak" between conventional and nuclear warfare.[32]

Bishop Quinn's most noted statement on the nuclear
issue was issued on 4 October 1981 in observance of the
800th birthday of St. Francis of Assisi. His pastoral
statement is entitled "Instruments of Peace--Weapons of
War."[33] Quinn asserted in this message that "the
weapons of nuclear war and our escalating race to produce
them" comprise "one of the greatest life or death issues
threatening us today." These weapons seriously endanger
the "continued existence of the human race . . . by the
threat of nuclear destruction." He affirmed the
statement of Pope John Paul II before the United Nations
in 1979 that "continual preparations" for nuclear war by
nations show "that there is a desire to be ready for war,
and being ready means being able to start
it. . . ."[34]

Quinn declared that nuclear weapons have introduced
a new and qualitatively different order of
destructiveness to warfare.

> Nuclear weapons are not simply conventional
> weapons on a larger scale. . . . Their
> tremendous explosive force, as well as their
> enormous and terrible side effects, will
> irrevocably alter our ecological system,
> genetic structures for generations to come
> and the fundamental fabric of our social
> systems.

He restated his critique of the neutron bomb and
more forcefully asserted that "it contributes to the
dangerous illusion that a 'limited' nuclear war can be

fought and won." Concerning current stockpiles, Quinn
claimed that the United States can destroy every major
Soviet city forty times over. In turn, the Soviet Union
can destroy every major American city seventeen times
over. Combined, the two arsenals "contain the equivalent
of twelve tons of TNT for every man, woman and child in
the entire world."

With Vatican Council II, Quinn recognized the right
of nations to protect themselves against unprincipled and
dangerous enemies. In the present world context,
defensive arms are necessary. But nuclear weapons and
the arms race, he said, "must be condemned as immoral."
These weapons violate the just-war principles of
proportionality and discrimination. After referring to
the effects of thermonuclear weapons, he asked: "What
good could possibly be proportionate to such
uncontrollable destruction and suffering?" Application
of the just-war principles to the arms race leads Quinn
to conclude "that a 'just' nuclear war is a contradiction
in terms." He affirmed that the Catholic Church clearly
teaches that "nuclear weapons and the arms race are
essentially evil. . . ."

Quinn recommended the following actions in response
to these evils:

> (1) Setting aside each month a day of
> prayer and fasting for an end to the arms
> race.
> (2) Instituting broad-based educational
> programs on the teaching of the Church
> regarding nuclear weapons and the arms
> race by parishes and schools.
> (3) Establishing in every parish peace
> and justice committees.
> (4) Supporting the national campaign for
> a "nuclear arms freeze" as a first realistic
> step toward a process of "bilateral
> disarmament."
> (5) Opposing the Department of Defense
> intentions to establish a "civilian-military
> contingency hospital system," if this system
> is based on the illusion that there can be
> an effective medical response in the case
> of nuclear war.
> (6) Supporting the development of creative
> proposals for converting military weapons
> technology to civilian production uses.

Archbishop Quinn addresses many of the crucial
questions in the nuclear debate. Are just-war principles
valid? Yes. Is national military defense a legitimate
right of nations? Yes. Are nuclear weapons

intrinsically different from conventional weapons? Yes.
Are nuclear weapons a force sufficient to imperil human
society and the natural order? Yes. Do counterforce
weapons destabilize deterrence and contribute to an
escalation of the arms race? Yes. Do tactical
counterforce weapons weaken the nuclear threshold? Yes.
Can vertical escalation in the use of nuclear weapons be
controlled? No. Can the effects of nuclear weapons be
controlled? No. Can a limited nuclear war be fought or
won? No. Should nuclear disarmament be mutual, rather
than unilateral? Yes. Though his approach is more
balanced than that of Hunthausen and Matthiesen, he, too,
fails to constructively address alternative means of
national defense to replace our current reliance on
nuclear weapons. Also, his critique of civil defense
fails to recognize that civil defense is a factor in
deterring the use of nuclear weapons. Even though the
effects of nuclear weapons can not be eliminated, any
reduction in the effects can diminish the advantages
gained by an adversary in using nuclear weapons.


Bishop Roger Mahony:   Stockton, California

     The editors of Commonweal describe Bishop Roger
Mahony as a representative of the "middle ground" among
those saying "no" to current U.S. military policy.[35]
Michael Novak responds that Mahony represents the
"middle" only if "one leaves out the right wing and the
center."[36]  Mahony's argument is more complete than
others we have examined in this section.  In his pastoral
letter dated 30 December 1981,[37] he acknowledges a
"real danger posed by Soviet policy" and affirms that "we
have a right to genuine security."  He does not advocate
"unilateral disarmament" or an "unqualified pacifism."
He does claim that the arms race, as represented in the
current policies of the United States and the Soviet
Union, exceeds the bounds of justice and moral legitimacy
defined in just-war theory.  He concludes that it "can no
longer be tolerated."  In his letter, Mahony seems to
support a "minimal deterrence policy" as a temporary
position, while pursuing nuclear disarmament through
negotiations.
     Mahony clearly describes his position as "nuclear
pacifism."  He also claims that the bishops of the Second
Vatican Council declared that nuclear pacifism is a
"weighty and unexceptional obligation of Christians."
Based on this interpretation of the Council's statements,
he concludes that:

          . . . any use of nuclear weapons, and by
          implication, any intention to use them, is
          always morally--and gravely--a serious

evil. No Catholic can ever support or
cooperate with the planning or executing
of policies to use, or which by implication
intend to use nuclear weapons, even in a
defensive posture, let alone in a "first
strike" against another nation.

Mahony proclaims that, because they are
indiscriminate and disproportionate, nuclear weapons are
unusable weapons, either in "first use" or in
retaliation. He then considers the question of
deterrence. If it is wrong to use these weapons, is it
also wrong to possess them as a deterrent to use by
others. Though his answer to this question is somewhat
ambiguous, he apparently accepts the argument that the
threat of retaliation is not as bad as actually using or
intending to use nuclear weapons, and that the threat
"may in fact be preventing the use of nuclear weapons."
He also cites the claim of some Christian moralists that
"condemning the possession of nuclear weapons as a
deterrent without suggesting practical political and
military alternatives is, at best, politically
inadequate, and at worst, dangerously naive." He hastens
to add, however, that not every national arms policy
advanced in the name of deterrence is morally acceptable.
For Mahony, the "only possible Catholic support for a
national nuclear deterrence policy" depends on the
following three "moral judgments:"

First, that the primary moral imperative is
to prevent any use of nuclear weapons under
any circumstances; secondly, that the
possession of nuclear weapons is always
an evil which could, at best, be tolerated,
but only if the deterrence strategy is used
in order to make progress on arms limitation
and reductions; and thirdly, that the
ultimate goal of what remains, at best, an
interim deterrence policy is the eventual
elimination of nuclear arms and of the
threat of mutual assured destruction.

Mahony concludes that the present policies of the
United States and the Soviet Union fail to meet any of
these conditions. He sees as the goal of these policies
nuclear "superiority," rather than sufficiency or parity.
This goal accelerates the arms race. He describes the
"counter-force" strategy announced by President Carter in
Presidential Directive 59 as an offensive or "first
strike" strategy. He believes that the cruise missile
will impede arms limitation agreements because this
weapon would elude verification. According to Mahony,
"it is not morally permissible to use nuclear weapons,"

such as tactical weapons (including the neutron warhead),
"to deter mere conventional warfare." His final judgment
on the current American policy of deterrence is as
follows:

> Since I believe the American arms policy has
> exceeded the moral limits of deterrence and
> has eroded our real security, and since there
> has been up until now no serious connection
> between American arms policy and a serious
> attempt to reduce arms world-wide, it is my
> conviction that Catholics no longer have a
> secure moral basis to support actively or
> cooperate passively in the current U.S.
> arms policy and escalating arms race.

Mahony's position is that no nuclear weapons are
morally usable and the present counter-force deterrent
strategy of "flexible response" is morally intolerable.
Therefore, he recommends the following:

> (1) Do not allow questions of policy to
> be decided by technical experts, who so
> often represent the "self-serving interests"
> of the industrial/military complex.
> (2) Pray for a "conversion of heart" to
> become peacemakers, and search for ways
> to become a "peace-advocate Church."
> (3) Educate ourselves on all relevant
> factors.
> (4) Use every political resource, including
> "peace lobbies and pressure on our
> Congressional Representatives," to ensure
> that the United States returns to a
> "minimal deterrence policy" and initiates
> "serious comprehensive proposals for arms
> limitation and reduction based on parity."[38]
> (5) Short of bilateral reduction in nuclear
> armaments, support a bilateral freeze on
> all research, construction, or testing of
> new nuclear weapons systems.

Mahony concludes that nothing short of "reduction in
half or a freeze" will be adequate strategies for the
present situation.

Mahony's argument is more balanced, yet more
restrictive than the positions advocated by the majority
of his associates in Pax Christi. He recognizes the
right of nations for security and the legitimacy of the
use of military force under conditions described by the
criteria of just-war theory. On the other hand, his
statement that "no Catholic can ever support or cooperate
with the planning or executing of policies to use, or

which by implication intend to use nuclear weapons" is
implicitly a call for Catholics in the national security
establishment to resign. His argument, which he
reiterated at a Congressional forum on the nuclear freeze
on 22 March 1982 reaches conclusions similar to those
published by Francis X. Winters in July 1981. Winters
holds that the recent pronouncements by American Catholic
episcopal authorities challenge civilian and military
officials whose position requires them to cooperate in
the planning or execution of nuclear policy to "stand
down." Winters continues:

> If the bishops are correct in their assess-
> ment of the damage to be expected from any
> strategic nuclear exchange, Catholics in the
> line of command for the use of, or threat to
> use, these weapons are now forbidden by
> conscience from meeting these constitutional
> responsibilities under pain of serious sin.
> Resignation of office is their only morally
> viable option.[39]

Mahony does not explicitly call for governmental
officials to resign, but, if they cannot change current
policies, this is the implication of his argument for
non-support and non-cooperation.

Mahony's discussion of deterrence leaves crucial
questions unresolved. He rejects counter-city warfare,
but then implies that the counter-value (counter-city)
strategy of mutual assured destruction is more acceptable
than a counter-forces strategy. Perhaps his point is
that counter-force weapons are more likely to be used
than the older, less accurate weapons. Or possibly his
argument is directed primarily against further spending
and the arms race, rather than on which weapons and
strategy most effectively deter. Also, he does not
explain why tactical or theater nuclear weapons are not
"morally permissible" for deterring "mere conventional
warfare." Are these weapons permissible for deterring
existing Soviet tactical and theater nuclear weapons,
such as the SS-20? Would he advocate increasing
conventional forces to achieve parity with the Soviet
Union for deterring conventional aggression? At least
three aspects are needed for effective deterrence to be
credible: capability, intention, and will. Mahony
rejects intention and the will to use nuclear weapons and
several categories of weapons. How does he expect the
concept of deterrence he envisions to be effective? Is
he suggesting a distinction between a "declared" policy
and an "actual" policy?

NATIONAL CONFERENCE OF CATHOLIC BISHOPS' PASTORAL
LETTER ON WAR AND PEACE, 1983

Pax Christi is an unofficial organization in the
Catholic Church. The positions of the peace advocates we
discussed in the last section represent individual
opinions. Thus far in this chapter we have not surveyed
the formal position held by the American Catholic
hierarchy. As pronouncements like those outlined above
have proliferated, however, greater attention has been
drawn to the National Conference of Catholic Bishops
(NCCB) pastoral letter, which does represent the formal
position of the American Catholic episcopacy. The
process through which the pastoral was developed is as
significant as the letter itself. An initial draft was
completed in June 1982 and was widely circulated for
comment. Following 700 responses amounting to over 1,000
pages, a revised draft was published in late October
1982. Again extensive reaction led to a third draft of
the letter, which, after further debate, was adopted on 3
May 1983. In this section we review the initial drafts
and some published reactions to them, and then we analyze
the final draft of the pastoral letter. By following
this approach we can identify some of the dynamic trends
surfacing in the Catholic dialogue, as well as the
current position of the church on nuclear issues. This
procedure is also consistent with the bishops' desire
that the letter contribute to a dialogical pursuit of
consensus on nuclear issues.

At the General Meeting of the NCCB in 1980,
Archbishop John Roach, the Conference president,
established the Ad Hoc Committee on War and Peace. This
committee was charged with the responsibility of
preparing a draft for a new pastoral letter on the
problem of war and the need for a theology of peace in
the nuclear age. Archbishop Joseph L. Bernardin was
selected to chair the committee which also included
Bishop George A. Fulcher, Bishop Daniel P. Reilly, Bishop
Thomas J. Gumbleton (president of Pax Christi U.S.A.) and
Bishop John J. O'Connor (Vicar General of the Military
Vicariate). Bruce Martin Russett, professor of political
science at Yale University, was engaged as a technical
consultant for the pastoral letter. Between July 1981
and June 1982, the committee interviewed over thirty
people including former and present governmental
officials, theologians, Scripture scholars, peace
advocates, and retired military personnel. The list of
those providing testimony is impressive: Harold Brown,
James Schlesinger, Casper Weinberger, Eugene Rostow,
Edward Rowny, Roger Molander, William O'Brien, Francis
Winters, Gordon Zahn, Ralph Potter, Paul Ramsey, Alan
Geyer, Charles Curran, James Finn, John Langan, Donald
Senior, Thomas Cornell, George Seignious, and others.

## The First Draft:   "God's Hope in a Time of Fear"

The committee published the first draft of the
letter, "God's Hope in a Time of Fear,"[40] with its
unanimous endorsement on 11 June 1982.    Endorsement
by Gumbleton of Pax Christi and O'Connor, a proponent of
the just-war tradition, suggests the strong desire of the
committee to develop a statement agreeable both to
pacifists and traditionalists.  In the first section of
the letter, the bishops recognize that in a world "marked
by sin" force has often been the method of resolving
conflict; "wars do and will occur."(p. 7)  They
acknowledge that at times, as a last resort, the use of
force is justifiable in defense of values.  The bishops
agree with the conclusion of the Second Vatican Council
that, "as long as the danger of war remains and there is
no competent and sufficiently powerful authority at the
international level, governments cannot be denied the
right to legitimate defense once every means of peaceful
settlement has been exhausted . . ." (p. 10)  They also
affirm, however, that not all reasons justify resorting
to war, and that violence is never the preferred method
for resolving conflict.  Concerning the role of the
church, "the whole force of Jesus' life and teaching
pointed toward peace." (p. 5)  Therefore, according to
the bishops, "the church is called to a ministry of peace
and reconciliation in history." (p. 7)
    The bishops recognize as equally valid two basic
responses to violence, the nonviolent, or pacifist,
tradition and the just-war tradition.  The framework
adopted for discussing war and nuclear weapons in
subsequent sections, however, is that of just-war theory.
Nuclear war and weapons are evaluated in reference to the
just-war criteria of discrimination, proportion,
intention and reasonable possibility of success.  Armed
with these criteria, and enlightened by pacifism, the
bishops set out to "think about war in an entirely new
way."(p. 20)[41]
    The third section of the letter contains the core of
the bishops' thought on war in the nuclear age.  They
preface this section with a clear statement of their
ultimate conclusions on these issues:

> There can be no place for weapons--especially
> weapons of mass destruction--in the world
> of peaceful reconciliation toward which we
> strive.  Even today, continued reliance on
> nuclear weapons is fundamentally abhorrent.
> If nuclear weapons had never been made, we
> could not condone their creation. . . .
>
> . . . Our goal must be to progress toward a
> world without weapons of mass destruction.

> We realize that progress will not be easy or
> rapid. Nor do we demand unilateral nuclear
> disarmament by the United States or its allies.
> But even in this immediate period of continued
> possession, certain minimal prohibitions on
> the use or threatened use of nuclear weapons
> are inescapable.(pp. 24, 25)

As indicated in this statement, the bishops' final
goal is nuclear disarmament through a process of
multilateral reductions. In the interim a policy of
deterrence limited by certain conditions is permitted.
Their argument is organized around three issues:
(1) counter-population use of nuclear weapons, (2) "first
use," and (3) deterrence policy. They strongly reject
the first two issues, and reluctantly "tolerate" the
third.

Regarding counter-value, or counter-population, use
of nuclear weapons, the bishops declare:

> Under no circumstances may nuclear weapons or
> other instruments of mass slaughter be used
> for the purpose of destroying population
> centers or other predominantly civilian
> targets.(p. 25)

This prohibition includes firing at military targets
when it is known that adjacent population centers will be
devastated as a side effect not directly intended. The
bishops also reject indiscriminate use of nuclear weapons
in retaliation. "No Christian," they conclude, "can
rightfully carry out orders or policies deliberately
aimed at killing noncombatants."(p. 26)

Concerning "first use," the bishops judged:

> We do not perceive any situation in which
> the deliberate initiation of nuclear warfare,
> on however restricted a scale, can be
> condoned. Non-nuclear attacks by another
> state must be deterred by other than
> nuclear means.(pp. 26-27)[42]

In making this pronouncement the bishops have the
European theater in mind. They are aware of NATO plans
to deter conventional warfare with nuclear weapons. They
also know that both NATO and the Warsaw Pact have large
numbers of tactical nuclear weapons. The bishops
conclude that NATO should not use nuclear weapons to
resist conventional aggression because the weapons would
"devastate the densely populated countries of Western and
Central Europe."(p. 27) They also reject the "first use"
of tactical weapons because of the lack of certainty in
preventing escalation from tactical to intermediate range

or strategic weapons.  The bishops do not specifically
advocate public announcement of a no "first use" policy.
They do strongly urge that "first use" not be threatened.
    The committee is not ready to renounce all use of
nuclear weapons; but neither is it ready to give
unambiguous indorsement to any use.  On this point the
letter reads:

> If nuclear weapons may be used at all, they
> may be used only after they have been used
> against our own country or our allies, and,
> even then, only in an extremely limited,
> discriminating manner against military
> targets.(p. 31)[43]

    The bishops choose not to condemn outright all
conceivable uses of nuclear weapons, because they are not
ready to reject the policy of deterrence.  They recognize
that "Soviet nuclear weapons provide fully as great a
threat to humanity as do our own," and "abandonment of
nuclear deterrence might invite an attack on the United
States." (p. 32)  The tension between these issues is
reflected in the bishops' unwillingness to fully endorse
a policy of nuclear deterrence.  They reaffirm their 1976
pastoral letter in which the NCCB declared:  "Not only is
it wrong to attack civilian populations but it is also
wrong to threaten to attack them as part of a strategy of
deterrence." (p. 28, underline added.)  The intention of
the bishops is not to approve of deterrence, but to avoid
rejecting it because of its possible value in preventing
nuclear war.  They declare: "A temporary toleration of
some aspects of nuclear deterrence must not be confused
with approval of such deterrence." (p. 32, underline
added.)  Deterrence is not approved, but "tolerated" as a
lesser evil than the use of nuclear weapons.  Because
they consider deterrence an evil, however, the bishops
affirm that their toleration "must be conditional upon
sincere, substantial efforts to modify current policy,"
and urgent pursuit of arms control, reductions and
disarmament.
    The committee calls for "multilateral abandoning" of
the strategy of nuclear deterrence under conditions which
allow monitoring, verification and maintenance of
adequate defenses during the period of reduction.  The
bishops also identify three measures which must be
prevented during the quest for arms control:  (1) the
development and deployment of destabilizing weapons
systems by either side; (2) the tendency to render
command and control systems more automatic and less open
to human intervention; and (3) the proliferation of
nuclear weapons in the international system.
    In summary, the bishops' position includes the
following points:

(1) Nuclear weapons cannot be used
directly against civilian populations
under any circumstances. Nor can their
use against populations be intended or
threatened.
(2) Nuclear weapons cannot be used first,
and the United States should abstain from
all preparations and threats to use them
first.
(3) Nuclear weapons can be used in
retaliation to a nuclear attack only
if their use can be limited in extent
and discriminating in effect.
(4) A policy of deterrence containing the
above three restrictions is "tolerated" as
a lesser evil.
(5) A policy of deterrence must be accompanied
by urgent and substantive efforts to achieve
multilateral, verifiable agreements to reduce
nuclear weaponry.

In recognition of the plurality of views in the
Christian community, the bishops seem almost apologetic
for not having rejected absolutely the policy of
deterrence. They do, however, recommend additional steps
for moving from reliance on deterrence to arms control
and the cultivation of world peace. They insist that
arms control efforts have been too limited. All states
should immediately end further development, production
and deployment of new nuclear weapons, and reduce the
number of existing weapons. The bishops "do not expect
any government to accept the risks of large-scale
unilateral disarmament." They do recommend "independent
initiatives" by the United States "to stimulate
reciprocal actions" by the Soviet Union. (pp. 39-40)
    Unlike most advocates of nuclear disarmament in the
current debate, the bishops acknowledge that a decision
to forego nuclear deterrence of non-nuclear attacks may
require other measures to maintain sufficient security
against aggression. These include increased conventional
forces, which may possibly necessitate conscription. The
bishops affirm: "It may well be . . . that a people must
be willing to make the sacrifices of strengthening
conventional forces if indeed this will reduce the
possibility of nuclear war." (p. 41) They also support
the principle of required military service for citizens
in times of necessity. They recognize the validity of
conscientious objection and advocate a policy permitting
selective conscientious objection to particular wars, a
position derived from the just-war principles. In
addition to military security measures, the pastoral
letter strongly encourages nonviolent means of conflict

resolution in the quest for a world order characterized
by "peace with justice." (p. 52)

## Responses to the First Draft

Following its completion in June, the Ad Hoc
Committee distributed the first draft for comments.  Over
700 responses were returned to the committee.  According
to one observer, there was a concerted effort by peace
groups to have a larger voice in the letter.  They called
for a more developed theology of peace and less reliance
on just-war concepts.  They also charged that there were
too many conservatives or traditionalists among those
providing testimony before the committee.  Others,
however, claimed that just the opposite was true.  These
reactions demonstrate that concensus was not reached
among American Catholics in the first draft.  In August,
1982 the Catholic periodical Commonweal published
responses from nine Catholics, which document the current
pluralism in the Church.[44]
      John Langan, a moral theologian from Georgetown
University, describes the document as a useful benchmark
in Catholic thinking.  In his view the draft "hovers
between nuclear pacifism and a restatement of just-war
theory for a nuclear age."[45]  Langan believes, however,
that the bishops should have devoted more space to the
moral qualities characterizing governing regimes.  He
suggests that moral justifications and criticisms of
national security policy need to include more realistic
assessment of Soviet resources, policies and intentions.
In considering Soviet threats, moral value must be given
to our preservation as a free political community.
Langan also stresses that strategy is needed for
political implementation of the NCCB position, and to
counter anticipated efforts by the Reagan Administration
to shuffle the letter "to the periphery of public
debate."
      James Finn praises the bishops for addressing
publicly the moral dimensions of political and strategic
issues.  In his view this action avoids the bifurcation
of politics and morality and requires the application of
reason in public discourse.  Finn thinks that the letter
helps to clarify the position of the Church, which has
been clouded in recent years by various Catholic
statements.  The letter confirms, he says, that Francis
Winters has "clearly overextended" the implications of
the Church's position by calling for governmental
officials to resign or violate Church teaching.[46]  Finn
criticizes the bishops, however, for posing a "moral
symmetry" between the superpowers.  He states that the
Soviet Union "is a tyranny" and it "behaves
tyrannically."  It has continued to build massive

armaments when the United States has slowed down. Soviet
leaders still seek to extend their empire by military
force. He concludes that an analysis that fails to make
moral distinctions between the democracies and the Soviet
bloc "cannot accurately set forth the circumstances
within which we must make decisions about a governed
international community nor can it offer the full moral
basis for the NATO deterrent system."[47]

Philip Odeen, a former Assistant Secretary of
Defense, is bothered by the heavy emphasis on pacifism in
the early portions of the letter. He indicates that it
is hard for him to imagine that "the greater good would
be served by a pacifist policy given Soviet military
actions in Hungary and Afghanistan, or Moscow's
suppression of the Poles and the Czechs."[48] Odeen
agrees with the bishops' call for non-nuclear deterrence
of non-nuclear attacks. He points out, however, that the
main opposition to this policy, as well as to a "no first
use" policy, comes from Western Europe, not Washington.
Odeen also appreciates the emphasis on arms control
presented in the letter. He agrees that the danger is
sufficient to justify "prudent risks" in disarmament
initiatives. The former assistant secretary is critical
of the bishops for accepting a caricature of American
nuclear strategy. He claims that the focus of our
strategy and targeting is "Soviet military power, not
Soviet population."[49] He does admit, however, that
millions of civilians would die if the policy were
implemented.

Gordon Zahn describes the pastoral letter as a
disappointment, but no disaster. In his view, it is
unquestionably the strongest statement yet by the
American Catholic hierarchy in opposition to nuclear
weapons and nuclear war. He is disappointed, however, by
the ambiguities in the letter and its failure to reject
outright nuclear deterrence. Zahn is highly critical of
the bishops for "too easy a readiness to settle for a
trade-off in the form of greater reliance on conventional
weapons and expanded forces, . . . including peacetime
conscription."[50] He clearly believes that the bishops
"tolerated" too much and urges them to be more prophetic
about deterrence and nuclear weapons. He does indicate,
however, that he is "generally well satisfied with the
tone and the thrust of the draft document."[51]

Sister Joan Chittester, president of the Conference
of American Benedictine Prioresses, clearly is not
satisfied with the draft letter. She criticizes the
bishops for tolerating the intolerable. The document,
according to Chittester, "is often a defense of war."[52]
She is disturbed by the letter's reaffirmation of
just-war theory and its failure to reject the policy of
deterrence. She calls upon the bishops in the final

draft to "say a clear no to nuclear war and the
possession and manufacture of nuclear weapons as well."
Let the bishops not be like the prophets of the court in
times past "who said what the government wanted to hear
them say but in the saying of it led whole nations to
death."[53]
    Charles Curran, noted professor of moral theology at
the Catholic University of America, is far less critical
of the document than is Chittester.  He believes that in
discussing deterrence the bishops should repudiate the
criterion of "superiority" or "equivalence" in favor of
"sufficiency" in nuclear strength.  Curran also advocates
incorporating into the letter explicit judgments against
the development of the neutron bomb.

The Second Draft:  "The Challenge of Peace:  God's
Promise and Our Response"

    The second draft of the pastoral letter is entitled,
"The Challenge of Peace:  God's Promise and Our
Response."[54]   It was released to the public in late
October and discussed at the annual meeting of the NCCB
in mid-November 1982.  In preparing the second draft, the
bishops sought to maintain consistency with recent papal
statements on war, and to integrate many of the thoughts
offered in the responses to the initial draft.  Many of
the criticisms we noted in the last section are reflected
in the revised draft.  Concerning the use of nuclear
weapons and deterrence policy, there is little
substantive change in the new draft.  The two drafts vary
significantly, however, in length, tone and emphasis.
The second draft relies less on the logic of just-war
theory and gives more attention to a "theology of peace"
and to nonviolent solutions to conflict.  The first
section, "Peace in the Modern World," and the last
section, "The Promotion of Peace," have been refined and
lengthened.  The revised draft is 70 percent longer than
the first draft, and most of the increase is an expanded
discussion of "peacemaking" (as opposed to
"peacekeeping") in the nuclear age.  In the middle
section, which focuses on nuclear weapons and deterrence,
the discussion is limited to U.S. weapons and strategy.
The bishops directed the letter to both the religious and
the political community. (p. 308)  As we will see below,
this draft was better received by the peace groups of the
Church, but less acceptable to Church traditionalists and
to policy makers in the government.
    The changed tone of the second draft is manifested
in subtle rewarding, minor additions or deletions, and in
reorganization of the material.  In the first draft, the
introduction states that we are in a "time of crisis" (p.
2) because of nuclear weapons.  In the revised draft, we

are in a "supreme crisis because nuclear war threatens
the existence of our planet."(p. 307) Further
identifying this crisis, the first draft speaks of "an
escalating arms race," "worldwide proliferation," and
"breakdown of relationships."(p. 1) The second draft
refers to the arms race and the intolerable fear it
creates, and then adds:

> As Americans, citizens of the first nation
> to produce atomic weapons, the only nation
> to use them and one of the handful of
> nations which today can directly affect
> the outcome of this supreme crisis, we have
> unique human, moral and political
> responsibilities to see that a "conscious
> choice" is made to save humanity.

In the preface to the first major section of the
letter, the statement "wars do and will occur" was
replaced by: "Wars mark the fabric of human history,
distort the life of nations today, and in the form of
nuclear weapons, threaten the destruction of the world
and the civilization which has been patiently constructed
over centuries."(p. 311) Also omitted is the
acknowledgement that at times, as a last resort, the use
of force is justified. The first draft organizes the
discussion in this section into three categories:
(1) "Nonviolence and Reconciliation;" (2) "The Right to
Legitimate Self-Defense;" and (3) "The Just War
Tradition." The positions of pacifism and just war are
recognized as equally legitimate traditions of the
Church. This presentation of the two positions is
maintained in the second draft. In the latter draft,
however, the right of national self-defense is eliminated
as a separate category and subsumed under the discussion
of just-war theory. This structural reorganization of
the material results in identifying non-pacific national
self-defense as an alternative for states equally
commendable with pacifism. No longer is "lawful
self-defense" specifically supported as a "right" of
states "once all peace efforts have failed." This change
not only differs from the first draft, it conflicts with
the Second Vatican Council and recent statements by Pope
John Paul II. Unquestionably, the Pope opposes nuclear
war and the arms race. In his message for the fifteenth
World Day of Peace, however, he affirmed:

> . . . Christians, even as they strive to
> resist and prevent every form of warfare,
> have no hesitation in recalling that, in
> the name of an elementary requirement of
> justice, peoples have a right and even
> a duty to protect their existence and

freedom by proportionate means against
an unjust aggressor.[55]

The first draft cites this same papal quotation in
the section entitled "The Right to Legitimate
Self-Defense." The statement does not appear in the
second draft. Perhaps it is no longer consistent with
the logic of the letter or the "new way" of thinking
about war to speak of a Christian "duty to protect." In
the final section of the letter, the bishops do
acknowledge again the right of governments to require
military service for "legitimate defense" and "the
protection of weaker states."(p. 319) They suggest that
citizens "may not casually disregard" the government's
conscientious call. But these statements are
inconsistent with the first section and exceptional to
the general tone of the letter.

The middle section of the second draft repeats
almost verbatim the major conclusions of the first draft
on nuclear warfare and deterrence policy. The bishops
say "no" to nuclear war, counter-population use of
nuclear weapons and "first use" of nuclear weapons.
Limited use in retaliation is even more questionable and
non-nuclear attacks still must be resisted by non-nuclear
means. Deterrence, or the "threat" to use nuclear
weapons, is viewed as a "lesser evil" than the actual use
of nuclear weapons.

The bishops have extended their discussion of
deterrence and sought closer correlation with papal
statements on the subject. Rather than using Cardinal
Krol's term, "toleration," they adopted the papal
description of deterrence as "morally acceptable."(pp.
316-17) This change, however, was only a semantic
adjustment. Even though the bishops use more accepting
terminology, the tone of the second draft is more severe
regarding the policy of deterrence. Perhaps because they
recognized that there are some within their ranks who are
even less tolerant of deterrent policy, they add:

> These judgments are meant to exemplify how
> a lack of unequivocal condemnation of
> deterrence is meant only to be an attempt
> to acknowledge the role attributed to
> deterrence, but not to support its extension
> beyond the prevention of use of nuclear
> weapons.(p. 317)

From its attributed role of preventing the use of
nuclear weapons, the bishops derive three criteria for a
"morally acceptable" deterrence policy. When they apply
these criteria to deterrent strategy, the bishops reach
the following general conclusions or principles:

(1) If deterrence exists only to prevent
the use of nuclear weapons by others, then
proposals to go beyond this objective to
encourage war-fighting capabilities must
be resisted. We must continually say "no"
to the idea of nuclear war.
(2) If deterrence is our goal, "sufficiency"
to deter is an adequate strategy; the quest
for superiority must be resisted.
(3) If deterrence is to be used as "a step
on the way toward progressive disarmament,"
then each proposed addition to our strategic
system or change in strategic doctrine must
be assessed precisely in light of whether it
will render steps toward arms control and
disarmament more or less likely. (p. 317)

These principles then lead the bishops to make the
following judgments:

In light of these general principles we oppose
some specific goals for our present deterrence
posture:

(1) The addition of weapons which are likely to
invite attack and therefore give credence to
the concept that the United States seeks a
first strike, "hard-target kill" capability;
the MX missile might fit into this category.
(2) The willingness to foster strategic
planning which seeks a nuclear-war fighting
capability.
(3) Proposals which have the effect of
lowering the nuclear threshold and blurring
the difference between nuclear and conventional weapons.

In support of the concept of "sufficiency" as
an adequate deterrent and in light of the
present size and composition of both the U.S.
and Soviet strategic arsenals, we recommend:

(1) Support for immediate, bilateral
verifiable agreements to halt the testing,
production and deployment of new strategic
systems;
(2) Support for negotiated bilateral deep
cuts in the arsenals of both superpowers,
particularly of those weapons systems which
have destabilizing characteristics;
(3) Support for a comprehensive test ban
treaty;
(4) Removal by all parties of nuclear weapons

from border areas and the strengthening of
command and control over tactical nuclear
weapons to prevent inadvertent and unauthorized
use.

In these principles and judgments, the bishops have
rejected the claim that our nuclear armaments are
insufficient or that the Soviets have superiority.  They
also condemn the continued arms race and developments
that might minimize the distinction between nuclear and
conventional weapons.  One of their stated objectives in
the letter is "to build a barrier against the concept of
nuclear war as a viable strategy for defense."(p.314)
The bishops insist that "there should be clear public
resistance to the rhetoric of 'winning' nuclear wars,
'surviving' nuclear exchanges and strategies of
'protracted nuclear war'."
In the last section of the draft, the bishops again
recognize that a reduced reliance on nuclear weapons
might require strengthening of conventional defenses.
They also add a segment on superpower relations.  In it
the bishops recognize "a Soviet threat" and "a Soviet
imperial drive for hegemony" as undeniable facts.  They
acknowledge that "the Soviet Union now possesses a huge
arsenal of strategic weapons as threatening to us as ours
may appear to them."  They also describe the Soviet
system as repressive and lacking in respect for human
rights.  The objective of this section, however, is to
urge Americans to see the Soviets as more than just
adversaries.  "Soviet behavior in some cases merits the
adjective monstrous," they conclude, "but neither the
Soviet people nor their leaders are monsters; they are
human beings created in the image and likeness of
God."(p. 321)
This additional material on the Soviet Union
responds to criticisms that the first draft isolated the
discussion of nuclear weapons from the Soviet threat and
actions.  This material, however, still is removed from
the basic discussion of deterrence.  It is in a different
section.  The discussion on weapons and deterrence
focuses almost exclusively on American weapons and
policy.  The first draft contains the following
statements in the section discussing deterrence:

"Abandonment of nuclear deterrence might
invite an attack on the United States.
. . . we cannot lightly demand abandonment
of possession of all nuclear weapons at
this moment. . . Rapid, abrupt, and one-
sided abandonment of all nuclear deterrents
might create dangerous political and
military instabilities in the world.

Soviet nuclear weapons provide fully as
great a threat to humanity as do our own.
We are strongly advised that if the United
States were to renounce its own weapons
unilaterally, it would greatly diminish
any incentive for the Soviet Union to
negotiate reduction or elimination of
its weapons. (p. 32)

Each of these statements has been displaced from
this section to another, or completely dropped from the
letter.

## Responses to the Second Draft

Following distribution of the second draft of the
NCCB pastoral letter, the bishops met in Washington,
15-18 November 1982, to discuss its contents. At the
beginning of this conference, the Washington Post
reported that a substantial number of bishops registered
significant disagreement over the proposed letter. What
was not clear, according to the Post, was whether the[56]
majority wanted the draft softened or toughened. The
New York Times, however, quoted Archbishop Bernardin as
saying: "My sense is that there is broad support for the
pastoral. . . . I would be very surprised if there is a
great deal of unhappiness."[57]
After the first "straw vote" of the conference, the
Times reported that more than two-thirds of the bishops
"basically agree with a proposed pastoral letter that
strongly opposes the use of nuclear weapons. . . ." In
the survey, 195 bishops were "basically in agreement"
with the letter, 71 had "major reservations," and 12 were
in "basic disagreement." On the question of nuclear
deterrence, 141 bishops affirmed basic agreement, while
114 expressed major reservations about the letter's
conclusions.[58] Concerning the document's tone, style,
length and intended audience, 110 basically agreed while
139 had major reservations. Following the conclusion of
the conference, New York's Daily News reported that only
six bishops opposed issuing a revised and final draft of
the letter in May 1983.[59] Though somewhat misleading
(see below, p. 100), these reports do accurately indicate
that a strong majority of the bishops favored publishing
a pastoral letter, but with revisions, especially
concerning the issue of deterrence policy.
Addresses by bishops on the first day of the
conference reflect basic reactions and changes advocated
by the bishops. As I suggested earlier, the peace
bishops were more pleased with the direction of the new
draft. Archbishop Hunthausen said concerning the second
draft: "I've read the document again and again and I am

convinced that the Spirit of Christ is at work among us."
He was "pleased to see" a restoration of the legitimacy
of pacifism and conscientious objection "to the center of
our Catholic tradition." He was also satisfied by the
letter's condemnation of counter-population use, "first
use," and limited use of nuclear weapons. Hunthausen was
disappointed, however, that the letter did not call upon
the government "to begin to lay down our nuclear arms
now, regardless of what others do." He also urged the
bishops to "say clearly" that "there is morally a
preferential option for noncooperation with the
preparation for nuclear war," and that the Church will
support all who choose this option.[60]

Archbishop Quinn described the second draft as
"strong and clear" and affirmed that "the strengths of
the pastoral far outweigh its weaknesses." He urged the
conference to amend the letter with a clear rejection of
the use of nuclear weapons in retaliation. He also
advocated stronger opposition to destabilizing weapons
such as the MX system.[61]

The address by Archbishop Bernardin was a defense of
the pastoral letter in which he outlined the Ad Hoc
Committee's intentions. In reaction to criticism of the
letter, he affirmed:

> We are conscious that there are two
> superpowers, that the policies of both
> create the arms race and that the history
> and posture of the Soviet Union is the
> principal reason why the United States
> maintains its nuclear arsenal. All of
> these facts are relevant, but none of
> them relieves us of the responsibility
> we have as American bishops to spell out
> the implications of Catholic teaching on
> modern warfare for our government and
> our society.

Bernardin also worked hard to convince his audience
that the pastoral letter was consistent with recent papal
statements.[62] Archbishop Pio Laghi, the papal
representative to the conference, seemed to disagree with
this assessment, however. He emphasized that the bishops
need to speak "with clarity and the greatest possible
unanimity." He further stated:

> . . . collegiality also requires that the
> members of the episcopal conference,
> recognizing their responsibility for
> and to the universal church, reach out
> beyond their ranks to achieve greater
> unity and collaboration with all the
> bishops of the world and the Holy Father.[63]

Archbishop Hannan of New Orleans clearly asserted
that the pastoral letter is inconsistent with papal
messages. He claimed that the letter also disregards the
Soviet or Communist threat, ignores "our duty to defend
Western Europe," misrepresents U.S. policy, and conflicts
with the position held by German Catholic bishops (see
below). Hannan concluded that the letter is "minimally
concerned with the horrible sufferings, physical and
spiritual, of those enslaved by communism and other
dictatorships which disregard human rights." He
advocated substituting the papal statement to the United
Nations on 11 June 1982 in place of drafting a new
pastoral letter.[64]

Cardinal Krol described the second draft of the
letter as "an acceptable working document." He advocated
a return to his description of deterrence as "tolerable"
(1976 Pastoral Letter), rather than "morally acceptable."
His strongest criticism of the letter, however, was its
failure to clearly recognize the right of nations to
defend their citizens. He affirmed:

> To allay the reasonable fears of some people
> in our country and more so of people in the
> free and occupied countries of Europe, it
> would help to emphasize that as religious
> leaders, we do not ignore the current harsh
> realities. We are aware of the communists
> avowed and never rescinded goal of subjugation
> of the world. Just recently Juri V. Andropov,
> before his designation as successor of
> Brezhnev, spoke of the triumph of communism.
> We do recognize the right of national self-
> defense, the necessity of defensive armaments,
> and the obligation to resist conquest of the
> world by a totalitarian system, and to resist
> tyranny and oppression by all lawful means.
> The statement rightly affirms that the
> dignity of the human person is at the center
> of the church's teaching on peace, it would
> help the average reader, to add that because
> of this dignity, the rights and freedoms
> which every human person claims must be
> defended.

Krol also suggested that the Gospel's ideal of
"offering the left cheek to the person who strikes you on
the right, cannot be invoked to deny governments the
right and duty to protect its citizens against unjust
aggressors. . . ."[sic][65]

Terence Cardinal Cooke urged the bishops to be more
consistent with papal statements, and to give more
emphasis to the just-war teaching of the Church. "It is
my hope," said Cooke, "that we reflect a realistic

attitude toward the evils of the loss of freedom, the oppression of faith, and the actual motivation of leaders of some nations to dominate." He advocated a more "balanced" recognition of the role of military personnel in contributing to the maintenance of peace. Cooke suggested that the comments he had received concerning the second draft "indicate the great potential which this draft has for seriously dividing our Church and our nation."[66]

### The Third Draft: "The Challenge of Peace"

Revisions incorporated in the third draft suggest that Archbishop Bernardin's preliminary assessment of the response to the second draft was not entirely accurate. There was less satisfaction with the draft than Bernardin predicted or the press reported. Concerning the "straw vote" taken at the Washington meeting (November 1982), Bishop O'Connor observed:

> In reality, analysis of the "votes" reveals that almost half the bishops felt serious reservations about the theological principles and the moral conclusions of the draft regarding preparations for nuclear war and preparedness, and that a majority had serious reservations, also, about the purpose, tone, style, length, and intended audience.

O'Connor added: "I would be personally surprised on the basis of what I seemed to be hearing at the November meeting, that had Draft II been up for vote at the meeting, it would have received the required two-thirds majority. . . ."[67]

Among those apparently not fully satisfied with the second draft were the Pope and some European bishops. Their objections centered on the document's imbalanced use of Biblical materials and the perspectives it presented on deterrence and the Soviet threat. In January the Pope "offered" to organize an "informal consultation" to discuss the draft letter, because "it seemed necessary" for the various national Episcopal Conferences "to act in concert" and "in fidelity to the tradition of the church and the teaching of Pope John Paul II."[68] The consultation was held 18-19 January 1983 at the Vatican and included bishops from the Federal Republic of Germany, England, Wales, Scotland, Belgium, Italy, France, Holland, the United States and several Vatican officials. The following April, the Catholic Bishops Conference of the Federal Republic of Germany issued a pastoral letter entitled, "Justice Creates Peace" which supports the NATO policy of "flexible

response." This policy holds that nuclear weapons might
be necessary to stop an overwhelming conventional attack.
The German bishops also refrain from advocating a "no
first use" policy. They do, however, agree with American[69]
bishops on the need to prevent nuclear war.

After the Rome meeting, further discussion with
governmental officials and a thorough review of other
responses, the Ad Hoc Committee issued a third draft of
the pastoral letter on 6 April 1983. This draft was
considered by the bishops at the NCCB meeting held in
Chicago, 2-3 May 1983. In responding to more than 400
proposed amendments to the draft, the Conference largely
resisted strong efforts either to move the letter closer
to the second draft or to soften criticism on nuclear
weapons and United States policy. The debate in Chicago
resulted in a toughening of the language opposing the use
of nuclear weapons and a more explicit endorsement of the
nuclear freeze movement. The NCCB approved the amended[70]
third draft by a resounding margin of 238 to 9.

The third draft is the longest yet, exceeding 150
double spaced pages. The cumbersome length of the
document is partially offset by an accompanying precis
which adroitly summarizes the intent and substance of the
letter. In the final draft the NCCB retained the title,
organization and structure of the second draft, except
for a significant addition in first part entitled, "The
Presumption Against War and the Principle of Legitimate
Self-Defense."(p. 32)[71] This addition is indicative of
the general content and the tone of the third draft. The
bishops continue their opposition to all war, especially
nuclear war. However, more than ten times they reaffirm
the right of legitimate national defense or the defense
of allies unjustly attacked. This dual emphasis on
nonviolence and the duty to resist aggression by force if
necessary is maintained throughout the text.

The third draft continues to recognize both pacifism
and the just-war position as legitimate moral options for
Christians. The discussion of these choices, however,
differs in tone and substance: "The Christian has no
choice but to defend peace, properly understood, against
aggression. This is an inalienable obligation. It is
the how of defending peace which offers moral options."
(p. 34) The two alternations envisioned by the bishops
are pacifism (active or passive nonviolence) and service
in the armed forces. The bishops affirm, however, that
pacifism is a right open only to individuals; and in
selecting this option, individuals may not "renounce
their obligations to others." The bishops point out that
Vatican Council II affirmed the legitimacy of pacifism
"as long as the rights and duties of others, or of the
community itself, are not injured." The NCCB also cites
the following words of Pope Pius XII:

>A people threatened with an unjust
>aggression, or already its victim, may
>not remain passively indifferent, it if
>would think and act as befits a Christian.
>All the more does the solidarity of the
>family of nations forbid others to behave
>as mere spectators, in any attitude of
>apathetic neutrality. (p. 36)

Concerning the actions of government, the third
draft affirms: "governments threatened by armed, unjust
aggression must defend their people. This includes
defense by armed force if necessary as a last resort."
(p. 35) In our previous discussion, we noted that a
quotation by Pope John Paul II, which recognized the
right of national defense, was included in the first
draft, but deleted from the second draft (above p. 93).
The papal statement has been reinserted in the third
draft, and even expanded. The quotation is from the
World Day of Peace Message (1 January 1982), in which the
Pope recognized that "totalitarian regimes" offer a
"false peace". He affirmed that Christians pursue peace
with a "realistic view" rather than a "utopian"
perspective. Then he concluded:

>This is why Christians, even as they strive
>to resist and prevent every form of warfare,
>have no hesitation in recalling that, in
>the name of an elementary requirement of
>justice, peoples have a right and even a
>duty to protect their existence and freedom
>by proportionate means against an unjust
>aggressor. (p. 39)

In this draft, the bishops unquestionably see the
"duty to protect" as consistent with their "new way" of
thinking about war. Along with the recognition of the
right of self-defense, the bishops have also acknowledged
the just-war tradition as the official position of the
Church regarding the duty of states. In fact, the
committee has introduced an innovation to this tradition
by identifying "comparative justice" as a separate
criterion (normally this idea is addressed under the
criterion of just cause). In discussing this principle,
the bishops recognize that propaganda is frequently used
to conceal injustice and to complicate the determination
of which adversary's cause is just, or "sufficiently
right" to resort to war. The bishops also affirm,
however, that "blatant aggression" and "subversion" are
often enough "readily identifiable by all reasonably fair
minded people." In such instances, justice can be
determined, and the "values at stake" may justify
overriding the presumption against war. Originally, the

third draft concluded the discussion of comparative
justice with the acknowledgement that a greater
recognition for human rights exists in our society than
in "totalitarian and tyrannical regimes." The
implication of this acknowledgement is that U.S. society
is more just than Soviet society. Therefore, the bishops
transferred this paragraph to the section in which they
compared the superpowers (p. 116).

In the third draft, the bishops add an extended
definition of the "moral authority" of the pastoral
letter. They differentiate between universal moral
principles and official Catholic doctrine, which are
binding, and "prudential judgments," which allow for
"diversity of opinion." The following statement reflects
their position:

> We do not intend that our treatment of each
> of these issues carry the same moral authority
> as our statement of universal moral principles
> and formal Church teaching. Indeed, we stress
> here at the beginning that not every statement
> in this letter has the same moral authority.
> At times we re-assert universally binding
> moral principles (e.g., non-combatant
> immunity and proportionality). At still
> other times we re-affirm statements of recent
> popes and the teaching of Vatican II. Again,
> at other times we apply moral principles
> to specific cases.
>
> When making applications of these principles
> we realize--and we wish readers to recognize
> --that prudential judgments are involved
> based on specific circumstances which can
> change or which can be interpreted differently
> by people of good will (e.g., the treatment
> of "No First Use"). However, the moral
> judgments that we make in specific cases,
> while not binding in conscience, are to be
> given serious attention and consideration
> . . . . (p. 5)

The substantive judgments of the bishops concerning
war and nuclear weapons have been modified in places, but
they remain essentially the same as those offered in the
first two drafts. The basic principles on war which the
bishops consider binding on conscience come directly from
just-war theory. They are summarized in the precis as
follows:

> (1) Catholic teaching begins in every case
> with a presumption against war and for
> peaceful settlement of disputes. In

exceptional cases, determined by the moral
principles of the Just War tradition, some
uses of force are permitted.
(2) Every nation has a right and duty to
to defend itself against unjust aggression.
(3) Offensive war of any kind is not
morally justifiable.
(4) It is never permitted to direct nuclear
or conventional weapons to "the
indiscriminate destruction of whole cities
or vast areas with their population. . . ."
(The Pastoral Constitution, #80).  The
intentional killing of innocent
civilians or non-combatants is always
wrong.
(5) Even defensive response to unjust attack
can cause destruction which violates the
principle of proportionality, going far
beyond the limits of legitimate defense.
This judgment is particularly important when
assessing planned use of nuclear weapons.
Any defensive strategy, nuclear or
conventional, which exceeds the limits
of proportionality is not morally
permissible. (p. iv)

Like the earlier statements, the third draft soundly
rejects the arms race because of its inherent dangers and
costs.  The bishops reaffirm a 1976 papal statement
before the United Nations which judged:  "The arms race
is to be condemned as a danger, an act of aggression
against the poor, and a folly which does not provide the
security it promises."  (p. 60)
The bishops again say "No" to total war and to
nuclear war.  In the second part, the bishops declare:

Today the possibilities for placing political
and moral limits on nuclear war are so
minimal that the moral task, like the
medical, is prevention:  As a people, we
must refuse to legitimate the idea of
nuclear war. (p. 61)

As in the second draft, the bishops see that their
task is to build a "barrier" against "the concept of
nuclear war as a viable strategy for defense" and to
marshal public resistance to the rhetoric of "winnable"
nuclear wars. (p. 65) They conclude:  "our 'no' to
nuclear war must, in the end, be definitive and
decisive." (p. 64) Perhaps their position is decisive,
but it is not unambiguous (the bishops describe it as
"nuanced").  They condemn "counter-population" warfare
and any indiscriminate or disproportionate use of nuclear

weapons, even in retaliation. They reject Archbishop
Quinn's amendment opposing "any use" of nuclear weapons,
but their "extreme skepticism" about all use of these
weapons leads them to judge "first use" and the use of
nuclear weapons to counter conventional attacks to be
"morally unjustifiable." Concerning "first use," they
affirm:

> We do not perceive any situation in which
> the deliberate initiation of nuclear war-
> fare, on however restricted a scale, can be
> morally justified. Therefore a serious
> moral obligation exists to develop non-
> nuclear defensive strategies as rapidly
> as possible to preclude any justification
> for using nuclear weapons in response to
> nonnuclear attacks. (p. 69)

This statement exemplifies the toughening of the
language of the third draft at the Chicago meeting.
Before the conference approved an amendment recommended
by Archbishop Quinn, the first two sentences of the
statement read:

> We abhor the concept of initiating nuclear
> war on however restricted a scale. Because
> of the probable effects, the deliberate
> initiation of nuclear war, in our judgment,
> would be an unjustifiable moral risk.

The bishops conclude that the possibilities of
limiting the use and effects of nuclear weapons are so
"remote" and the danger of escalation so great that "it
would be morally unjustifiable to initiate nuclear war in
any form." (p. 70) However, they also acknowledge a
continuing responsibility of the United States to protect
itself and to assist in the defense of its allies against
either conventional or nuclear attack. Furthermore, they
recognize that developing adequate conventional forces is
a lengthy process. Therefore, they conclude, that "the
deterrence of a nuclear attack may require nuclear
weapons for a time, even though their possession and
deployment must be subject to rigid restrictions."
(p. 71) The bishops are aware that NATO's refusal to
adopt a "No First Use" pledge "is to some extent limited
to the deterrent effect of this inherent ambiguity."
Nonetheless, they "urge NATO to move rapidly toward the
adoption of a 'No First Use' policy, but doing so in
tandem with development of an adequate alternative
defense posture." (p. 72) Clearly the bishops prefer
reductions in both nuclear and conventional forces. They
admit, however, that increases in conventional defenses

would be a "proportionate price to pay, if this will
reduce the possibility of a nuclear war." (p. 101)
       As the above observations imply, the third draft
again recognizes that, as an interim position only, a
policy of nuclear deterrence is "morally acceptable."
Still, their acceptance is "strictly conditioned" and
tied to "progressive disarmament." (p. 80f) Deterrence
policy must not directly intend the destruction of enemy
populations. Plans must include only military targets.
Weapons systems should enhance the stability of
deterrence by not being vulnerable to preemptive strikes
and not possessing a first strike threat. The bishops
acknowledge that U.S. targeting policy is guided by the
principle of discrimination, and they recognize that the
new, highly-accurate, counterforce weapons provide a
greater capacity for discriminating use than the older
systems. They also judge, however, that even properly
targeted nuclear weapons would likely cause
disproportionate noncombatant destruction, and
counterforce weapons threaten to make the adversary's
retaliatory forces vulnerable because they possess a
"prompt hard target kill" capability. (p. 89) This
threat may more likely result in preemptive use of
nuclear weapons. Therefore, the bishops oppose
deployment of these weapons by both the United States and
the Soviet Union.
       The criteria which the bishops offer for evaluating
deterrence policy are essentially the same as those
presented in the second draft (above, p. 94-95). The
bishops' policy recommendations also resemble those of
the earlier drafts. They support immediate, bilateral
negotiations for "deep cuts" in nuclear arsenals, a
comprehensive test ban treaty, the removal of tactical
nuclear weapons from areas where they are likely to be
captured, and the strengthening of command and control
measures. The bishops refrain from endorsing any
specific political initiatives, but they again support
agreements "to halt the testing, production, and
deployment of new nuclear weapons systems." (p. 90) As
originally written, the third draft called for a "curb"
on new weapons. During the Chicago meeting the bishops
also considered using the terms "cease," "freeze," and
"stop." In the end, they returned to their terminology
of the first two drafts and urged a "halt" in the arms
race, which for them is a "moral imperative."
       The last third of this draft is concerned with the
"promotion of peace," or "peacemaking." Though expanded
and slightly modified, this section generally reaffirms
the positions of earlier drafts on arms control, civil
defense and peace education programs. The bishops urge
serious negotiations, summit meetings and "independent"
initiatives to (1) "halt" the development of new weapons,
(2) end the arms race, and (3) reduce arsenals. They

also criticize the credibility of the government's
efforts in civil defense and they endorse the
establishment of an academy of peace. The bishops
support the principles of conscientious objection and
selective conscientious objection to particular wars, and
they urge that these principles be recognized by legal
statutes.
The third draft is far more critical of the Soviet
Union than earlier drafts (see above, pp. 96). In the
section entitled, "The Promotion of Peace," the following
statements are among those added:

> Many peoples are forcibly kept under
> communist domination despite their manifest
> wishes to be free. Soviet power is very
> great. Whether the Soviet Union's
> pursuit of military might is motivated
> primarily by defensive or aggressive aims
> might be debated, but the effect is
> nevertheless to leave profoundly insecure
> those who must live in the shadow of
> that might. . . .

> . . . NATO is an alliance of democratic
> countries which have freely chosen their
> association; the Warsaw Pact is not.

> To pretend that as a nation we have lived up
> to all our own ideals would be patently
> dishonest. To pretend that all evils in
> the world have been or are now being
> perpetuated by dictatorial regimes would
> be both dishonest and absurd. But having
> said this, and admitting our own faults,
> it is imperative that we confront reality.
> The facts simply do not support the
> invidious comparisons made at times even
> in our own society between our way of
> life, in which most basic human rights
> are at least recognized even if they are
> not always adequately supported, and
> those totalitarian and tyrannical regimes
> in which such rights are either denied
> or systematically supresses. . . .

> A glory of the United States is the
> range of political freedoms its system
> permits us. We, as bishops, as Catholics,
> as citizens, exercise those freedoms in
> writing this letter, with its share of
> criticisms of our government. We have
> true freedom of religion, freedom of
> speech, and access to a free press.
> We could not exercise the same freedoms

in contemporary Eastern Europe or in the
Soviet Union. . . . (p. 116)

In this comparison of the superpowers, the Soviet
Union is described as a deceiving, imperialistic threat
to humanity. Still, however, the assessment of the
"Soviet threat" excludes significant reference to Soviet
forces and weapons, and the threat is discussed after all
judgments have been made concerning national security,
defense policies, and the use of nuclear weapons. The
structural arrangement of the pastoral letter implies,
therefore, that either weapons systems and defense policy
have little to do with the perceived threat to security,
or nuclear weapons are a greater threat than the Soviet
Union. William O'Brien points out that this is an
erroneous application of just-war theory, to determine
justifiable means prior to an assessment of the cause
("threat").[72]

CONCLUSION

The evolutionary process through which the NCCB
pastoral letter was developed indicates that the Catholic
episcopacy is tremendously concerned about the moral
issues associated with war and nuclear weapons. American
bishops are more critical of nuclear weapons than the
German bishops and their position goes beyond that of
Pope John Paul II. The overwhelming approval of the
pastoral letter indicates the level of the bishops'
concern. The fact that over 400 amendments were proposed
for the third draft even after two years of debate also
reveals that a wide diversity of opinion still exists
among the clergy. Nevertheless, some general
observations can be drawn from the position presented in
the pastoral letter.

The Catholic Church in America recognizes the
legitimacy of both pacifism and the just-war tradition
for individual believers. Indeed, the pastoral itself is
a somewhat awkward consolidation of these two moral
points of view. After some wavering, the Church strongly
reaffirmed the just-war principles as the right moral
philosophy for governments. It is the right and duty of
governments to defend their citizens against unjust
aggression.

Concerning nuclear weapons issues, the bishops are
willing to increase conventional forces if this will lead
to a reduced reliance on nuclear forces for deterrence.
The bishops have not affirmed Hunthausen's call for
unilateral nuclear disarmament, withholding of taxes, and
ceasing all arms sales to other nations. They do not
specifically endorse Matthiesen's call for workers to
resign from industries constructing nuclear weapons; they

do, however, recommend careful evaluation by employees.
The bishops have not reached Francis Winters' conclusion
that civilian and military officials in positions of
planning or executing nuclear weapons policy face the
choice of resignation or violating the Church's teaching.
They do conclude that no Christian should follow orders
to perform immoral acts, such as indiscriminate bombing.
With Quinn, the bishops strongly question the
government's civil defense policy. The bishops
essentially subscribe to Mahony's position on the
"non-use" of nuclear weapons. They reject indiscriminate
use and first use of these weapons, and they are
skeptical that any use can be morally justified.

With Pope John Paul II, the bishops have declared a
policy of deterrence "morally acceptable." They insist,
however, that deterrence must be based on "sufficient"
rather than "superior" nuclear forces. They oppose the
deployment of destabilizing, "counterforce" nuclear
weapons. They also urge a "halt" on the development of
new weapons and call for "deep cuts" in existing
arsenals. The bishops strongly condemn the arms race and
they encourage unilateral initiatives to stimulate
productive negotiations toward balanced, mutual,
verifiable nuclear disarmament.

The NCCB letter raises difficult questions, to which
critics like James Schall, Michael Novak and William
O'Brien are quick to respond. Where is the line to be
drawn between the church's responsibility as a moral
critic and the government's responsibility as
policy maker? Should the church address specific
strategies and weapons, or should its discussion be
limited to general moral principles? Can an assessment
that largely ignores Soviet weapons, policies and
practices provide effective analysis for American
security plans and policies? By moving from a
description of the effects of nuclear weapons to a
critique almost exclusively focused on American weapons
and policies, have the bishops neglected a central
feature of deterrence, that is, that both the Soviets and
Americans must be deterred? One must wonder how credible
a deterrence policy is that unilaterally rejects most
uses and threats to use nuclear weapons, and limits
weapons development to a criterion of contribution toward
progressive disarmament rather than the requisites for
deterring adversarial capabilities. Finally, one must
question the consistency with which the pastoral letter
will be applied. The NCCB clearly distinguishes between
binding principles and prudential judgments.
Nevertheless, within two days of the letter's approval,
some bishops were insisting that "faithful Catholics"
ought to consider the prudential judgments binding.

110

NOTES

1. Michael Novak in "Arms and the Church,"
Commentary 73 (March 1982): 39, describes Pax Christi as
an "international Catholic disarmament movement."

2. Personal interview, Spring Lake, N.J., 27 April
1982.

3. J. Bryan Hehir, "The Catholic Church and the
Arms Race," Worldview (July-August 1978):13-14; and "The
Pope's Delicate Balance," Commonweal 109 (26 March 1982):
168.

4. "The Catholic Church and Witness Against War,"
in War or Peace?, pp. 200-213.

5. Ibid., p. 200.

6. Ibid., p. 206.

7. Ibid., p. 209.

8. Joseph Fahey, "Pax Christi," in Shannon, War or
Peace?, p. 60.

9. Ibid., p. 62.

10. These priorities are discussed by Fahey, ibid.,
pp. 63-64; the quotations are cited from an undated
brochure entitled "Pax Christi U.S.A.: International
Catholic Movement for Peace." This brochure indicates
that Pax Christi offers support for pacificsts and
selective conscientious objectors; but unlike Vatican II,
does not also offer support for those who for reasons of
conscience choose to bear arms in defense of their
country.

11. Fahey, ibid., p. 65-66.

12. Ibid., pp. 66, 69.

13. Ibid., pp. 69-70.

14. Unpublished letter dated 13 March 81, submitted
to Archbishop Bernardin by Mary Evelyn Jegen, SND,
National Coordinator, Pax Christi U.S.A.

15. Ibid., p. 5.

16. Christianity and Crisis, 41 (17 August 1981):
218-31.

17. "Ecclesiastical Wars Over Peace," National Review (25 June 1982): 760.

18. This address, entitled "Faith and Disarmament," is reprinted in Christianity and Crisis, 41(17 August 1981): 229-31.

19. Ibid., p. 229.

20. Ibid.

21. Unpublished manuscript of "The Church, The Gospel and the Arms Race," p. 4, distributed by Archbishop Raymond Hunthausen, 907 Terry Avenue, Seattle, Washington 98104.

22. Ibid. In a pastoral letter published in the Catholic Northwest Progress, the newspaper of the Catholic Archdiocese of Seattle, 2 July 1981, Hunthausen implied that the Soviet threat was more alleged than actual.

23. "The Church, The Gospel and the Arms Race," p. 3.

24. In "American Bishops and Nuclear Disarmament," The Wall Street Journal, 14 January 1982, Michael Novak pointed out that not 50 percent, but less than 10 percent of the defense budget was allocated to strategic arms, which Hunthausen claimed to be protesting. The total defense budget amounts to less than 50 percent of federal budget. According to Wallace Turner, the $125 Hunthausen withheld equalled 50 percent of his quarterly tax. The remaining $125 was sent to World Peace Tax Fund of Bellpoint, Long Island, "which accepts money from those who object to supporting the military with taxes." Cf. "Tax Refusal Completes Prelate's Moral Journey," New York Times, 19 April 1982.

25. Cf. Editor, "A Catholic Antinuclear Protest," The Christian Century 32 (14 October 1981): 1011-12; "The Religious 'Peace' Offensive," MINDSZENTY REPORT (October 1981); Catholics Take to the Ramparts," Time (19 April 1982).

26. "Antinuclear Position Proves Costly in Amarillo, Home of Weapons Plant," The New York Times, 21 March 1982. Despite Matthiesen's advice to the contrary the man did resign from Pantex. As of December 1982, he was the only one to do so in protest against nuclear weapons.

27. Leroy T. Matthiesen, "Nuclear Arms Buildup," 21 August 1982, in Nuclear Disarmament: Key Statements of

Popes, Bishops, Councils and Churches, edited by Robert
Heyer (New York: Paulist Press, 1982), pp. 155-56.
(Here after cited as Nuclear Disarmament.)

28. Ibid., p. 156.

29. Editor, "The Price of Apostleship," National
Catholic Reporter (12 March 1982).

30. Novak, "American Bishops and Nuclear
Disarmament," The Wall Street Journal, 14 January 1982.

31. Heyer, Nuclear Disarmament, p. 96.

32. Hehir, "The Catholic Church and the Arms Race,"
Worldview, pp. 16-17.

33. All of the following citations from Quinn in
this section are from a reprint of this message in Catholic Update: Today's Faith in Focus (Cincinnati: St.
Anthony Press, April 1982), passim. The message is also
published in Heyer, Nuclear Disarmament, pp. 156-64. St.
Francis has in recent years become a symbol of peace for
many in the peace movement.

34. The address by Pope John Paul II is reprinted in
Heyer, Nuclear Disarmament, pp. 45-46.

35. Commonweal 90 (12 March 1982): 137.

36. Michael Novak, "Mahonyism," National Review (9
July 1982):838.

37. The following quotations are cited from this
unpublished letter entitled "The Call of Christ, Prince
of Peace: Becoming a Church of Peace Advocacy." This
letter is reprinted in Commonweal 109 (12 March 1982):
137-43.

38. Mahony here equates "minimal deterrence" and
"parity." Normally these are seen as different
positions. "Minimal deterrence" advocates "sufficiency,"
not "parity" in military strength. Mahony encourages a
reduction of current armaments by "one half on both
sides."

39. Francis X. Winters, "The Bow or the Cloud?:
American Bishops Challenge the Arms Race," America 145
(18-25 July 1981): 29.

40. The following quotations are cited from this 11
June 1982 draft. Page numbers of the draft are included
parenthetically in the text following the quotations.

41.  This quest for a "new way" of thinking follows
the admonition of the Second Vatican Council, as noted
previously.  The difficulty of this endeavor is
illustrated by the use of traditional just-war criteria
as the terminology in this "new way" thinking.  Though
the second draft does move more toward a "theology of
peace," this inconsistency remains.  The juxtaposition of
pacifism and just-war theory as equally valid positions
also continues to be problematic in the second draft.  It
may well not be possible to think about issues in ways
equally acceptable to pacifists and just-war supporters.

42.  This statement, like the previous one concerning
counter-population use, was retained verbatim in the
second draft, except "condoned" was changed to "morally
justified" and "deterred" became "resisted."

43.  This statement, along with all talk permitting
the use of nuclear weapons, was omitted from the second
draft.

44.  Commonweal 109 (13 August 1982): 424-40.

45.  Ibid., p. 424.

46.  Ibid., p. 433.

47.  Ibid., p. 434.

48.  Ibid., p. 429.

49.  Ibid., p. 430.

50.  Ibid., p. 435.  Zahn's pacifism is reflected in
this objection.

51.  Ibid., p. 436.

52.  Ibid., p. 428.

53.  Ibid., p. 429.

54.  The second draft was printed in full by the
National Catholic News Service, Origins:  NC Documentary
Service 12 (28 October 1982): 307-28.  Origins is
sponsored by the NCCB, 1312 Massachusetts Avenue, N.W.,
Washington, DC  20005.  Quotations from the second draft
cited herein are from the Origins printing and page
numbers are included in the text parenthetically
following the quotation.

114

55. Pope John Paul II, "Peace: A Gift of God Entrusted to Us!" Day of Peace message, 1 January 1982. Reprinted by the Knights of Columbus.

56. "Bishops Appear Divided on Proposed A-War Letter," The Washington Post, 16 November 1982, p. A2.

57. "Catholic Bishops Are to Open Nuclear Arms Debate Today," The New York Times, 15 November 1982, p. B6.

58. "Majority of Bishops Back Draft of Arms Letter," The New York Times, 17 November 1982, p. B4.

59. "Bishops Slap Nukes," Daily News, 19 November 1982, p. 2.

60. Raymond G. Hunthausen, "A Statement in Response to the Pastoral Letter on War and Peace," God's Peace: His Promise and Our Work, 15 November 1982. This document is an unpublished draft of Hunthausen's address to the NCCB Conference.

61. "Comments of Archbishop John R. Quinn," an unpublished draft of Quinn's address to the conference, 15 November 1982.

62. Joseph L. Bernardin, "Remarks on the Pastoral Letter on War and Peace," an unpublished draft presented to the conference, 15 November 1982. Bernardin is chairman of the Ad Hoc Committee drafting the pastoral letter.

63. "Remarks by Most Reverend Pio Laghi," an unpublished draft of the Apostolic Delegate's remarks to the NCCB, 15 November 1982.

64. "Statement of Archbishop Philip M. Hannan of New Orleans at the NCCB Meeting in Washington, D.C., November 15, 1982," an unpublished draft of Hannan's address.

65. "Comments on the 2nd draft of the Pastoral, 'The Challenge of Peace'; by Cardinal Krol, at the Plenary meeting of the Catholic Bishops in Washington, November 15, 1982." This document is an unpublished draft of Krol's address.

66. "Intervention of His Eminence, Terence Cardinal Cooke, at the meeting of the National Conference of Catholic Bishops," Washington, D.C., Monday, November 15, 1982, unpublished draft of Cooke's address. Cooke is the Military Vicar for U.S. military service personnel.

67.  Bishop John J. O'Connor, "The Bishop's Pastoral:
An Overview," National Catholic Register, 26 December
1982; reprinted in OPS Review special issue entitled "The
Bishop's Proposed Pastoral on War and Peace:  Some
Perspectives," (December 1982, pp. 20-21) by the Office
of Pastoral Support, Military Vicariate (1011 First
Avenue, New York, New York, 10022).

68.  "Vatican Issues Communique on War and Peace
Pastoral," Catholic Voice, 31 January 1983, p. 7.

69.  "German Bishops Uphold a Case for A-Arms," The
New York Times, 28 April 1983, p. A8; "Justice Creates
Peace," The Week in Germany 14 (29 April 1983): 1.

70.  Kenneth A. Briggs, "Bishops Endorse Stand
Opposed to Nuclear War," The New York Times, 4 May 1983,
p. A1.

71.  Page numbers cited parenthetically in the text
are from the "Third Draft:  The Challenge of Peace:
God's Promise and Our Response," May 1983, copyrighted by
the United States Catholic Conference, Inc.  Amendments
to this draft at the Chicago NCCB Meeting, 2-3 May 1983,
have been incorporated into the text.

72.  Lecture presented at the U.S. Army War College,
Carlisle Barracks, Pennsylvania, 14 April 1983.

# [ 5 ]
# Protestant Peacemaking:
# The National Council of Churches

## INTRODUCTION

In this chapter we turn our attention to recent
statements from the Protestant tradition.  I am using the
term "Protestant" in a general sense to identify
"non-Roman Catholic" Christians.  Included in this
chapter are churches other than those which originated
during the Reformation or which adhere to a "reformed"
theology.

Another point also is important to recognize in
discussing Protestants.  The Catholic bishops suggest
that we receive their pastoral letters as "moral
guidance" rather than absolute statements of moral
doctrine.  This caution is even more warranted among most
Protestant groups.  Protestant moral statements generally
represent the opinions of those individuals or groups
making pronouncements.  Rarely, if ever, are such
statements fashioned as creeds to which accent is
requisite for membership.  For example, among Southern
Baptists the Christian Life Commission is the agency
tasked with publishing ethical statements on social
issues.  No Southern Baptist would contend, however, that
the Commission's statements are official policy, or even
that they represent the majority opinion within the
domination.  The same is true of statements issued by
leaders of most other Protestant churches.  With this
caution, however, it should also be recognized that
leadership opinion is a significant indicator of trends
and may represent the views of the majority of a church's
membership.

My research in this chapter and the next depends
heavily on the responses by denominations to the
questionnaire I sent in early 1982 (see Appendix A).
This approach allows each denomination to identify the
documents it considers most relevant to the discussion.
I begin by looking at some of the churches affiliated
with the National Council of Churches, and then, in the
next chapter I consider other Protestant groups.  This

chapter and Chapter 6 form a unit on "Protestant peacemaking." I have not thematically grouped the churches in these two chapters. In general the National Council of Churches is more aggressive in its pursuit of peacemaking than its member churches. These churches are, however, more assertive than the Lutheran bodies or the Southern Baptist Convention. Also, of the National Council churches, the positions of the Presbyterian Church in the United States and the Episcopal Church more closely resemble the Lutheran positions in their continued use of just-war concepts. The least active of the major denominations are the Lutheran Church--Missouri Synod and the Southern Baptist Convention. Both of these denominations have expressed concern over nuclear weapons issues, however, and generally affirm just-war principles.

## THE NATIONAL COUNCIL OF CHURCHES

The National Council of the Churches of Christ in the U.S.A. (NCC) is a "cooperative federation" of 32 Protestant and Orthodox Churches. The aggregate membership of these churches is approximately 40 million, or 18 percent of the national population. Almost half of the 75 million Protestants in the United States are members of churches associated with the NCC. The NCC is not a governing body and has no control over affiliate churches, however, its statements on war and nuclear weapons have strongly influenced the positions adopted by many larger Protestant denominations in the NCC.

More than a decade before Randall Forsberg issued her <u>Call to Halt the Nuclear Arms Race</u> (1980),[1] identified as the "founding document of the nuclear weapons freeze movement" by Senators Kennedy and Hatfield,[2] the NCC called for a mutual halt to testing, production, and deployment of nuclear weapons. A policy statement adopted in 1968 and entitled "Defense and Disarmament: New Requirements for Security" has become a basic position paper of the NCC.[3] This document favors a new world order of "global interdependence," rather than nationalism, which it says presently guides U.S. defense policies. The statement also calls for a new perspective on national security. The massive accumulation of military power by the United States has not provided the security intended by this arms buildup. National security has decreased as the nuclear arms race has increased. Present defense policies "threaten to destroy the created order," and they subordinate all other values to "military necessity." Our understanding of national security should recognize the need for relying on international processes, meeting the needs of the underdeveloped world, and supporting human rights and

values.  We must acknowledge the "ultimate futility of
the attempt to maintain nuclear superiority."
    Based on these propositions the NCC urges the United
States to seek the following:

A.  In arms control and arms limitation--

    - a mutual halt in the further production
      and deployment of strategic offensive
      and defensive missile systems, including
      the anti-ballistic missile system;
    - widespread support for the non-
      proliferation treaty;
    - a mutual cessation of production of
      fissionable material for military
      purposes;
    - a comprehensive test ban treaty, taking
      into full account available national
      means of detection and inspection;
    - A United Nations declaration forbidding
      nations to place weapons of mass
      destruction on the seabed;
    - continued study and planning in
      problems related to conversion from
      defense to nondefense production;
    - the strengthening of international
      revulsion against the production and
      use of chemical and bacteriological
      weapons and the development of effective
      control and verification measures to
      reinforce international restraints.

B.  In defense spending and use of resources--

    - significant reductions in defense
      spending and the channeling of the
      funds into development projects at
      home and abroad;
    - a radical curtailing and strict
      controlling of the supply of arms
      to other countries.

C.  In peace-keeping, peace-making, and
    disarmament--

    - the strengthening of the United Nations
      as a peace-keeping and peace-making
      agency, including the training by
      member nations of special forces to be
      available for United Nations peace-
      keeping operations;
    - a major and sustained effort, in
      conjunction with other nations, for
      substantial and rapid progress toward

arms control and general disarmament
through international agreement.

The General Board of the NCC adopted this 1968
policy statement by a vote of eighty-eight to zero, with
two abstentions. In it we find the basic issues and
objective goals advocated by many Protestant disarmament
statements over the last fifteen years. These include
ending the arms race, terminating our reliance on nuclear
weapons, the "freeze" proposal, reduced defense spending,
and increased support for international agencies and
developing nations. The statement recognizes the need
for defense and security, but affirms that means other
than military are also essential to attain these
objectives. Only U.S. policy is addressed directly; the
actions or policies of other nations are ignored.
However, the heavy emphasis on treaty agreements
implicitly recognizes bilateral or multilateral
responsibilities in arms control and limitation.

In 1973 the NCC again urged the United States to
suspend underground nuclear testing, for as long as the
Soviet Union abstained from such testing, and to pursue
agreement on a comprehensive test ban treaty.[4]  By late
1977 the NCC had begun to criticize specific U.S.
policies and weapons. In November of that year, noting
that nuclear weapons "pose an increasing threat of utter
devastation if ever used," the NCC called for a goal of
"general and comprehensive disarmament." The Council
also supported a "halt in further production of nuclear
weapons and a roll-back of existing nuclear weapons,
toward the ultimate goal of eliminating nuclear weapons
from the arsenals of all nations. . . ." Specifically,
the NCC urged the United States to cease funding the
development of the neutron bomb, cruise missile, Trident
submarine, MX missile, and the Mark 12A warhead. Our
government was asked to renounce military doctrines and
strategies "which lead to the use of nuclear weapons."
The Council called for negotiated reductions rather than
unilateral disarmament; however, as a unilateral
"initiative," it again recommended the suspension of
underground testing, coupled with an invitation to the
Soviet Union to do the same.[5]

The following year the NCC advocated "new
initiatives" by the United States. These included
announcing a "no first-strike" policy, adopting a policy
of "no threat or use of nuclear weapons against
non-nuclear states," and initiating a "moratorium" on new
strategic weapons systems. The Council also urged its
member churches to fulfill their vocation as
"peacemakers" by allocating increased resources "to
education and action on the disarmament agenda," and
increasing efforts "to change the institutions in our
society which are obstacles to peace." This 1978
resolution was entitled "Swords into Plowshares." As the

title implies, the NCC asked its members to turn to the
task of developing "non-violent forms of political power"
for resolving international conflict.[6]
        Perhaps in pursuit of this last injunction,
representatives of the NCC met with officials from
Orthodox and Protestant churches of the Soviet Union in a
Consultation on Disarmament on 27-29 March 1979.
Following this Geneva meeting, a joint statement was
published entitled Choose Life. "With one voice"--and in
words similar to previous NCC statements--the delegates
rejected the arms race. They "confessed that seeking our
security through arms is in fact a false and idolatrous
hope and that true security can be found only in
relationships of trust." The representatives called upon
their "brothers and sisters" to press for approval of
SALT II accords and for a general prohibition of nuclear
arms testing, development and deployment.[7] Two years
later the NCC cited this consultation as a part of its
rationale for fully endorsing the nuclear freeze campaign
in the United States.[8]
        During the 1970s the NCC was fairly complimentary in
its remarks to President Carter. However, the Council
strongly denounced early Reagan policies in "a message to
the churches" entitled "The Re-Making of America?"[9]
This message characterizes Reagan's proposal "to get
America back on track," as "a reversal of direction for
this country" which threatens "the vision of America as
the model and embodiment of a just and humane society."
The statement provides the following evaluation of the
Administration's military policy:

> Since the end of World War II and the
> concurrent beginning of the nuclear age,
> this nation has attempted to seek and
> maintain peace through diplomatic rather
> than military means, through multilateral
> more than unilateral channels, through
> negotiation rather than coercion (the
> exception of Vietnam notwithstanding).
> It has relied on the concept of "mutual
> assured destruction" to provide an uneasy
> umbrella for this fragile enterprise
> in the world--the assurance that the
> consequences of nuclear exchange are
> too devastatingly costly for any
> nation to risk it. Now all that is
> to be reversed. Nuclear superiority
> and the capacity to project overwhelming
> military power anywhere in the world
> are proposed as basic national policies.
> Resources that previously contributed,
> however inadequately, to efforts to
> improve life are now to be diverted
> to produce more weapons of death,

increasing inflation and accelerating
the international arms race. Although
the United States and the Soviet Union
both have more than enough strategic
nuclear warheads to kill the earth's
people several times over, yet
further weapons escalation is proposed.

Reversing an increasing willingness to
see the world in its real diversity
and pluralism, the new administration
is determined to turn away from the
uneasy detente of the past decade and
revive the distorted vision of the bi-
polar Cold War world, in which all
adverse occurrences, at home or abroad,
are attributed to the machinations of
a single force--Communism. Turning
from the growing satisfaction of being
one of a worldwide community of
nations, this administration proposes
to make America "Number One" in the
world. Not number one in literacy,
life expectancy, or assistance to
less developed nations. Not number
one in freedom from infant morality,
drug addiction, crime or suicide.
But, rather number one in military
dominance, in the ability to impose
our will on others or to kill
multitudes in the attempt.

In this statement, the NCC offers the following
observation concerning the international military
context: "There are real dangers in the world, and the
behavior of other nations sometimes threatens peace and
justice--witness Afghanistan. Those dangers are not
lessened by this nation's turning from the path of
patient strength." It is noteworthy in this statement
that the NCC seems to regret turning from "mutual assured
destruction," a policy so frequently criticized for
indiscriminately targeting population centers. This
suggests that the NCC considers current policy more
dangerous than MAD, because it offers greater risk of
nuclear war.

In the last several years, the Council has become
the target of increasing attacks from the religious and
political right. Recently, theologians and political
analysts who consider themselves "political centrists"
have also severely criticized its statements and actions,
associating the Council with leftist and even Marxist
movements.[10] One of the organizations leading the
assault on the NCC is the Institute for Religion and
Democracy (IRD), formed in 1980 by a small group of

United Methodists as an attempt to move their
denomination away from what they considered its
"leftward" pattern. The organization's current president
is United Methodist evangelist Ed Robb from Marshall,
Texas. He concurs that a principal goal of the IRD is to
shift the emphasis of the NCC and "mainline" Protestant
denominations to a centrist position.[11] The IRD is
closely associated with the "neoconservative" political
organization Coalition for a Democratic Majority,
organized in 1972 by Edmund Muskie, Hubert Humphrey,
Henry Jackson, Daniel Moynihan, and others.[12]

The membership of the IRD is small; however its
advisory board includes many well known figures. In
addition to prominent United Methodist clergy, the board
includes Michael Novak, Peter Berger, Julian Hartt, Carl
Henry, James Finn, and Richard John Neuhaus.[13] Neuhaus
has concluded that NCC and mainline Protestant leaders
are no longer "sympathic critics" of the nation and,
thus, cannot provide effective moral leadership for the
American public.[14]

The NCC has taken seriously these criticisms. They
were among the central issues discussed by the governing
board of the NCC in its annual meeting, 10-13 May 1983.
Thus far, the Council has not materially changed the tone
or substance of its position, and it appears that a
majority of the leaders among member denominations
continues strongly to support the Council. In fact, the
statements adopted by member churches in recent years
reflect positions similar to that of the NCC. However,
in May 1983 the Council of Bishops of the United
Methodist Church voted to conduct an internal
investigation into allegations concerning NCC funding of
Third World revolutionary movements. The bishops also
expressed their continuing support of the NCC, as well as
the World Council of Churches.

## THE MAINLINE PROTESTANT DENOMINATIONS

There is no formal agreement as to which churches
are considered "mainline" Protestant denominations. I am
using the term in reference to the older, well
established denominations affiliated with the National
Council of Churches. As indicated in the last section,
there is close similarity between the positions on war
and nuclear weapons adopted by these churches and the
NCC.

## The United Methodist Church

The United Methodist Church (UMC) is the second
largest Protestant denomination in the United States, and
the largest member of the NCC. Approximately one-fourth

of the forty million members claimed by the NCC are members of the UMC. It is ironic that in 1982 the president of the Institute for Religion and Democracy was a United Methodist, as was the president of NCC, James Armstrong. Armstrong's position, however, is clearly more representative of the views held by Methodist bishops. At their annual meeting in November 1981, the Council of Bishops of the UMC issued "A Call to Nuclear Disarmament and Peace with Justice." This document described the "threat of nuclear holocaust" as the most crucial issue facing humanity today. This theme was continued in a pastoral letter published by the bishops in April 1982. The Council requested that the letter be read in all churches on 16 May 1982. In this letter the bishops affirm: "One issue transcends all others as we look into the uncertain future. It is the issue of human survival."[15] Noting the existence of 50,000 nuclear weapons in the world, the bishops judge that "arguments concerning parity have become irrelevant because of the frightening overkill capacities of both the United States and the Soviet Union." "With the push of a button" superpower leaders could provide "a 'final solution' to the human story." Because of this threat, the bishops endorse the Joint Resolution on Nuclear Freeze and Arms Reduction. In the April letter they urge:

> Governments must stop manufacturing nuclear weapons. Deployed weapons must be removed. Stockpiles must be reduced and dismantled. Verification procedures must be agreed upon. Eventual nuclear disarmament is necessary if the human race, as we know it, is to survive.

The bishops do not call for unilateral disarmament. They urge mutual efforts by the superpowers. They also acknowledge the lack of trust between the two nations and, therefore, call for serious negotiations on the basis of "mutual self-interest" and a "commitment to a global future."

John B. Warman is a Methodist bishop from Harrisburg, Pennsylvania. His rejection of the use of nuclear weapons is more graphic than the letter by the Council of Bishops. He specifically criticizes the neutron bomb and the Trident submarine. He asserts that no nuclear weapon can be used in Christian love. "You cannot boil seven million human beings in their own juices and then speak of Christian love. It would be far better for us to trust the God of the Resurrection and suffer death than to use such a weapon."[16] Warman does not explain his figure of "seven million." The tone of his article, however, is not factual. He seems more intent on increasing emotional rage toward nuclear weapons than presenting a reasoned discussion.

Alan Geyer, a Methodist minister, employs considerably more reason and factual data in his approach to nuclear disarmament. He is currently the executive director of the Churches' Center for Theology and Public Policy in Washington. He has studied and written on disarmament issues for more than a decade and has been a member of the prestigious International Institute for Strategic Studies (London) since 1965. His book, The Idea of Disarmament! Rethinking the Unthinkable (1982),[17] is an argument for the necessity of nuclear disarmament. In Geyer's words: "It is an argument for affirming the primacy of American responsibility for reversing the arms race, without minimizing Soviet complicity in it or the shenanigans of many other states."[18] Geyer strongly criticizes the policy of deterrence, counterforce strategy, and U.S. efforts at arms control.

Geyer is exceedingly pessimistic about past trends in arms control. The McCloy-Zorin Agreement of 1961 committed both superpowers to work for general and complete nuclear disarmament. This commitment was renewed in the Test Ban Treaty of 1963, the Nuclear Non-Proliferation Treaty of 1968, and the SALT I Treaty of 1972. The tremendous increase in nuclear weapons during this same period leads Geyer to conclude that the arms race is out of control. He sees deterrence as a policy which rationalizes the unending production of nuclear weapons[19] and cites twenty-one reasons for rejecting it. He claims that the "missile crisis" of the 1950s and the "ICBM vulnerability" of the 1980s are hawkish scenarios for justifying new weapons systems. Nevertheless, he concludes that in the short-run a minimalist deterrence policy may be necessary.

He contends, however, that our policy should not include "counterforce" strategy, which he considers to be a "first strike" and "war fighting" doctrine. He also believes that this strategy, with its more accurate and smaller weapons, reduces the distinction between nuclear and conventional weapons, thus, making nuclear warfare more psychologically plausible.[20] Because of the proximity of military targets to population centers and the likelihood of escalation, Geyer rejects claims that counterforce warfare could be conducted discriminately.

The last chapters of The Idea of Disarmament are Geyer's scenarios for pushing beyond deterrence in a phased process to arms control (e.g., SALT II), arms reductions and, finally, nuclear disarmament.[21] Geyer supports the negotiating concepts like those of Charles Osgood who advocates unilateral initiatives to stimulate reciprocal reductions.[22] He calls for objective descriptions of the Soviet Union. He insists that Soviet brutality, aggression, and arms buildup should not be ignored; but he also urges that prevelent myths about the Soviet Union should be discredited. Geyer claims, for

example, that Soviet power is not growing all over the
world; that the Soviet Union has a good record of
complying with arms treaties, and that they are more
transigent than the United States in arms negotiations.
He affirms that "the Soviets, through most of the
Brezhnev era, were deeply serious about arms
limitations."[23]

Geyer concludes his book with sketchy outlines for a
"Theology of Peacemaking" based on religious humanism, a
humanized technology, and a demythologized concept of
security.[24] He claims that the traditional theories of
pacifism and just war are war theories, not peace
theories. He sees some validity in just-war theory as an
ethic for when and how to fight a war. What is also
needed, he claims, is a peace theory, a "theology of
peacemaking," which for Christians should be a higher
priority than a war ethic.[25]

Alan Geyer's work is not an official Methodist
position. However, it is a sophisticated statement
consistent with the pastoral letter of the Council of
Bishops.


## American Baptist Churches

The denomination of American Baptist Churches
(ABC)[26] has approximately one and one-quarter million
members. It is closely affiliated with the National
Council of Churches and its position on nuclear weapons
is similar to that of the United Methodist Church.

In 1964 the ABC adopted a "Resolution on Peace with
Justice." This resolution addressed two issues which are
now common concerns in ABC statements: nuclear weapons
and underdeveloped countries of the Third World. The
resolution warned against nuclear proliferation and urged
American Baptists to be agents of peace and
reconciliation. "As Christ was concerned for mankind in
his hunger, sorrow and nakedness, so must we be concerned
for men caught in a world of conflict and need and must
work for a world of peace with justice and freedom."[27]
This last phrase, "peace with justice and freedom," has
become a common theme of many denominations in recent
years, Protestant and Catholic.

By the late 1970s American Baptist statements on war
were longer and more specific. In 1978 the General Board
adopted a "Resolution on Disarmament" closely resembling
the NCC resolution of that year, "Swords into
Plowshares." In it the Board stated: "As Christians we
believe that armaments and military force are
inconsistent with the ways of Jesus Christ and the
biblical hope of justice and peace. We seek to convert
armaments into implements that affirm life rather than
deny it."[28] The resolution condemned the arms race for
threatening world peace and diverting limited resources

from meeting human needs. It then expressed support for the United Nations' Special Session on Disarmament and called for a strong declaration on disarmament. In addition to encouraging bilateral efforts to limit arms through a SALT II agreement, the resolution urged the United States to "work tirelessly" for a Comprehensive Test Ban Treaty. The document concluded by calling American Baptists to a "vocation as peacemakers." It urged them to greater commitment in prayer and allocation of resources to the disarmament agenda.

In December 1978 the General Board adopted a "Policy Statement on Military and Foreign Policy," which continued to call for arms control and disarmament measures. "These goals must be pursued multilaterally and bilaterally where possible and with safeguards, but nations must, at times, also take some unilateral steps to halt the arms race in order to encourage trust and reduce the likelihood and destructiveness of war." The Board again advocated nonproliferation agreements and a global ban on nuclear testing. The United States was urged to pursue the development of a stronger United Nations, one capable of providing global enforcement systems.

In a 1981 resolution, the General Board launched a direct attack on the arms race and President Reagan's proposals for rebuilding the nation's defense. The Board expressed dismay over the growing reliance by many countries on military expenditures as a substitute for negotiations and diplomacy. Then it focused directly on Reagan Administration policy:

> We are alarmed at the enormous
> increases in military spending both
> planned and enacted into law by our
> own government. It is now projected
> that the United States will spend more
> than one trillion dollars on its
> military over the next five years,
> while making major reductions in
> expenditures for health, education,
> welfare, transportation and
> housing. . . . Meanwhile, our
> government places low priority on
> negotiations with our adversaries
> for arms control. This emphasis on
> military spending as a means to
> national security ignores the fact that
> the security of a nation is weakened
> when its own people are treated unjustly.
> Cutting expenditures for human needs
> decreases our nation's security by
> increasing class conflict, racism,
> poverty, and illiteracy.

This ABC resolution also stated that "with the
development of strategic nuclear weapons with
first-strike capabilities, the assumption that mutually
assured destruction will deter war has been supplemented
by a dangerous new doctrine of limited nuclear war as a
legitimate foreign policy option." Based on these
observations, the ABC resolution urged the Administration
and Congress to identify and eliminate all weapons which
"destabilize the current military balance and needlessly
escalate the arms race." Especially the cruise missile,
neutron bomb, and the MX missile system should be closely
examined in this regard. The resolution also called on
the Administration to increase its efforts to negotiate
with the Soviet Union "an immediate freeze at present
levels of stockpiles of nuclear warheads and delivery
systems and future reductions in strategic nuclear arms
and other types of weapons."[29]

In a rare and, therefore, significant action on
9 December 1981, the American Baptist Executive Ministers
issued a "Call for Elimination of Nuclear Weapons." The
denomination's thirty-six chief executive officers
endorsed this document, which declared:

> Believing there is no justification for
> the use of nuclear weapons on any people
> under any circumstances, we call on the
> nations of the world to stop the produc-
> tion of nuclear weapons, to dismantle
> those that exist, and to join in a
> program of mutual inspection. We call
> upon the President, Congress, and the
> leaders of other nations, to take bold
> initiatives to reach these goals.

The statement by the executive ministers falls
clearly in the position of nuclear pacifism. The ABC
documents cited in this section were sent to me by Larry
Pullen of the ABC Peace Concerns Program. In his cover
letter, Pullen offered the following comments:

> As Manager of the Peace Concerns Program,
> I give sermons, talks, seminars and
> workshops, and in each of those contexts
> I call into question the traditional
> Just-War Theory. I believe that the use
> of nuclear weapons would violate both
> the tenet of discrimination (military
> vs. civilian population) and the tenet
> of proportionality (good gained greater
> than evil incurred). The development
> of tactical nuclear weapons and a
> counter-force strategy may seem to
> enhance the credibility of the nuclear
> deterrent, but such an erosion of the

threshold between conventional and
nuclear weapons greatly increases the
probability that a war involving the
major powers would become an all-out
nuclear war.[30]

Like the Executive Ministers, Pullen also seems to
advocate a position of nuclear pacifism. His statement,
however, contains an inconsistency common in recent
church literature on disarmament. He questions the
validity of just-war theory, but then applies its
criteria to proscribe the use of nuclear weapons. His
logic would be more consistent if he affirmed the
just-war criteria as his rationale for rejecting the use
of nuclear weapons. Otherwise, he is rejecting the
criteria by which he judges.

## Christian Church (Disciples of Christ)

The Christian Church, known as the Disciples of
Christ, is approximately the same size as the American
Baptist Churches, with over 1,200,000 members. The
Disciples Church actively supports and defends the
National Council of Churches' position. With the NCC, it
has for years adopted resolutions on the arms race and
nuclear weapons. The denomination's principal statements
on these issues were approved by the General Assembly in
1979 and in 1981. One of the resolutions adopted in 1981
designated "Peace with Justice" as the area of primary
concern and focus for the years 1982-1985. This means
that educational programs, worship services, and action
programs in the next four years will be devoted to issues
such as arms control and disarmament, peacekeeping,
peacemaking, world hunger, human rights, freedom,
injustice, and economic inequality.

In 1979 the General Assembly approved a resolution
calling on the Senate to ratify the second Strategic Arms
Limitation Treaty (SALT II) as a step toward arms
reductions. The Assembly asked President Carter and the
Congress "to question the role of the United States as
the world's largest producer and exporter of arms," to
intensify their efforts to reverse the dangerous and
burdensome arms race, and to pursue "with urgency" a
comprehensive ban on nuclear testing. Also, the Assembly
suggested that church members consider joining Disciples
Peace Fellowship, "a fellowship of members . . . who
reject war as a method of settling international disputes
and work together toward the elimination of war and the
creation of conditions of peace among peoples and
nations."[31]

The General Assembly endorsed several resolutions in
1981 concerning the issues of war and peace. The Church
recognized the right of conscientious objection, and even

encouraged consideration of this option in conjunction
with its support for "the peace testimony of the
Christian Church."[32]   In opposition to the preparation
of students for war by the military academies, and to the
futility and cost of war as a means of resolving
international conflict, the Assembly endorsed the
formation of a National Peace Academy to train persons in
peaceful methods of conflict resolution.[33]
     The Disciples fully endorsed a nuclear arms freeze
in 1981.  As rationale for this proposal, the Assembly
cited the existence of American and Soviet arsenals
sufficient "to kill hundreds of millions of people," new
forms of technology which encourage a "first strike
mentality," and discussions of "limited nuclear war"
among military and political leaders.  The freeze
resolution is stated as follows:

> Therefore, be it resolved, that the
> General Assembly of the Christian Church
> (Disciples of Christ) meeting in Anaheim,
> California July 31-August 5, 1981 endorse
> the following position:  To improve
> national and international security, the
> United States and the Soviet Union should
> stop the nuclear arms race.  Specifically,
> they should adopt a mutual freeze on the
> testing, production and deployment of
> nuclear weapons and of missiles and new
> aircraft designed primarily to deliver
> nuclear weapons.  This is an essential,
> verifiable first step toward lessening
> the risk of nuclear war and reducing the
> nuclear arsenals.[34]

     The Assembly further resolved that congregations be
encouraged to collect signatures supporting the freeze,
which would be sent to Presidents Reagan and Brezhnev.
In a separate resolution that same year, the Assembly
voiced its "deep conviction that this most heinous
obscenity of the continuing nuclear armaments research,
development, and production be brought to an immediate
end."  The Assembly urged the leaders of nations "to stop
this madness and get on with those things that make for
peace."
     The forty-nine executive officers who comprise the
Council of Ministers of the Christian Church in the
United States and Canada prepared a message to be read to
all congregations on 20 December 1981.  This message
called on Disciples to renew their faith and hope in
Christ as the means of peace, and to pray, study, and
risk in the interest in true peace.  Included in this
statement was the following paragraph:

In such a situation we are reminded that
the church especially is called to pursue
peace because our Lord is the Prince of
Peace. We are concerned that where any
nuclear war once was unthinkable, some
speak now of limited nuclear war as an
option. We are concerned that while
peace demands arms limitation at the
very least, the world's arsenals are
growing at an alarming rate. We are
concerned that the military expenditures
of East, West and the Third World are
coming at the expense of a poor and
hungry humanity. We are concerned that
world economic woes might cause some
leaders to believe they can solve
internal problems by waging war.[36]

Robert Steffer is a Disciples minister and an
educational specialist employed at the denominational
offices in Indianapolis, Indiana. One of his functions
is to assist in establishing "shalom" congregations among
Christian churches. In the spring of 1982 we discussed
his views on just-war theory and the responsibility of
Christians in the nuclear age. He tended to equate just
war with the medieval crusade mentality; that is, a
theory which only affirms warfare, not a two-edged
evaluation guided by the principles of justice. Though
Steffer does not claim to be a pacifist, he affirmed that
the church can no longer voice its approval of warfare
and military force as a means of conflict resolution
among nations. The church, he said, must stand for
peace, not war. Steffer did not, however, address what
the church's response should be when external aggression
disrupts the peace with justice which the Christian
Church advocates. Steffer's views seem to characterize
the position taken by Disciples in their recent
statements on war and peace.[37]

## The United Presbyterian Church in the United States of America

In 1946 the United Presbyterian Church in the U.S.A.
(UPC) declared: "Christians know that war is evil. The
use of the atomic bomb means that war reaches a degree of
destruction which multiplies this evil beyond human
concept." The General Assembly then called for "the
immediate cessation of the manufacture of atomic
bombs."[38] Since that time the General Assembly of this
2,500,000 member denomination has endorsed statements on
nuclear disarmament and arms control on at least fifteen
occasions. UPC pronouncements closely resemble those of
the National Council of Churches.

The UPC has advocated negotiated and verifiable multilateral reductions and arms control through the aegis of the United Nations. In 1963, and again in 1971, the Church supported the goal of "general and complete disarmament." UPC pronouncements have urged ratification of a comprehensive nuclear test ban, a nuclear nonproliferation treaty, the Chemical Ban Treaty, and the SALT II Treaty. In 1979 the General Assembly adopted the Choose Life statement issued jointly by representatives of the National Council of Churches and churches of the Soviet Union. The next year the UPC opposed the development of the MX missile system. In 1981 the General Assembly requested that the President, Secretary of State, and members of Congress "make a solemn public commitment never again to be the first to employ nuclear weapons as an instrument of warfare."[39] In discussing this issue the Assembly affirmed:

> . . . with the issuance of Presidential Directive 59 in 1980, the basic policy of the United States in regard to nuclear war has been shifted from a policy of mutual deterrence commonly known as Mutual Assured Destruction to a policy of "flexibility," which offers a first-strike option and allows the President, when he considers the enemy threat sufficiently serious, to order a "limited" nuclear attack on enemy targets.[40]

This statement is an inaccurate assessment of "Countervailing Strategy," unveiled by President Carter in P.D. 59, and the development of nuclear strategy. The Presbyterians are correct, however, in recognizing the increase in public statements by administrative officials concerning the "limited" use of nuclear weapons, and "fighting" and "winning" a nuclear war. Also, the question of "first use" of nuclear weapons has become a hotly contested issue in the United States and Europe, and has been rejected by many of the churches surveyed in this study.

In 1981 the General Assembly endorsed Randall Forsberg's Call To Halt the Nuclear Arms Race. It distributed this document and a study guide to congregations, presbyteries and synods throughout the denomination and urged its support by them. The Assembly also sent copies of this nuclear freeze proposal with a statement of its endorsement to the President, members of Congress, and to persons in the Russian Orthodox Church.[41]

The study guide distributed with the freeze proposal explores twenty-three questions relevant to the risks of nuclear war, the arms race, weapons systems of the United

States and the Soviet Union, and previous treaty
agreements. The document presents factual data, laced
occasionally with simple slogans, to prepare
Presbyterians for the nuclear debate. For example, "The
best way to destroy an enemy is to make the enemy your
friend." "To disarm means," among other things, "to turn
suspicion or hostility into friendliness."[42] The study
guide seeks, as Geyer suggested, to demythologize beliefs
about the arms race and the Soviet Union. It recognizes
that Soviet influence has not constantly expanded since
World War II. In the arms race the Soviets are portrayed
as playing "catch-up" with the United States. The guide
judges that the United States and the Soviet Union "are
roughly in parity," therefore, now is an appropriate time
to seek a mutual nuclear weapons freeze. The guide also
suggests that it is U.S. weapons development and policy
that perpetuates the arms race and impedes nuclear arms
control.

Peacemaking has become a principal emphasis of the
UPC. In 1980 the Church approved a report of the
Advisory Council on Church and Society entitled
"Peacemaking: The Believers' Calling." As the Council
underscores, this report is not the usual analysis of
specific social policy issues. It is a call for the
Church to adopt "peacemaking" as a "fundamental
dimension" of Christian living and church ministry.[43]
It is no longer adequate, the document states, to simply
issue pronouncements in response to the "world's peril,
our nation's policies, and God's promise." Peacemaking
must be the vocation of the church. "We are at a turning
point. We are faced with the decision either to serve
the Rule of God or to side with the powers of death
through our complacency and silence."[44] The report
then calls on the UPC "to mobilize at every level for
maximum involvement and influence in peacemaking."[45]
This suggests that now Presbyterians are studying,
debating, and organizing for political action on nuclear
issues from congregational to denominational levels.

Robert F. Smylie, of the Office of Peace and
International Affairs, responded to my request for UPC
statements by forwarding Church documents and his
personal observations. Concerning the various types or
classifications of weapons, he suggested: "An overall
concern for ending the arms race and a constant
opposition to nuclear weapons do not lend themselves to
debating fine points of the particular nuclear weapons
doctrine governing such use."[46]

The general thrust of the UPC position is clear.
One point, however, needs explanation. In "Peacemaking:
The Believers' Calling," the UPC claims that peacemaking
is a fundamental duty of Christians and the church. The
document affirms that we must choose between serving the
"Rule of God" or the "powers of death." It also implies
that "our nation's policies" are a part of the problem

causing the "world's peril." Thus, the document places
in opposition U.S. national policies and the "Rule of
God." By deduction, this means that U.S. policy is part
of the "powers of death." Does this also mean that one
cannot be a Christian, or at least a Christian doing his
duty, if he supports national policy? Should we conclude
from this that one must agree with the UPC position on
national policy to be in right standing with God and the
church? Is this document affirming, like Francis
Winters, that those employed in positions related to
nuclear policies face the choice of resignation or
violating basic church policy?

## Presbyterian Church in the United States

The position of the Presbyterian Church in the
United States (PCUS), a denomination of 870,000 members,
is similar, though not identical, to that held by the
United Presbyterian Church and the National Council of
Churches. In 1978 the PCUS called for a multilateral
"halt" to further production and testing of nuclear
weapons through negotiated agreements. The General
Assembly also acknowledged peacemaking as a Christian
vocation and urged members to be more serious about
disarmament efforts. In 1981 the PCUS endorsed
"Peacemaking: The Believers' Calling" (reviewed in the
previous section). In that same year the General
Assembly also adopted a paper entitled "The Nature and
Value of Human Life."[47] This document employs the
criteria of just-war theory in evaluating war in the
nuclear age. Its discussion resembles the first draft of
the recent NCCB pastoral letter. The document reaches
three general conclusions. Conventional war, if it
corresponds with the criteria of just war, is in
principle justified. The document states as follows:

> Within our framework, justifications of
> such war can be understood as representing
> a judgment that an irreducible conflict
> of the obligations to do no harm and to
> protect from harm does exist. Especially
> in situations where one nation acts as
> aggressor against another, the fulfill-
> ment of the obligation to protect human
> life from such unwarranted aggression
> has been taken as more consistent with
> respect for human life than the obliga-
> tion to do no harm.

The paper, however, warns that such judgments are
extremely difficult to make, and "in all but the most
blatant and widely acknowledged acts of aggression it is
dubious as to whether any nation can transcend its own

subjective interests in making the judgment about
aggression."[48]
The second conclusion reached in the paper is that
nuclear war is not justified; nuclear weapons "are
indiscriminate in their effects and virtually
unconfineable in their destructive impact"
(disproportionate).[49]   It is highly improbable that
nuclear war can be "limited."

The last conclusion advanced in this document is
that the issues of conventional war and nuclear war
cannot be compartmentalized.  "Even if abstractly we are
persuaded that conventional war may be justifiable while
also persuaded that nuclear war is not justifiable, we
are not at liberty to turn to the question of
conventional war as though it were isolated from that of
nuclear war."  In a war between nations possessing
nuclear weapons, progression to the use of these weapons
"may be less than inevitable, but it certainly is nothing
less than highly probable."  Therefore, the document
concludes, any resort to war in the present age must be
seriously questioned.

In the cover letter accompanying materials sent to
me by the PCUS, Gasper B. Langella cites the following
statement adopted by the church in 1929:  ". . . the
church should never again bless a war, or be used as an
instrument in the promotion of war."[50]  He moves from
this quotation to point out that in "Peacemaking:  The
Believers' Calling" the categories of the church's policy
statement no longer belong to the just-war theory.  He
suggests that in adopting this statement the 1981
Assembly "theologizes in terms of what one could call a
'Just Peace Theory'."  It does not appear, however, that
in this action the PCUS has rejected just-war theory as
Langella infers.  The same Assembly adopted "The Nature
and Value of Human Life," statement which clearly does
use just-war categories to proscribe nuclear warfare as
indiscriminate and disproportionate.  This is an
affirmation of the applicability of just-war theory.

The endorsement of both of these documents by the
1981 Assembly may be an inconsistency.  More likely,
however, the PCUS is recognizing the justice of resisting
aggression, by force if necessary, while also rejecting
the use of nuclear weapons as justifiable means of
resistance.  This apparent acknowledgement of the
validity of just-war theory differs from the position
statements of other churches affiliated with the NCC
which we have thus far surveyed.

The PCUS position varies in another regard.  The
1981 Assembly elected to endorse ratification of the SALT
II Agreement rather than the nuclear freeze as a means
toward nuclear arms control.  In 1978, however, the
Church adopted a resolution that called for a
multilateral "halt" in production and testing of nuclear
weapons.

## The Episcopal Church

The Episcopal Church (EC)[51] has traditionally formed a supportive alliance with national government, albeit, at times as a loyal critic. In response to my request for materials, Charles A. Casaretti, Public Issues Officer for the Episcopal Church, affirmed this point as follows: "on the broader issues of ethics and morals, we have always assumed a role as partner with the political sector in the policy dialogue."[52] Because of this relationship the influence of the Episcopal Church on national policy has normally exceeded its numerical size, which currently equals nearly three million members.

In 1962 the House of Bishops issued a Pastoral Letter on "War and Peace" which committed the Episcopal Church "to put into practice the Christian mission of peacemaking."[53] There was little sustained action on the issue of the arms race, however, until 1979. In that year the General Convention of the EC took several relevant steps. It endorsed the statement on "War and Violence" adopted by the bishops of the Anglican Communion at the recent Lambeth Conference. This statement affirmed that the many forms of violence, including oppression, revolution, terrorism and war, were incompatible with the teaching and example of Jesus. The bishops called on Christians everywhere "to engage themselves in non-violent action for justice and peace," and, furthermore,

> to protest in whatever way possible at the escalation of the sale of armaments of war by the producing nations to the developing and dependent nations, and to support with every effort all international proposals and conferences designed to place limitations on, or arrange reductions in, the armaments of war of the nations and of the world.[54]

The 1979 General Convention also established the three-year Joint Commission on Peace and authorized it to present to the Church a comprehensive program for addressing the issues of war and pace. The responsibility of the Commission was to identify the international and domestic implications of U.S. policy, and to suggest educational and pastoral programs for the Episcopal Church which would facilitate its ministry of peace and reconciliation. As advocated by the Commission's chairman, Bishop William C. Frey, the 1982 General Convention established the Commission as a continuing organization of the Church. Frey believes that the question of war and peace should be placed at

the center of church life.  In reflecting on the work of
the Commission, Frey significantly observed:  "There is a
lot of heat but very little light on this question--I'd
like to see the Commission shed some of that light.
Everyone in the Church says:  'I'm against war and for
peace.'  But my question is:  How?"[55]
     In addition to the Commission on Peace, two other
groups of Episcopalians are seeking to answer Frey's
question of how to be against war and for peace.  One of
these is the Arms Race Task Force of the Episcopal Urban
Caucus, organized in 1980.  George Regas, the Task Force
leader, wants this group to be an "action oriented"
grass-roots movement within the Church.  "'We in the
Church must be protagonists in the struggle to reorder
our country's priorities,'" according to Regas.[56]
     The other group fighting nonviolently for peace is
the Episcopal Peace Fellowship (EPF), organized in 1939.
This 1,200 member organization was instrumental in
bringing the "peace issue" before the 1979 General
Convention.  The appointment of a full time executive
secretary to this organization indicates an
intensification of efforts by the Church in this area.
One of the primary functions of the Peace Fellowship is
"to educate the Church in all the ramifications of the
arms race issue."[57]
     The 1982 General Convention went beyond the 1979
Convention in its disarmament actions.  In addition to
extending the life of the Joint Commission on Peace, the
Convention advocated a freeze on production of nuclear
weapons by the United States and the Soviet Union and a
reduction of existing nuclear arsenals.  The Convention
also urged the United States to adopt a "no first strike"
nuclear policy.  At the conclusion of the annual session,
the bishops issued a strongly worded pastoral letter
reaffirming the role of the Church as peacemaker and
calling the arms race the most compelling moral issue in
the world public order.  The Convention also asked the
U.S. government to end military support to El Salvador
and other Central American countries.


## United Church of Christ

     The United Church of Christ (UCC) has been a leading
advocate of nuclear disarmament among the National
Council churches.  Many of its statements predate those
of other denominations and the NCC.  In 1958 the UCC
endorsed arms reduction negotiations and the development
of a United Nations police force.  During the 1960s the
Church supported a nuclear test ban treaty, urged a
moratorium on anti-ballistic missile systems and Multiple
Independently-Trageted Reentry Vehicles (MIRVs), and
favored SALT negotiations.  In 1971 the UCC called for
new education for peace ministries, and expressed thanks

"for the witness in opposition to war of all those who have opposed with sacrifice and nonviolent civil disobedience the use of U.S. power in Indochina, especially Philip and Daniel [Berrigan]."[58]  In that year the UCC also stated its support for both "indigenous liberation movements" and "non-military solutions to problems."[59]  The juxtaposition of these two issues is somewhat puzzling.  Is the UCC suggesting that liberation movements should be nonviolent?

In 1977, more than five years before the National Conference of Catholic Bishops published its pastoral letter on war and peace, the Office of Church in Society of the UCC called for a moratorium on nuclear-fission weapons and new strategic weapons systems, a "no first strike" policy, a policy of "nonuse" of nuclear weapons against non-nuclear states, and establishment of a World Peace Tax Fund.

The General Synod of the UCC in 1981 adopted world peace as its priority issue for the next four years.  In conjunction with this action, the Synod urged nuclear disarmament through multilateral negotiations and encouraged unilateral initiatives by the United States. The Synod recognized "the need, in the world's present circumstances, for defense forces well-chosen, well-equipped, well-trained, well-led and well-rewarded."[60] It also supported the establishment of a National Academy of Peace and Conflict Resolution and the development of means other than military for resolving international tensions.  The Synod called on "all segments" of the 1,750,000 member UCC to become a peace church.

Associated with the call to become a peace church, M. Douglass Meeks developed for the Office for Church in Society a draft document entitled "Is the United Church of Christ a Peace Church?"  After discussion and revision, this document may provide the basis for a General Synod pronouncement in 1983.  In it Meeks suggests that the UCC is not becoming a peace church like historic pacifist churches such as the Brethren, Quakers, or Mennonites.  He describes these churches as "sectarian," that is, basically separated from the world. The ethic of the UCC is one of "solidarity with and involvement in the world."  Meeks affirms that because the UCC does not have a sectarian view of the state, "it cannot as a matter of principle or ethical rule reject all civil and political exercises of force."  Therefore the UCC is not a pacifist church.

Meeks also declares that Reinhold Niebuhr's cold war language of "ethical realism" is insufficient for the church in the age of nuclear parity.  In this age "all human beings must become 'pacifists' as regards to the use of nuclear weapons."  Therefore, Meeks implies that in becoming a peace church, the UCC is not a "pacifist," but a "nuclear pacifist" church.  Meeks suggests that a peace church is one that refuses to accept war as an

inevitability, or an essential function of the state.  A
peace church is one that seeks nonviolent alternatives to
international conflict.[61]
     The United Church of Christ is clearly one of the
leading Protestant churches in the peace and disarmament
movement.  It is study and action oriented.  The UCC has
established a fund specifically designated for support of
peace literature and activities.  Among its actions is a
weekly vigil at the Cambridge Common in the Boston area
in support of nuclear disarmament.  Though not yet an
official document, "Is the United Church of Christ a
Peace Church?" indicates the trend in the UCC position
and is helpful in distinguishing between the contemporary
"peace church" and the historic "pacifist" churches.  In
Meeks' thought a peace church is a politically involved
"nuclear pacifist" organization that seeks to alter
social conceptions and governmental policies.


Reformed Church in America

     With a membership of approximately 350,000, the
Reformed Church in America (RCA) is the smallest of the
traditional Protestant denominations in the United
States.  Like the Presbyterian churches, the RCA is a
part of Calvinist theological tradition, which,
historically, has supported the just-war position.  Karl
Barth was the most influencial Reformed theologican in
the twentieth century.  Since this Swiss scholar's call
in 1959 to outlaw nuclear weapons, the Reformed Church
has increasingly employed just-war criteria to renounce
the use of nuclear weapons and the arms race.
     In 1979 the Reformed General Synod adopted a "Call
to Action" that advocated "a full and general
prohibition" of further nuclear arms testing, development
and deployment.  The Synod also urged its member churches
to emphasize the "biblical vision of peace" and the
"devastating social and personal consequences of the arms
race."[62]  In support of this action, the 1980 Synod
distributed to churches a Theological Commission study
entitled "Christian Faith and the Nuclear Arms Race:  A
Reformed Perspective."
     The first section of this study focuses on nuclear
arsenals and the arms race, and presents a very alarming
picture of the current world context.  Relying primarily
on disarmament literature[63] for sources, the document
compares United States and Soviet arsenals and reaches
the conclusion that the superpowers are at a position of
"essential equivalence."  Each of the superpowers has the
capacity to destroy the world's population many times
over.  The present balance of power provides a rare
opportunity for initiating a process of multilateral
disarmament.  Recent events, however, suggest that this
"historic opportunity" may be missed.  The Commission

argues that new U.S. weapons such as the Trident
submarine, cruise missiles and MX missiles pose "grave
threats to the existing balance of power" and are certain
to escalate the arms race.  These weapons are
"particularly ominous" in that they make possible a shift
"from a defensive strategy of deterrence to an offensive,
'first strike' or 'counterforce' strategy."  The authors
of the RCA document conclude that "the defensive
strategies of previous decades seem almost benign
compared to the insidious technologies and aggressive
policies that threaten the future."  In the age of
nuclear weapons, "the word 'war' has become obsolete. . .
. Today the accurate terms are holocaust, doomsday,
apocalypse.  Armageddon is no longer a figure of speech,
nor the Book of Revelation a tract for other times."

Based on this ominous assessment of world
conditions, the RCA study draws several conclusions.
Nuclear war is unwinable.  The nuclear arms race is a
false religion which fails to provide lasting security.
There is no defense against nuclear war.

In discussing Christian attitudes toward war, the
RCA document supports the just-war views of Calvin and
Luther, and the right of states for national defense.
The study affirms, however, that because nuclear weapons
are indiscriminate and disproportionate means of warfare,
"they make a just war impossible."  In the nuclear age
"deterrence is nothing more than a massive hostage system
with whole populations compelled to live under the
constant threat of genocide."  The following quotation
summarizes the RCA position as reflected in this study:

> It is not the purpose of this paper to
> argue against every use of military
> force.  One need not accept the pacifist
> position, however, in order to recognize
> the false morality inherent in any
> recourse to nuclear weapons.  Ronald S.
> Wallace, a Calvin scholar, offers a
> noteworthy if understated speculation:
> "Judging by Calvin's language about
> war in his sermons it is possible that
> he might have been a pacifist in face
> of the possibility of modern nuclear
> war."  False religion leads to immorality
> as well as insecurity.  Nuclear war and
> the preparations for it violate every
> code by which historic Christianity has
> determined a war to be just.

In addition to rejecting the use of nuclear weapons
and the arms race, the RCA study condemns the
technological determinism, profit motives, and "demonic
power of nationalism" which drive the armaments
escalation.  The document concludes with a call to the

Church to stand against both "an exploitative capitalism and an aggressive communism wherever these systems oppress humanity." It affirms:

> The faithful church today will stand in the power of love against the false gods of this world. She will condemn any preparation or use of nuclear force and the godless morality of security through might. Inspired by a unity already manifested in Christ, she will call the nations to forge new, non-violent security systems based not on narrow nationalisms but on the vision of global community and world order. A faithful church will resist runaway technology, rapacious profit motives, and the mad presumptions of the nations that compel the arms race.

In addition to distributing the "Christian Faith and the Nuclear Arms Race: A Reformed Perspective" to Reformed churches, the 1980 Synod approved sending the document to the churches of the Soviet Union. The Synod also voted to give priority attention to the nuclear arms race. The following year the Synod reaffirmed the report of the Theological Commission and issued a new warning against a growing "militarism" in the world. The Christian Action Commission of the RCA also identified the following peace and disarmament groups which, evidently, it found helpful in addressing the nuclear issues: Mobilization for Survival's Religious Task Force, The Riverside Church Disarmament Program, Fellowship of Reconciliation[64] and The World Peacemakers of the Church of the Savior.

Robert A. White, the RCA Minister for Social Witness, prefaced the materials he sent me with the following observation: "There is a growing sentiment within our denomination that nuclear proliferation and the resurgence of militarism generally in our country must be opposed by people of faith."[65]

## A Summary of the Mainline Protestant Positions

In this section we have surveyed the views of the larger Protestant denominations affiliated with the National Council of Churches.[66] The aggregate membership of these eight denominations is over twenty million. Several features are immediately apparent concerning their positions. There is much similarity in the positions, literature and even language adopted by these denominations, the NCC and the Catholic bishops. All advocate a vocation of "peacemaking" for Christians.

Three of these churches retain the language or logic of
just-war theory; all call for nuclear disarmament and
emphasize the need for developing nonviolent techniques
for resolving international conflict. Each of the
Protestant denominations expresses grave reservations
about the use of nuclear weapons. Of the eight churches,
four proscribe "any use" (nuclear pacifist), and seven
call for a "no-first-use" policy.

The sense of urgency among these religious bodies is
depicted in the recent work of the Reformed Church,
described above. The denominations insist that it is
time now to make significant steps in disarmament. Since
1978 concern over nuclear issues has greatly increased.
In this regard the nuclear weapons freeze proposal is
more a manifestation than a catalyst of disarmament
sentiment. Several years before Forsberg or Kennedy and
Hatfield made their proposals, Protestant (and Catholic)
churches were calling for a "moratorium" or a "halt" to
nuclear weapons testing, production, and deployment.
Each of these churches endorsed the freeze resolution,
except the PCUS; and it has approved a statement with the
same intent.

The reasons for the increased concern over nuclear
issues include: (1) mounting expenditures for defense;
(2) the development of new and accurate weapons systems;
(3) failure of arms negotiations; (4) rhetoric by
American leaders about "fighting" and "winning" a
"limited" nuclear war; (5) realization that the United
States has not renounced a "first use" policy; (6)
East-West tensions resulting from Soviet arms deployment
and actions in Afghanistan and Poland; and (7) North-
South tensions prompted by the economic needs of the
lesser developed countries.

It should also be noted that the Protestant churches
have not always done their work well. There are elements
of a religious crusade in many of their statements.
Slogans and motive imagery are at times substituted for
factual data. At other times the selective presentation
of facts creates incomplete or inaccurate perspectives.
Because the focus has been primarily on the effects of
nuclear weapons, especially American weapons, there has
been inadequate attention given to relations, force
structures, and the problems of negotiations in the
international arena. For example, not one of the church
documents reviewed in this chapter addressed the balance
of forces problem in Europe. Several churches asked the
United States to reduce arms sales or grants to the Third
World; but none of these, however, discussed the fact
that when the United States did reduce military aid in
the 1970s to some Latin American countries, other nations
supplied them with even more modern weapons. The United
States does export a large amount of arms, but it is
highly questionable to say, as the Christian Church does,
that the United States is the world's largest exporter.

The Soviet Union and European nations supply more weapons to the Third World than the United States. Also, none of the Protestant churches considered increasing conventional forces as a means of reducing reliance on nuclear weapons.

The question by Episcopal Bishop Frey still stands as a challenge to the Protestant churches: "Everyone in the church says: 'I'm against war and for peace.' But my question is: How?" The recent statements, educational programs, and actions by the churches, however, will also place increasing demands on the government for acceptable answers to this question, especially as it relates to nuclear war and the arms race.

## NOTES

1. Forsberg, a former defense analyst with the Stockholm International Peace Research Institute, founded the Institute for Defense and Disarmament Studies, 251 Harvard Street, Brookline, Massachusetts, 02146, in 1979. The American Security Council, in Washington Report (June 1982): p. 6, claims that Forsberg is a part of a "Soviet Connection" because of her trip to the Soviet Union in December 1981 to confer with disarmament experts. This charge is questionable; however, Forsberg's work is often less critical of the U.S.S.R. than the U.S.

2. Freeze! How You Can Help Prevent Nuclear War (New York: Bantam Books, 1982), pp. 115-16.

3. This policy statement is available at the NCC, 475 Riverside Drive, New York, New York, 10027. The document is cited frequently by member churches and subsequent NCC documents.

4. This "Resolution on Senate Resolution 67 on Suspension of Nuclear Testing" was adopted on 14 October 1973. A similar proposal entitled "Resolution on the Complete Cessation of All Explosive Nuclear Testing" was adopted on 4 May 1977. Both of these resolutions referred to the 1968 policy statement on defense and disarmament.

5. "Resolution on Nuclear Weapons," adopted on 10 November 1977.

6. "Swords into Plowshares: The Churches' Witness for Disarmament," adopted 10 May 1978.

7. Choose Life was endorsed by the NCC on 10 May 1979. The American delegation to this consultation included leaders from American Baptist Churches, United Presbyterian Church, Lutheran Church in America,

Christian Methodist Episcopal Church, Reformed Church in America, United Methodist Church, and the United Church of Christ.

8.  "Resolution on a Nuclear Weapons Freeze," adopted 14 May 1981.

9.  "The Re-Making of America?" was adopted by the NCC on 15 May 1981.

10.  Cf. "National Church Council Faces New Type of Critic," The New York Times, 3 November 1982, p. A19; Rael Jean Isaac, "Do You Know Where Your Church Offerings Go?" Readers Digest 122 (January 1983): 120-25.

11.  James M. Wall, "Neoconservatives Aim at Liberals," The Christian Century 99 (4 November 1982): 115-17.  Cf. Eric Hochstein and Ronald O'Rouke, "A Report on the Institute of Religion and Democracy," commissioned and distributed by the United Methodist Church in 1981.

12.  Wall, ibid., p. 116.

13.  Carl Henry is the former editor of Christianity Today, a conservative evangelical periodical.  James Finn, previous editor of Worldview, and Michael Novak are well published Catholic laymen.  Julian Hartt is a professor and author from Duke University.  Richard John Neuhaus is an Evangelical Lutheran, former editor of Worldview, and current editor of Forum Letter.

14.  Neuhaus presented these ideas in an address entitled "War, Peace and the Churches," at the Tenth Annual FORSCOM/TRADOC Professional Training Workshop, Atlanta, Georgia, 13 October 1982.  Neuhaus was himself a leader of the Vietnam protest movement, and a leading social critic in the 1970s.  Thus, his would not seem to be an attack from the "far right."

15.  The "Pastoral Letter to A People Called United Methodist," issued on 29 April 1982 by the Council of Bishops of the United Methodist Church, was published in The United Methodist Reporter, 7 May 1982.

16.  John B. Warman, "A Quiet Shout," Circuit Rider (May 1982), p. 5.

17.  Alan Geyer, The Idea of Disarmament:  Rethinking the Unthinkable.  Elgin, Illinois:  The Brethren Press, 1982.

18.  Geyer, The Idea of Disarmament, p. 12.

19.  Ibid., p. 61.

20. Ibid., pp. 66-68.

21. Ibid., p. 170.

22. Ibid., p. 172-73.

23. Ibid., p. 183.

24. Ibid., p. 209.

25. Ibid., p. 199. A more concise statement by Geyer is his article "The Arms Race is Serious. Theology, to Date, Isn't," Christianity and Crisis 42 (1 November 1982): 336-41.

26. The American Baptist Churches were formerly named the American Baptist Convention.

27. "American Baptist Resolution on Peace with Justice," adopted by the ABC in May 1964. This statement was reaffirmed in 1966 and 1979.

28. "Resolution on Disarmament," passed by the General Board of the ABC in June 1978.

29. "Resolution on Military Spending," adopted by the General Board in late 1981.

30. Personal letter, 19 January 1982.

31. Resolution No. 7936, "Concerning Ending The Arms Race," adopted by the General Assembly of the Christian Church, 26-30 October 1979.

32. Resolution No. 8120, "Resolution Concerning Support for the Conscientious Objector to War," adopted in 1981.

33. Resolution No. 8143, "Resolution Concerning a National Peace Academy," adopted in 1981.

34. Resolution No. 8129, "Resolution Concerning a Nuclear Arms Freeze," adopted in 1981.

35. Resolution No. 8136, "Resolution Concerning Nuclear Arms," adopted in 1981.

36. The Council of Ministers, Christian Church (Disciples of Christ) in the United States and Canada, "A Message to the Congregations of Christian Church (Disciples of Christ), 8 December 1981.

37. Robert Steffer, personal interview, Ocean Township, N.J., 11 May 1982.

38. The Peacemaking Project of the Program Agency, United Presbyterian Church in the U.S.A., "A Study and Action Guide on the Nuclear Arms Race and the 'Call to Halt the Nuclear Arms Race'," endorsed by the UPC in 1981, p. 32. This document reproduces Randall Forsberg's nuclear weapons freeze proposal along with a study guide. Section four of the document, prepared by Robert Smylie, is a collection of UPC General Assembly statements on nuclear armaments. Hereafter cited as "Study and Action Guide."

39. Church and Society 72 (September/October 1981): 13.

40. Ibid., p. 12. Though the policy announced by President Carter in P.D. 59 had a new name, "Countervailing Strategy," and it did reflect movement away from MAD, it was not a new strategy in the sense claimed by the UPC and others. See policy statements by McNamara in 1962 and Schlesinger in the mid 1970s; Henry S. Rowen, "The Evolution of Strategic Nuclear Doctrine," in Strategic Thought in the Nuclear Age, edited by Laurence Martin (Baltimore: Johns Hopkins Press, 1980; U.S., Department of the Defense, Report of Secretary Harold Brown to the Congress on the FY 1981 Budget, FY 1982 Authorization Request and FY 1981-1985 Defense Programs, 29 January 1980, pp. 65f. Countervailing Strategy, if supplemented by many accurate weapons, has the capacity for "first strike," as does each strategy employed in the nuclear age, including MAD. The intent behind Countervailing Strategy, according to proponents, is to deter aggression at various levels. Therefore, "limited" nuclear war is an associated concept; deterrence, however, not offensive action, remains the goal of defense policy in this strategy. Another observation is in order that differs with, but would perhaps be even more alarming to the Presbyterians. National security policy did not prevent the first use of nuclear weapons; and within this policy, since the dawn of the nuclear age, the President has had the authority to use nuclear weapons "when he considers the enemy threat sufficiently serious." This is not a new change in policy. There is, however, agreement among NATO nations to consult before resorting to nuclear weapons.

41. Church and Society 72 (September/October 1981):10-11.

42. "Study and Action Guide," p. 5.

43. The United Presbyterian Church in the United States of America, "Peacemaking: The Believers Calling," 1980, p. 2.

44. Ibid., p. 4.

45. Ibid., p. 7.

46. Robert F. Smylie, personal letter to Donald L. Davidson, 4 March 1982.

47. "The Nature and Value of Human Life, A Paper Adopted by the 121st General Assembly and Commended to the Church for Study," The Presbyterian Church in the United States, 1981.

48. Ibid., pp. 25-26.

49. Ibid.

50. Gaspar B. Langella, personal letter to Donald L. Davidson, 28 January 1982.

51. Formerly known as The Protestant Episcopal Church in the United States of America.

52. Charles A. Casaretti, personal letter to Donald L. Davidson, 20 January 1982.

53. "The Episcopal Church Looks at Issues: The Arms Race," a brochure distributed by the Public Issues Office, the Episcopal Church Center, 815 Second Avenue, New York, New York, 10017. This brochure, prepared in late 1980 or early 1981 contains three articles which discuss the arms race and response to the arms race by the Episcopal Church, and laity. Hereafter cited as "Issues: The Arms Race."

54. The "War and Violence" Lambeth Resolution was reproduced in a document identified as "Church in Public Affairs, Church and Society, Social Policy of the Episcopal Church," pp. 136-38 distributed by Charles Casaretti of the Episcopal Church Center.

55. "Issues: The Arms Race."

56. Ibid.

57. Ibid.

58. See United Church of Christ, Minutes of the General Synod, 29 June 1971, p. 76.

59. Ibid., 28 June 1971, p. 4.

60. The resolutions of the 1981 General Synod concerning war and peace were reprinted in UCC Network, 4 (July 1981): pp. 2-3.

61. "Is the United Church of Christ a Peace Church?" is distributed by the Office for Church in Society, 105 Madison Avenue, New York, New York, 10016.

62. Reformed Church in America, Minutes of the General Synod, 1979, pp. 95-97.

63. In recent years a number of writers and organizations have produced literature that have become standard sources for peace and disarmament advocates. These include books and articles of Jim Wallis and Sojourners Magazine, Richard J. Barnet, Sidney Lens, The Defense Monitor, Robert C. Aldridge, The Institute for Policy Studies, Bulletin of the Atomic Scientists and others. Some of these sources represent the "minimal deterrence" position; a few advocate unilateral disarmament and pacifist positions. All of this literature is highly critical of recent U.S. policy.

64. Minutes of the General Synod, 1981, pp. 66-68.

65. Robert A. White, personal letter to Donald L. Davidson, 13 January 1982.

66. Several smaller denominations affiliated with the NCC were not included in this study because of their relatively small size. The larger Black denominations affiliated with the NCC were omitted for several reasons: First, none of them responded to the request for information and materials and time limitations prevented researching their church documents. Second, there is little reference to the positions of these denominations in the religious press. This suggests that, like many denominations, they may not have articulated extensive views on the arms race. It should be recognized, however, that the larger Black denominations, such as the National Baptist Convention, U.S.A., Inc. and the African Methodist Episcopal Church, are a sizable portion of the nation's population, with a combined membership of well over ten million. These denominations represent about one-fourth of the NCC affiliate members.

67. See "Conventional Arms Transfer in the Third World, 1972-81," U.S, Department of State Bulletin 82 (October 1982): 50-65; Andrew J. Pierre, The Global Politics of Arms Sales (Princeton, New Jersey: Princeton University Press, 1981).

# [ 6 ]
# Protestant Peacemaking: Lutherans, Southern Baptists, and Others

## THE LUTHERAN CHURCHES

The five Lutheran bodies in America report a combined membership of almost 8,500,000. The largest of these, the Lutheran Church in America, The American Lutheran Church, and the Lutheran Church--Missouri Synod, are fairly equal in size and together account for eight million members. Each of these denominations is heir to the theology of Martin Luther and has, therefore, traditionally advocated the just-war position on questions of war and peace. Of these churches, only the Lutheran Church in America is affiliated with the National Council of Churches. However, the Lutherans have councils of their own, the Lutheran World Federation (LWF) and the Lutheran Council in the USA. After a quick review of recent joint statements, we will begin our discussion of the churches with an assessment of the Lutheran Church in America.

It should be recognized that the concern for nuclear disarmament is international in scope. Particularly is this true among Christian churches in the world community. Undoubtedly President Reagan's claim is true that communist agents have participated in and perhaps orchestrated and funded anti-nuclear activities. It is also certainly true that the Soviet Union promotes disarmament propaganda in the West, while forcefully suppressing it in the East. Communist actions in the West, however, may be seen as opportunistic rather than causal, at least among Christian groups.

In the spring of 1981 a delegation from the Evangelical Church in Germany (EKD) met for a week in Washington, D.C. with leaders of the Association of Evangelical Lutheran Churches, The American Lutheran Church, and the Lutheran Church in America. Following this meeting a joint statement was issued which expressed regret over increasing arms buildup by East and West and the worsening of relations between the power blocs.[1]

149

In August 1981 the Lutheran World Federation
Executive Committee met in Turku, Finland. At this
meeting the Committee unanimously adopted a "Statement on
Peace" which expressed awareness of increased tensions
between NATO and Warsaw Pact countries and especially
between the United States and the Soviet Union. The
statement explicitly deplored the following factors
because of their contribution to these tensions:

-- the large-scale increase in military
spending on both sides, the escalation
of the arms race, and the development of
new weapons, such as neutron warheads,
in various countries;
-- the massive buildup of intermediate
range nuclear missiles by the U.S.S.R.
and the U.S.A.;
-- the slow progress of the Madrid follow-up
conference on the Helsinki Final Acts
(Conference of Security and Cooperation
in Europe); [sic]
-- the consequent spread of dread, fear,
and resignation among peoples;
-- the continuation of numerous armed
conflicts in different parts of the world;
-- the prolongation and intensification of
such conflicts by big power involvement
in them on the basis of ideological
self-interests;
-- the use of the world's limited resources
on arms, which sharply curtails resources
available for development work and for
attempts to eliminate social and economic
injustices.[2]

The Executive Committee also affirmed in this
statement that the Christian community transcends
national ideological and political boundaries. It called
on all Christians, and especially Lutherans, to intensify
direct personal communications between churches living
under different social systems. Through such contact it
was hoped that Christians might displace cold war
attitudes and collaborate on the issues of disarmament,
nonproliferation of nuclear weapons, support for arms
negotiations, and human rights.

The Lutheran World Federation convened a subsequent
meeting on peace issues in Geneva, 6-8 November 1981.[3]
Bishop Josiah Kibira of Tanzania, the LWF president, was
joined at this meeting by nineteen other bishops from the
United States, Scandinavia, East and West Germany,
Romania, Latvia, Czechoslovakia, Poland, France, the
Netherlands, Hungary, and Africa. Attending from the
United States was Bishop James R. Crumley, Jr., of The

Lutheran Church in America. The purpose of this meeting, according to Crumley, was to begin the process recommended by the Executive Committee of the LWF; that is, sharing across ideological and national boundaries mutual concerns on peace and disarmament. In describing the Geneva conference to members of his own denomination, Crumley reflected:

> Lutherans are not pacifists, and the Lutheran Church has not been known as one of the historic "peace" churches of the Christian family. Our theology views humanity as fallen and has recognized that force may be necessary in the maintenance of order. We also hold that government has the right and duty to use power for the protection of its citizens. But isn't it true that the nuclear age has altered the way we are to apply our theological and ethical presuppositions? The consequences of nuclear warfare are so drastic as to summon us all to unprecedented efforts on behalf of peace. Between governments the tool is negotiation. We can urge our governments to negotiate with their adversaries to put an end to the proliferation of nuclear weapons, to accomplish a reduction in the level of arms, to continue to work patiently for a surveillance system that will ensure the keeping of treaties. It is in everyone's self-interest that this be done, but Christians can promise support for such negotiations out of a faith that sees peace as God's loving will for the world.

Crumley concluded his observations by affirming: "The nuclear weapons issue seems to me to be one which has to be separated from all others as of peculiar urgency. We can delay no longer."[4]

## Lutheran Church in America

Bishop Crumley's observations provide an introduction to the position held by the Lutheran Church in America (LCA). The LCA is the largest of the Lutheran bodies with nearly three million members. As observed earlier, it is the only Lutheran body affiliated with the National Council of Churches.

The LCA Biennial Convention adopted a Social Statement in 1970 which Richard J. Niebanck describes as "the official statement" of the Church.[5] The statement

is entitled "World Community:  Ethical Imperatives in an
Age of Interdependence."[6]  It discussed human rights
and security in the context of a "world neighborhood."
It recognizes that the technologies of communication,
transportation, and weaponry "are drawing men into an
increasingly intimate neighborhood where the action of
any nation or interest can lead to instantaneous and
irreversible consequences for all." (p.1)  Concerning the
function of government, this statement affirms:  "The
classical Christian tradition views civil authority as a
sign of God's loving activity of advancing human justice
and well-being and of preserving man from his tendency to
violence and self-destruction.  Just government performs
the double function of promoting the welfare of men and
restraining wickedness." (p.1)  In "World Community" the
LCA hopes that this function can be increasingly
performed by the "emerging forms of world civil
authority."  Accordingly, the Church calls for support of
the United Nations and international law.

In the section on security and war prevention, the
1970 statement indicates that Christian tradition
acknowledges "the human tendency to destructive
aggressiveness and the component of force required by
political authority for the purpose of maintaining peace
within and among nations." (p.4)  The statement also
concludes, however, that it is clearly time for a
rethinking of the meaning of national security.  "In view
of the overkill capacity now possessed by the
super-powers, national security can no longer be defined
in terms of either nuclear superiority or even nuclear
stalemate."(p.4)  The LCA then advocates a stronger
international legal framework for arms control and
security.  It calls on the United States to undertake
"unilateral initiatives" in nuclear arms limitation to
improve the climate for negotiations.  The LCA also urges
churches to work "for a lessening of the nuclear peril
and the realization of greater degrees of justice for the
poor of the world." (p.5)  The following observation is
characteristic of the basic LCA perspective in "World
Community:"

> The present Christian attitude toward armed
> violence must of necessity be a two-sided
> one.  On the one hand, it must recognize
> the suicidal character of nuclear war
> among the Great Powers; on the other, it
> must accept the fact that while injustice
> persists there will continue to be
> violent conflicts within and among nations.

The 1970 statement concludes by calling on churches
to support national policies "which contribute to the
building of a world community."  Specifically the church

should encourage governmental policies in the areas of development assistance, support for the United Nations, and arms limitation.

Lutheran thought in the last two decades has been significantly influenced by two other works. These are A Theory of Politics by William H. Lazareth and Conscience, War and the Selective Objector by Richard J. Niebanck. Both of these books are steeped in Luther's theology and just-war theory. Lazareth acknowledges that a "just" war is "a necessary evil in the world as a means of restraining and punishing those who would challenge and disrupt God's created order of peace and justice." He also affirms the opposite pole in just-war logic, that "all is not fair in either love or war for Christian non-pacifists."[8] The political end does not justify all military means. When Lazareth applies this logic to nuclear weapons, he asks: "Even if we grant that 'just wars' against aggressors are permissible in principle, would nuclear retaliation be justifiable in practice?" He concludes as follows:

> War has always been hell, but in a nuclear age it could easily become a suidical exercise in mutual annihilation. . . .
>
> Our nuclear weapons have attained such an awesome destructive capacity that controlled arms reduction has now become the most moral (as well as the safest and cheapest) means of national defense.[9]

Niebanck's thought is similar to that of Lazareth. He quotes Lazareth in his SALT II: Strategic Arms Limitation Treaty, written in 1979 in support of ratifying the treaty.

The delegates to the LCA Convention, 3-10 September 1982, moved beyond earlier Church positions by endorsing a nuclear weapons freeze proposal. In a resolution to be read in every congregation, the Convention declared its support for "a multilateral, verifiable freeze of the testing, production, stockpiling, and deployment of nuclear weapons and delivery systems as a step toward the eventual elimination of nuclear weapons."[10] The Convention delegates further resolved to urge the leaders of the United States and the Soviet Union to initiate steps toward the reduction and elimination of nuclear weapons and to "consider taking reasonable and appropriate risks in the search for greater trust and understanding among nations. The delegates also decided that the LCA resolution should be communicated to the United Nations, the President of the United States, and to other nations possessing nuclear weapons. Other issues raised by local synods, but not acted on by the

Convention, included the adequacy of just-war theory, withholding of "war taxes," a peace tax fund and a peace academy. According to Niebanck, this 1982 resolution emerged from the Convention floor rather than the Division for Mission or the Church hierarchy. He suggests that support for the freeze resolution is part of a popular movement within the Church that goes beyond positions advocated by himself and other leaders.[11]

The general conclusions of the LCA are similar to those adopted by other denominations affiliated with the NCC. The Church raised the issues of "first strike," deterrence strategies, and new weapons systems in studies prepared in 1982, but has not discussed them in official documents. The eventual elimination of nuclear weapons is stated clearly as the goal; but the Church does not formally proscribe all use of nuclear weapons or the policy of deterrence prior to achieving this goal.[12] The LCA affirms more readily than the other mainline denominations surveyed above the just-war tradition and the responsibility of governments for national defense. Its position is guided by what may be called "ethical realism" and "nuclear realism." The Church acknowledges aggressive tendencies in people and nations and, thus, the need for security (ethical realism). However, it does not approve of every available means to achieve political ends, and it affirms that nuclear weapons are so destructive that arms control and limitation is the only moral political option (nuclear realism).

## The American Lutheran Church

The statements published by the 2,363,000 member American Lutheran Church (ALC) closely resemble those of the Lutheran Church in America. The General Convention of the ALC adopted a statement in 1966 which continues to guide Church pronouncements. This statement is entitled "War, Peace, and Freedom: A Statement Commended by the Church."[13] This document acknowledges the possibility of conditions in which a nation may be forced to choose between basic values.

> It is possible that a nation and its people cannot have peace, security "and" freedom. Under some circumstances their only alternatives may be "either" the peace of surrender to tyranny and totalitarianism "or" the security and freedom bought by risking and engaging in war.[14]

It is within the context of these tensions that the ALC statement addresses the issues of war, peace, and freedom. Using the logic of just-war theory, the

document affirms several conclusions. War is an evil
scourge and cannot be called good, righteous or holy.
"Christians are sure that the seeds of conflict and war
never can be totally eliminated from this present world.
They dare not, however, take the position that a specific
war is inevitable."[15] In times of national emergency,
Christians should support their government's call to
military service unless prohibited by conscience.
Christians should also work for justice, good will,
freedom, and peace by communicating and assisting across
cultural boundaries. They should support multilateral
and verifiable reductions in armaments and work toward
stronger international controls. Concerning these
efforts for peace, the ALC observes:

> Neither "peace at any price," nor naive
> reliance on the words of the enemy, nor
> allegiance to Utopian goals can bring war
> under control. Voluntary, governmental,
> and intergovernmental measures, built upon
> the foundations of good will and mutual
> understanding between people, can help.[16]

This statement also advances the opinion that war
"is least likely to erupt" when potential adversaries are
equal in military power.

In 1972 the ALC General Convention approved another
statement entitled "Peace, Justice, and Human Rights."
This statement reaffirms the 1966 position on the control
of war and again urges greater efforts toward peace and
universal human rights. The Convention approved a
resolution in 1979 that expressed "strong opposition to
the international arms race, and especially the
proliferation of nuclear weapons." This Convention urged
support of the SALT II Treaty and other steps to limit
and reduce nuclear armaments.

Since 1980 the ALC has devoted increased attention
to nuclear disarmament issues. In 1981 Presiding Bishop
David W. Preus declared peacemaking a vocation of the
church second only to evangelism. Preus also has become
a leader in efforts to improve communications and
understanding between Lutherans of the Eastern and
Western blocs. The ALC Church Council in 1981 adopted a
resolution encouraging the U.S. government to resume SALT
negotiations and to voluntarily comply with the SALT II
Treaty "as a sign of good faith to the Soviet Union and
the global community." The Church Council further
resolved to encourage members to participate in Ground
Zero (18-25 April 1982) and other educational programs on
nuclear disarmament.

In 1980 the General Convention requested the Office
of Church in Society to prepare a study on militarism and
the arms race for presentation to the 1982 Convention.

This office was assisted in its work by suggestions from
a consulting group of thirty-eight persons. The results
of the study were adopted by the General Convention on 10
September 1982 in the form of a statement entitled
"Mandate for Peacemaking." The statement affirmed the
following points. Peacemaking is a Christian mandate and
should be a central task of the Church. This function
includes efforts to curb the arms race and establish
international justice. Nations have legitimate security
interests, but escalation in nuclear weaponry has made
nations less secure and imperiled the world. There is no
need for nations to possess weapons sufficient to destroy
enemy targets many times over. Christians in the Soviet
Union and its allied states have the same yearning for
peace as we do. They are eager to speak against arms
escalation policies of their government, but do not enjoy
the same freedom as Americans to do so. Our impassioned
call for restraint must, therefore, be addressed to both
sides of the East-West confrontation. Nevertheless, we
have a "special calling" to address our own society and
government and a "special competence" to influence our
political processes concerning the arms race and the
"threat of nuclear annihilation."

Based on these affirmations, the statement offers
several recommendations. "The peacemaking task in our
time requires a mass movement of social change, the
building of a solid majority in our nation and other
nations who will insist that national security be defined
in less militaristic terms." To enable people to become
more active participants in the task of peacemaking, the
statement recommends preparation of liturgical and
educational materials on the mandate of peacemaking, the
arms race, and military spending. Concerning United
States nuclear policies, the ALC statement declares that
any use of nuclear weapons is immoral because these
weapons cannot comply with the just-war criteria of
discrimination, due proportion, and reasonable prospect
of victory. The "threat" to use nuclear weapons implicit
in the policy of deterrence is also immoral. In the
present dilemma, however, deterrence is essential for
preventing the use of these weapons until they can be
eliminated. The long-term goal of United States policy
must be the "elimination of nuclear weapons from the
earth." To achieve this goal the statement urges the
government to take the following steps:

> (1) Invite the Soviet Union and other
> nations to join us in a freeze on the
> development of any new nuclear weapons
> systems and on the production of any
> additional warheads or delivery vehicles
> within already-developed weapons systems.
> (2) Invite the Soviet Union and other

nations to join us in a step-by-step
reduction of the number of warheads and
delivery vehicles which now exist.
(3) Invite the Soviet Union and other
nations to agree with us not to deploy
nuclear weapons in a manner that makes
warheads unverifiable, since the
philosophy of security through deterrence
requires that all parties be able to know
the capabilities of all parties.
(4) Show a willingness to take some
risks through specific unilateral steps,
inviting adversary nations to reciprocate
--understanding that continuation on the
present course of nuclear terror carries
exceedingly high risks.

At the conclusion of the statement the ALC again
affirms its support for members who, on the basis of
conscience, choose not to serve in any war or in
particular wars. The Church also supports those who
elect to serve in the armed forces and affirms the
government's right of conscription in times of declared
national emergencies.

The ALC, like the LCA, has reaffirmed its support
for the principles of the just-war tradition. Based on
these principles, the Church has declared that nuclear
weapons are unusable. Therefore, it considers
multilateral, verifiable nuclear disarmament imperative.
Until this occurs, a policy of deterrence is necessary as
a lesser evil. The Church does not advocate unilateral
disarmament. But neither does it deal with its own
acknowledgement, that people of the Eastern Bloc have far
less freedom to agitate for disarmament than people in
the West. Of what value, in terms of multilateral
disarmament, is sharing mutual fears of nuclear
annihilation with citizens of the East, if these citizens
have little influence on the policy of their governments?
Does this action have a positive or negative affect on
Soviet willingness to negotiate nuclear arms reductions?
If Eastern bloc leadership is responsive to its people,
however, then American Lutherans may be providing a most
valuable service in their cross cultural communications
with Lutherans of Eastern and Western Europe.


The Lutheran Church--Missouri Synod

In response to my request for material on the
Lutheran Church--Missouri Synod's position on peace and
war, Jerald C. Joersz sent a document entitled,
"Guidelines for Crucial Issues in Christian Citizenship."
This paper was prepared by the Commission on Theology and

Church Relations of the Missouri Synod in 1968. It
discusses the Synod's view of the Christian's
relationship to government, civic order, and war.

The paper affirms that government is ordained by God
for the purpose of upholding order and providing justice.
Civic order is to be maintained by government to provide
the opportunity for men to work together in the task of
expanding justice and freedom. The maintenance of order
sometimes requires the responsible application of force.
At these times, it is the Christian's duty as citizen to
support the government's efforts to provide order and
security, unless these efforts conflict with the will of
God. The Christian's choice concerning participation in
the use of violent force should be guided by the criteria
of just war, as specified in the Augsburg Confession,
Art. XVI (1530 A.D.).

This paper contains the following statement on
modern weapons of war:

> The destructive potential of modern weaponry
> and the impersonality of contemporary
> techniques of warfare lay upon the
> Christian citizen the special burden of
> reminding himself and others that human
> life is a sacred trust from man's Creator
> and that the temptation to rely on and
> resort to the kind of massive violence
> made possible by these inventions has
> introduced into the human situation a
> new factor of incalculable moral magnitude.
> It is therefore imperative for him to
> work together with all men of goodwill
> for the responsible limitation of
> armaments, the eradication of sources
> of conflict, and an aggressive interest
> in the preservation and expansion of the
> conditions of peace.

In addition to the passage cited above, individual
pastors and scholars have commented on nuclear issues.
According to Joersz, however, "the Synod has not taken an
official position through convention action on the matter
of nuclear warfare."[17]

## Wisconsin Evangelical Lutheran Synod

The position of the Wisconsin Evangelical Lutheran
Synod may be stated quickly. According to President Carl
H. Mischke, the following is the only official statement
taken by the Synod on the issues of war and peace.

We believe the proper relation is preserved

between the church and the state and the
welfare of all is properly served only when
each, the church and the state, remains within
its divinely assigned sphere and uses its
divinely entrusted means.  The church is not
to exercise civil authority nor to interfere
with the state as the state carries out
its reponsibilities.  The state is not to
become a messenger of the gospel nor to
interfere with the church in its preaching
mission.  The church is not to attempt to
use the civil law and force in leading people
to Christ.  The state is not to seek to
govern by means of the gospel.  On the
other hand, the church and the state may
participate in one and the same endeavors
as long as each remains within its assigned
place and uses its entrusted means.

We reject any attempt on the part of the
state to restrict the free exercise of
religion.

We reject any views that look to the church
to guide and influence the state directly
in the conduct of its affairs.

We reject any attempt on the part of the
church to seek the financial assistance
of the state in carrying out its saving
purpose.

We reject any views that hold that a
citizen is free to disobey such laws of
the state with which he disagrees on the
basis of personal judgment.

This is what Scripture teaches about the
church and the state.[18]  This we believe,
teach and confess.

## Summary of the Lutheran Positions

Denominations representing three of the eight and
one-half million Lutherans in America have taken no
official position on nuclear warfare, other than a
reaffirmation of the just-war tradition as understood by
Martin Luther.

The positions adopted by the LCA are more general in
content than the statements of other mainline Protestant
denominations.  The 1982 statement of the ALC resembles
in tone and content the second draft of the NCCB pastoral
letter.  It does not, however, specifically endorse

announcement of a "no-first-strike" policy. These
Lutheran denominations do not address individual weapons
systems or strategic policies. They continue to affirm
just-war theory and the right and responsibility of
government to provide for national defense.
     Both the LCA and the ALC have called for serious
progress in nuclear arms reductions and advocate the
eventual elimination of these weapons. The statements of
each church reflect a significantly heightened concern in
the last three years. Both have endorsed a multilateral,
verifiable moratorium or freeze on new weapon systems
until reductions can be negotiated. The LCA and ALC have
also urged the United States to take low risk unilateral
initiatives to encourage the process of disarmament. The
ALC has concluded that nuclear weapons cannot actually be
used in fighting. The LCA has not advocated specifically
that these weapons are unusable in any circumstance.


THE SOUTHERN BAPTIST CONVENTION

     The Southern Baptist Convention (SBC) is by far the
largest Protestant denomination in the United States with
over 13,500,000 members. It is larger than all the
Lutheran groups combined. The SBC membership
approximately equals that of the mainline churches
affiliated with the NCC, less the United Methodist
Church. Though the SBC has churches in all states, its
strength is in the South. The SBC traditionally has
supported a strong defense. It has adopted statements
affirming the importance of peace, but its activities in
this area have been limited.[19]
     In 1978 the Annual Convention acknowledged "the
complexities of maintaining adequate military strength in
a divided world and at the same time pressing for peace
and freedom from the threat of nuclear holocaust."
Nonetheless, the delegates expressed their support for
mutual agreements to slow the nuclear arms race. They
urged national leaders to continue striving for strategic
arms limitations and encouraged multilateral shifting of
funds to meet basic human needs.[20] The following year
the Convention expressed its conviction that multilateral
nuclear arms control is essential and urged the Senate to
ratify the SALT II Treaty.
     With the winds of political change in the nation and
the denomination, the SBC resolution "On Peace and
National Security" in 1980 was significantly different in
tone. The Convention delegates affirmed as follows:

          WHEREAS Dastardly acts of terrorists like
          those in Iran and blatant violations of
          international law like those of Russia in
          Afghanistan remind us that we live in a

sinful and dangerous world, and

WHEREAS, We realistically acknowledge the
timely reassessment of our nation's security
needs and we appreciate the attention given
to spend for defense and

WHEREAS, Christians are, by definition,
followers of the Prince of Peace and
dedicated to "follow after the things
which make for peace,"

Be it therefore Resolved, That we openly
admit to the conflict within our own beings
between the longing for world peace and
the gnawing need to prepare deterrents to
war, and

Be it further Resolved, That we work at ways
actively to wage peace in the world, teaching
and praying in our homes and churches.[21]

The following year the Convention passed a similar,
though milder, resolution:

WHEREAS, The Bible gives a clear mandate for
Christians to be peacemakers in a world where
hostility and war are present realities; and

WHEREAS, We acknowledge the timely reassessment of our nation's security needs and
appreciate the renewed commitment to a
strong national defense;

Be it therefore Resolved, That we express our
longing for world peace; and

Be it further Resolved, That we affirm the
pursuit of negotiations with other nations
for the consideration of appropriate mutual
agreements on arms control, while recognizing
the necessity of defense preparedness that
will serve as a deterrent to war; and

Be it finally Resolved, That we work actively
to encourage peace in the world by teaching
and praying in our homes and churches, and
that we be reminded of the importance of
our witness to the world in proclaiming the
hope we all have in Christ, the Prince of
Peace.[22]

In 1982 the SBC continued to emphasize both "a
strong defense" and " a responsible limitation of nuclear
weapons." As an amendment to the resolution "On Peace
with Justice" the Convention added: "That we support a
program of mutually verifiable disarmament, including
nuclear disarmament; and, we assure the United Nations
Special Session on Disarmament of our prayers and hopes
for progress toward peace."[23]

This resolution, with its amendment, illustrates the
basic thrust of the SBC position. A strong majority
acknowledges the need for nuclear arms control, but
focuses more on the need for a strong defense. A small
but growing minority encourages greater efforts in
peacemaking. In 1981 five state conventions passed
resolutions which included the following statements:
Nuclear war "would be indiscriminate in its victims and
uncontrollable in its devastation (Mississippi); "there
is no military strategy more insane than that which is
based on the belief that a limited nuclear war can be
fought and won" (Virginia); the superpowers are engaged
in "a dangerous and wicked escalation of nuclear arms"
(South Carolina). Nuclear freeze resolutions were
introduced in two state conventions but these were not
passed. Each of the conventions called for greater
efforts in peacemaking.[24] In 1982, after "spirited
debate," a nuclear freeze resolution was adopted on a
divided vote by the New York convention.[25]

E. Glenn Hinson, a Harvard educated professor of
church history at Southern Baptist Theological Seminary,
has been a principal leader of the nascent peace effort
among Southern Baptists. In addition to teaching and
writing on peace issues, Hinson is a coordinating editor
of the new periodical Baptist Peacemaking. In its first
year this periodical grew from 9,000 to 23,000 copies per
edition.[26]

The Christian Life Commission is the SBC agency
responsible for addressing social issues. In 1981 the
Commission published a pamphlet entitled "Issues and
Answers: War and Peace."[27] This document provides a
discussion of modern warfare and the traditional
Christian responses of pacifism, holy war or crusader,
and just war. The pamphlet clearly reflects a reliance
on just-war logic. It stresses the value of peace and
justice, and the responsible use of power by governments.
It affirms that there are times when states must use
power to maintain order between nations, but only as a
last resort. Peace is defined as wholeness, health,
security, and harmonious relationship with God, humanity,
and nature. Peace is always the goal of the Christian.
The pamphlet affirms, however, that peace "can never be
bought at the price of justice." Peace is not a
superficial tranquility that conceals injustice,
violence, and corruption." Therefore, as the just-war

tradition acknowledges, "there are times when injustices
become so blatant and cruel that they must be resisted
with physical force." This necessity, however, does not
diminish our commitment to the ideal of peace, and "any
necessary use of force is always restrained by a deep
longing for peace."
     Concerning the issues of modern war, the pamphlet
urges Christians to:  Support arms limitation efforts;
resist the military-industrial complex "that lobbies to
increase its profits;" resist "national idolatry;"
support the United Nations; and, while recognizing that
arms are sometimes necessary in defense of freedom and
justice, maintain the conviction that "peace with justice
ought always to be a major goal of the world's political
leaders."
     Southern Baptists support nuclear arms control and a
strong national defense. Denominational statements fall
generally toward the "conservative" end of the just-war
position. The SBC has not endorsed a freeze resolution
or rejected "all use" of nuclear weapons. Official
statements have not addressed specific weapons systems or
strategies of deterrence. There is a small but growing
peace effort among Southern Baptists. A final
observation on this denomination is in order. Billy
Graham is a Southern Baptist. Certainly his opinions are
not "official" statements. However, no individual has
greater influence on Southern Baptist thought than Billy
Graham. In recent years Graham has combined with his
call for Christian rebirth an urgent plea for nuclear
disarmament. He has described the arms race as
"madness."[28]


OTHER CHURCH BODIES

     Among the religious bodies in America there is a
large number of churches sometimes referred to as "free
churches." Some of these churches have formed
associations or conferences because of their similarity
in faith and practice. Even then, however, each church
remains autonomous, hence the name "free church." When I
requested information concerning their position on war,
thirteen of these loosely connected denominations or
associations responded with letters. The aggregate
membership of these groups equals five and one-half
million. Most of those responding indicated that because
of the autonomy of member churches no "official"
statements on war and nuclear weapons had been adopted.
The vast majority of those churches who did not respond
to my request for information, those representing
twenty-seven million Protestants, also fall into this
category. Perhaps they too have adopted no formal
position on these issues.

The letters from the thirteen churches who did
respond suggest a plurality of opinion.  Melvin
Worthington, executive secretary, indicated that the
National Association of Free Will Baptists (231,000
members) "has not adopted a position as a denomination"
on nuclear weapons.   He suggests that there is a
"diversity of ideas" among Free Will Baptists.[29]
    Joseph R. Flower is the general secretary of the
General Council of the Assemblies of God (1,630,000
members).  He indicates that "no official statements"
have been made, except for the following on "Military
Service."

> As a Movement we affirm our loyalty to the
> government of the United States in war or
> peace.
>
> We shall continue to insist, as we have
> historically, on the right of each member
> to choose for himself whether to declare
> his position as a combatant, or noncombatant,
> or a conscientious objector.[30]

    Paul A. Tanner, executive secretary of the Church of
God (Anderson, Indiana:   175,000 members) suggests that
positions on nuclear weapons vary considerably within the
membership.[31]   The Independent Fundamental Churches of
America report no record of any statements on these
issues.[32]
    The stated clerk of the Christian Reformed Church
(213,000 members) writes:  "I am confident that from a
Christian point of view there lies in all Christians a
deep abhorrence at the thought of using nuclear weapons
against our fellow men."  Concerning nuclear weapons, he
states that "the assemblies of the Christian Reformed
Church have not to this date spoken specifically on this
matter."[33]  In 1939 the annual Synod meeting adopted a
firm statement on war that is consistent with just-war
theory.  The Banner, a publication of this Church,
published several articles in its 28 September 1981
edition that reflect a variety of opinions on nuclear
weapons.[34]
    The response of the Seventh-day Adventists and the
Conservative Baptist Association of America graphically
reflect the diversity of opinion among the free churches.
Both write that their groups have taken "no position" on
the subject of nuclear weapons.  The Adventists (553,000
members) letter also states that "we believe deeply that
the separation of church and state is truly that."  Each
has its own sphere of action and "each should refrain
from reaching over into the other's sphere of
action."[35]  An earlier Adventists statement affirms
that, based on this separation, "it is not its

prerogative to make a judgment as to whether or not a
nation should enter into war." The Church also teaches,
however, that war is God's judgment and only He has the
power to take life. Therefore, the Church advises its[36]
members to "follow noncombatant life-saving service."

By way of contrast the letter from the Conservative
Baptist Association (225,000 members) affirms that a
small minority of members are discussing the possibility
of unilateral disarmament. "The movement as a whole"
however, would "undoubtedly" identify with the following
statement:

> Living in a world flawed by sin, the United
> States must adapt itself to the realities
> of international relationships entered upon
> and fostered from a negotiating position of
> strength. A powerful defense establishment
> posture is one element of such strength.
> The will of the nation to use that powerful
> defense establishment is another element of
> that strength. And finally, a believable
> determination never to use the power
> available to it in a preemptive strike, but
> the equal determination to respond if
> struck with a full range of weapon options
> up to and including nuclear, is the
> necessary undergriding of the United States'
> position.

The letter concludes:

> We struggle with most of the items in the
> statement above. Currently we are not sure
> of our will, and currently have not persuaded
> the world wide community that we will respond
> if struck a first blow, but I sense that we
> are working on these potential weaknesses
> and if potential enemies will wait until we
> restore our strength, we may again soon be
> negotiating from a strength posture.[37]

The Morman churches include the congregations of the
Church of Jesus Christ of Latter-Day Saints (2,700,000
members) and the Reorganized Church of Jesus Christ of
Latter-Day Saints (190,000 members). They are neither
"free churches" or "mainline" Protestant churches. Their
growing membership has considerable influence in Utah and
other western states. Traditionally, Mormons have been
strong supporters of the national defense program. This
apparently is still true. In recent years, however, they
have protested the basing of additional missile systems
(e.g., the MX) in western states. The MX basing
proposals have prompted serious reflection on nuclear

issues by many Mormans.  Recent statements recognize the
need for strong defense, but also urge increased efforts
in nuclear arms control.  Mormon statements are generally
consistent with the just-war position.
   I have observed elsewhere that none of the black
churches responded to my request for information and
that, apparently, they had published few (if any)
statements on the issues of nuclear war.  According to T.
J. Jemison, the National Baptist Convention, U.S.A.,
Incorporated (NBC) is beginning to alter this pattern.
At the 1983 annual meeting of the National Council of
Churches governing board, Jemison, who is the recently
elected president of the NBC, pledged that his
denomination is becoming more active in social issues.
He reported that the NBC executive board endorsed a
nuclear weapons freeze in May 1983.  Furthermore, Jemison
affirmed:  "We are joining other religious leaders of
this nation in opposing the nuclear arms race."[58]  The
NBC is the largest of the black denominations, with over
five million members.


THE HISTORIC PEACE CHURCHES

   The majority of the historic peace churches
descended from the "Radical Reformation" of sixteenth
century Europe.  They were called, primarily by their
adversaries, "Munsterites" and "anabaptists," or
"rebaptizers."  They identified themselves as "Bruder"
(Brethren), and formed such groups as the Swiss Brethren,
the Hutterite Brethren, the South German Brethren, and
Mennonites (Dutch Anabaptists).[59]  The sixteenth
century Anabaptists advocated a repristination of church
structure, that is, a return to the pre-Constantinian era
of the church.  In part because they were persecuted by
Catholics and the major reformers (Luther, Calvin,
Zwingli), the Anabaptists advocated a separation of
church and state.  Their theology was informed by a
rather literal interpretation and direct application of
the Scriptures, which led them to reject infant baptism,
coercion of faith, state requirements concerning church
membership and forms of worship, and the use of force in
human relationships.  The "Bruder" were pacifists.[40]
   The other major sources of the historic peace
churches were the movement of George Fox (Quakers) and
the separatists in seventeenth century England, and the
Pietist movement of the eighteenth century.  Today the
most prominent of the historic peace churches are the
Quakers (Society of Friends), the Mennonites, the Amish
and the Church of the Brethren.  These churches are
"sectarian" in the sense that, in varying degrees, they
form societies separate from the general culture and are
generally uninvolved with the affairs of government.

These Christians are pacifists.[41]  It is largely
through their agitation that the classification of
"conscientious objection" to military service has been
established.  The historic peace churches are numerically
insignificant as a percent of the national population.
In 1979 the following membership figures were reported by
these churches:

| | |
|---|---:|
| The Mennonite Church | 98,000 |
| The Older Order Amish Church | 80,000 |
| The Church of the Brethren | 172,000 |
| The Friends (Quakers) United Meeting | <u>61,000</u> |
| Total | 411,000 |

The influence of the pacifist churches, however, far
exceeds their numerical strength.  Their profile has
elevated in direct proportion to the force of the
contemporary peace movement.  Robert Steffer of the
Christian Church (Disciples) commented that, in seeking
to develop literature and educational programs for
"peacemaking," he turned to those long experienced in the
field, the historic peace churches.  No doubt this is
also true of other denominations and disarmament groups.
Appendix C of <u>Freeze!  How You Can Help Prevent Nuclear
War</u>, by Senators Kennedy and Hatfield, is a list of some
two-hundred coordinators of the nuclear freeze campaign.
At least seventy of these are religious groups, and over
twenty of them are local organizations of the American
Friends Service Committee (Quakers).[42]
     As complete pacifists these churches have always
advocated nonviolence and disarmament.  It is not
unexpected that they have been involved in the
contemporary movement.  In addition to organizing
opposition to the arms race and nuclear policies, these
churches have been particularly active in developing new
literature.[43]   The Mennonite and Brethren in Christ
churches participate in an organization called New Call
to Peacemaking.  This group has joined with other
Catholic and Protestant pacifist organizations in
endorsing a statement entitled "New Abolitionist
Convenant."[44]  This document is widely distributed in
the contemporary peace movement.  It is not so much a
statement as a call for all Christians to covenant
together for the abolition of nuclear weapons.  The
document states that, like slavery, nuclear weapons must
be abolished before they annihilate the world.  The "New
Abolitionist Covenant" makes the following affirmation:

     Nuclear war is total war.  Unlimited in their
     violence, indiscriminate in their victims,
     uncontrollable in their devastation, nuclear
     weapons have brought humanity to a historical

crossroads. More than at any previous time
in history, the alternatives are peace or
destruction. In nuclear war there are no
winners.

Nuclear weapons, the document continues, present a
test of survival and a test of faith. "At stake is
whether we trust in God or the bomb. We can no longer
confess Jesus as Lord and depend on nuclear weapons to
save us. Conversion in our day must include turning away
from nuclear weapons as we turn to Jesus Christ." The
building and threatened use of nuclear weapons is a sin
against God and his creation. We refuse to cooperate any
longer with the preparations for total war. Furthermore,
those who adopt this statement affirm:

> We covenant together to work to stop the arms
> race. In light of our faith, we are prepared
> to live without nuclear weapons. We will
> publicly advocate a nuclear weapon freeze as
> the first step toward abolishing nuclear
> weapons altogether. We will act in our
> local communities to place the call for a
> nuclear weapon freeze on the public agenda.
> We will press our government and the other
> nuclear powers to halt all further testing,
> production, and deployment of nuclear weapons,
> and then move steadily and rapidly to
> eliminate them completely.

The New Call to Peacemaking goes beyond the "New
Abolitionist Covenant." This group calls for tax
withholding and draft resistance if necessary; it urges a
unilateral freeze on nuclear weapons by the United
States, with the hope that the Soviet Union will follow
our example.[45]

In 1981 the Friends General Conference (Quakers)
addressed a statement to President Reagan and Premier
Brezhnev. This statement appealed to both "to take
immediate steps to initiate a bilateral freeze of the
development, production, and deployment of all nuclear
weapons. The two leaders were especially urged to
renounce the "first use of nuclear weapons," and
encouraged to consider George Kennan's proposal for "an
immediate fifty percent reduction in nuclear arms." The
Friends Committee on National Legislation, four years
earlier approved a statement which affirmed: "we also
believe that unilateral disarmament by the United States
together with other far-reaching revisions of its foreign
policy is required by Christian principles and would
encourage other nations to disarm."[46]

As noted earlier, the historic peace churches
constitute only a small part of American society. There

is, however, an increasing similarity between their statements and those of the churches committed to peacemaking; and these latter churches represent a very large segment of the American populous.

CONCLUSION

In the last two chapters we have reviewed the positions (or nonpositions) held by churches representing nearly 50 million United States citizens. When we add to this figure the number of Roman Catholics in America, we have surveyed the positions advocated by the religious leaders of almost 100 million Americans. We again caution the reader that this kind of statistical assessment is fraught with problems. Church membership figures are not always accurate. The percentage of church leaders supporting the positions adopted by their denominations varies. We have noted counter movements within the Catholic Church and the United Methodist Church which advocate more conservative or traditional positions; and in the Southern Baptist Convention there is a small minority that urges greater peacemaking efforts than those adopted by the majority. Also, it should be acknowledged that some church members are influenced very little by the opinions of church leaders or the official positions adopted by their churches. If we arbitrarily reduce all the figures in half, however, we are still talking about 50 million Americans--a sizable percentage of the American public. I would suggest that the positions reflected in this study at least demonstrate trends and possibly represent the thought of a majority of church members. Most of the statements have been approved by wide representation from the denominations in general church meetings. Compared with recent polls and electoral results on the nuclear freeze resolution, this may well be a conservative estimate.[47] In at least one church, the Lutheran Church in America, delegates to the convention adopted a stronger position on nuclear disarmament than was advocated by denominational leaders.
Virtually all groups surveyed advocate "peacemaking." It is highly unlikely that a Christian church would not hold this position when it was Jesus who said, "Blessed are the peacemakers, for they will be called sons of God" (Matthew 5:9). Understanding what churches mean by "peacemaking," however, is perhaps the most difficult problem in this study. To Southern Baptists, peacemaking seems to mean maintaining a strong defense, while seeking mutual reductions in nuclear weapons. Their position falls toward the right end of the just-war spectrum. Lutheran peacemaking favors the retention of adequate defense forces while actively

cultivating disarmament sentiment in the international
Lutheran fora. The Lutherans also support the just-war
tradition, though these principles lead one group, The
American Lutheran Church, to renounce "all use" of
nuclear weapons. Peacemaking to the National Council
Protestant bodies means acknowledging the need for
security, at least in principle, while devoting all
efforts toward a reduction in defense spending and an end
to the arms race. The position of these denominations is
generally nuclear pacifism, though some reach this
position through the just-war criteria. To the historic
peace churches, peacemaking equals pacifism and general
disarmament.

A few things are clear. All of the denominations
that have adopted positions (that is the great majority)
recognize the need for nuclear arms control and they
advocate stronger efforts to negotiate reductions in
nuclear weapons. It is also transparent that concern
over these issues has mushroomed in the last three years
and, increasingly, more resources are allocated to
peacemaking and disarmament. Several denominations have
designated nuclear weapons issues as their primary social
concern in the coming years.

Of the twelve major Protestant denominations
discussed in the last two chapters, ten endorsed
resolutions supporting a nuclear weapons freeze; nine
advocated ratification of the SALT II Treaty; five urged
unilateral initiatives by the United States in nuclear
disarmament; five affirmed that nuclear weapons should
not be used under any circumstances and two more
seriously questioned any use of these weapons; and seven
advocated adoption of a "no-first-use" policy by the
United States. Only the historic pacifist churches
officially urged complete unilateral nuclear disarmament
by the United States. (See chart at Appendix B.)


NOTES


1. "March 1981 Statement on International Tensions
by West German Protestant Leaders and U.S. Lutheran
Leaders," an unpublished statement dated 9 March 1981 and
sent to the writer by the Office for Governmental
Affairs, Lutheran Council in the U.S.A.

2. This statement was reprinted under the title
"Lutheran Leaders and the Arms Race," Rocky Mountain
Newsletter, January 1982.

3. This meeting was held two weeks prior to The
World Council of Churches' "Public Hearing on Nuclear

Weapons and Disarmament," 23-27 November 1981 in
Amsterdam. Cf. World Council of Churches, Executive
Committee, Document No. 12, undated.

4. James R. Crumley, Jr., unpublished pastoral
letter addressed "Dear Partners," 8 November 1981.

5. Richard J. Niebanck, personal letter to Donald
L. Davidson, 1 February 1981. Niebanck is Secretary for
Social Concerns, Department for Church in Society of the
LCA.

6. This statement, hereafter referred to as "World
Community," has been reproduced as a pamphlet and is
available from the Division for Mission in North America,
LCA, 231 Madison Avenue, New York, New York, 10016.

7. A Theology of Politics was originally written in
1960. Conscience, War, and the Selective Objector was
written in 1968. Both books were published by the Board
of Social Ministry, Lutheran Church in America. These
documents have been frequently quoted in Lutheran
literature. Lazareth's work was quoted as late as 1979
by Niebanck and George H. Brand in SALT II: Strategic
Arms Limitation Treaty, Division for Mission in North
America, LCA, 1979.

8. Lazareth, ibid., pp. 17-18.

9. Ibid., pp. 25 and 26.

10. "War and Peace in a Nuclear Age," a resolution
adopted by the LCA Convention, 3-10 September 1982.

11. Richard J. Niebanck, telephone conversation with
Donald L. Davidson, 29 November 1982.

12. Cf. "Peace and War: Some Theological and
Political Perspectives," and George H. Brand, "Arms
Control and Reduction in the 1980s; Problems and
Prospects." Both documents were published by the
Division for Mission in North America, LCA, 1982.

13. Produced by the Commission on Research and
Social Action, the ALC, 422 South Fifth Street,
Minneapolis, Minnesota, 55415.

14. Ibid., p. 2.

15. Ibid., p. 7.

16. Ibid., p. 9.

17.  Jerald C. Joersz, assistant executive secretary, personal letter to Donald L. Davidson, 15 January 1982.

18.  Commission on Inter-Church Relations, Wisconsin Evangelical Lutheran Synod, This We Believe:  A Statement of Belief of the Wisconsin Evangelical Lutheran Synod (Milwaukee, Wisconsin:  Northwestern Publishing House, 1980), pp. 22-23.  The comment by Carl H. Mischke is in a personal letter to Donald L. Davidson, 12 January 1982.

19.  Cf.  observations by Dan Magee in "25 Probe Baptist Response to Peacemaking," Baptist Standard 94 (15 September 1982): 4.

20.  Annual of the Southern Baptist Convention, 1978, p. 54.

21.  Ibid., 1980, p. 54.

22.  Ibid., 1981, p. 54.

23.  Ibid., 1982, p. 59.

24.  Cf. Charles Johnson, "Peacemaking SBC Style," Baptist Peacemaker 2 (January 1982): 12.

25.  Cf. Baptist Standard 94 (17 November 1982): 9.

26.  "Peacemaking Partners," Baptist Peacemaker 2 (January 1982): 2.

27.  "Issues and Answers" is a series of pamphlets published by The Christian Life Commission of the Southern Baptist Convention, 460 James Robertson Parkway, Nashville, Tennessee, 37219.  Foy Valentine, the executive director, is also a consulting editor for Baptist Peacemaker.

28.  Cf. reports of Graham's speeches and activities at Harvard, the Soviet Union and elsewhere in the Boston Globe, New York Times, Sojourners Magazine, and Graham's periodical, Decision.

29.  Melvin Worthington, personal letter to Donald L. Davidson, 18 January 1982.

30.  Joseph R. Flower, personal letter to Donald L. Davidson, 25 January 1982.

31.  Paul A. Tanner, personal letter to Donald L. Davidson, 20 January 1982.

32.   Harold F. Freeman, National Executive Director, IFCA, personal letter to Donald L. Davidson, 15 January 1982.

33.   William P. Brink, personal letter to Donald L. Davidson, 22 January 1982.

34.   The most extensive treatment I have seen on nuclear weapons by a member of the Christian Reformed Church is by Mark R. Amstutz, "The Christian and Nuclear Arms," The Reformed Journal (February 1982):11-16. Amstutz's approach is from the just war perspective.   He suggests that the crucial question today is how to prevent the use of nuclear weapons.  He concludes that maintaining "rough equivalence" while seeking a mutual moratorium and then reduction of weapons is the most promising approach.

35.   Clark Smith, personal letter to Donald L. Davidson, 13 January 1982.

36.   "Seventh-day Adventist Teachings on Governmental Relationships and Noncombatancy," undated booklet published by the National Service Organization of the General Conference of Seventh-day Adventists.

37.   Ralph R. Monsen, personal letter to Donald L. Davidson, 13 January 1982.  Mr. Monsen reaffirms at the conclusion of his letter that his remarks are "not official pronouncements."

38.   Charles Austin, "New Leader Steers Black Baptist Church into Activist Course," The New York Times, 16 May 1983, p. A10.

39.   Cf. Franklin Hamlin Littell, The Origins of Sectarian Protestantism:  A Study of the Anabaptist View of the Church (New York:  The Macmillan Company, 1964), pp. xv-xviii.

40.   Some groups called "Anabaptists," such as the Munsterites and the followers of Thomas Muntzer, advocated revolution.  The historic peace churches of today, however, did not descend from these groups.

41.   An excellent spokesman for the position advocated by the historic peace churches is John Howard Yoder, a Mennonite scholar.  See his The Politics of Jesus (Grand Rapids, Michigan:  William B. Eerdmans Publishing Co., 1972) and The Original Revolution: Essays on Christian Pacifism (Scottdale, Pennsylvania: Herald Press, 1977).

174

42.  Freeze!  How You Can Help Prevent Nuclear War,
pp. 238-51.  Many more than seventy of these
organizations may be religious groups.  At least seventy
of them are known to be religiously affiliated from their
names.

43.  See J. C. Wenger's The Way of Peace, adopted by
the General Conference Mennonite Church in 1971; "An
Agenda on Militarism and Development," adopted by the
Mennonite Central Committee, 27 January 1979; "Resolution
on the World Arms Race," adopted by the Peace Section
(U.S.), Mennonite Central Committee, 1 December 1978;
"Church of the Brethren Statements on Disarmament and the
United Nations," Church of the Brethren General Board,
1451 Dundee Avenue, Elgin, Illinois, 60120.

44.  The "New Abolitionist Covenant," ca.1981 is
jointly distributed by Fellowship of Reconciliation (an
interdenominational organization), New Call to
Peacemaking, Pax Christi U.S.A. (a Catholic group),
Sojourners (an evangelical Protestant organization), and
World Peacemakers.

45.  New Call to Peacemaking, Second National
Conference, "Statement of the Findings Committee," 2-5
October 1980, Green Lake, Wisconsin.

46.  These two statements by the Friends are cited
from To Proclaim Peace:  Religious Statements on the Arms
Race, compiled and edited by John Donaghy for The
Fellowship of Reconciliation, Fall 1981.

47.  Several public opinion polls between March and
June 1982 reflect that from 73 percent to 91 percent of
the respondents supported a verifiable mutual freeze of
nuclear weapons if the U.S. and U.S.S.R. were about equal
in strength.  However, 67 percent to 86 percent opposed
U.S. unilateral reductions, an unverifiable freeze or any
freeze that would result in Soviet nuclear superiority.
See Public Opinion 5 (August/September, 1982):33-40.

# [ 7 ]
# The Nuclear Debate: Final Comments

## INTRODUCTION

I began this study with the goal of documenting the positions of leading ethicists and the major religious denominations in America concerning the moral issues of war. Specifically, I wished to describe views on the validity of the just-war tradition in the nuclear age, the use of strategic and theater nuclear weapons, and the policy of nuclear deterrence. While I was researching this subject, there was an explosion of interest and information which has reshaped my questions to some extent. Ethicists do, but churches often do not, distinguish between the types or levels of nuclear weapons (i.e., strategic, intermediate, and tactical). Consequently, I have been unable to fully differentiate denominational positions on the various types of weapons. In contemporary literature the distinction is more often made between "old" weapons associated with the strategy of Mutual Assured Destruction (MAD) and the "new" weapons of counterforce or countervailing strategy ("flexible response"). Also, I have expanded my research to incorporate responses to additional issues of high interest this past year, including the nuclear weapons "freeze" campaign, "unilateral initiatives" in arms reductions, and the policy of "first use" of nuclear weapons.

In the preceding chapters I have surveyed the positions of several ethicists, the Roman Catholic Church, and the major Protestant denominations. The combined memberships of these churches represent roughly 45 percent of the U.S. population. A noteworthy feature of most church positions is that, presently, they are quite fluid. No denomination better illustrates this fact than the Catholic Church. It is fair to say that the churches have thought more about nuclear issues in the past two years than at any time in the last twenty.

In this final chapter, I provide a summary analysis
of positions documented in this study and offer general
observations concerning the current nuclear debate. I
conclude by suggesting considerations for a moral defense
policy. Before we turn to the summary, however, a brief
survey of the Jewish position is warranted.

JEWISH VIEWS: A RELUCTANT CRITICISM

Jewish bodies have published few statements on the
issues of nuclear weapons. The support of American Jews
for the defense of Israel, combined with their general
reaction to the Beirut massacre, would suggest that their
views fall within the just-war position. Though Michael
Walzer does not write in the name of Judaism, his position
could be considered "a" Jewish view. The Union of
American Hebrew Congregations has adopted over the years
several resolutions supporting the SALT Treaties and a ban
on nuclear testing. In 1981 the Union approved a
resolution which urged a verifiable, 50 percent reduction
of nuclear stockpiles by the United States and Soviet
Union; a "freeze" on the testing, production, and
deployment of nuclear weapons; and adoption of nuclear
nonproliferation treaties. The Union also vigorously
protested oppression of Jews in the Soviet Union.[1]

In November 1982 the Union of Orthodox Jewish
Congregations of America became the first Orthodox Jewish
organization to publically criticize the Reagan
Administration's nuclear policies. The Union adopted a
statement at its 84th Biennial Convention which called
upon all nations to seek alternatives to armed conflict in
resolving international violence because of the "specter
of total destruction." Carefully avoiding the word
"freeze," the Union affirmed: "We support the ultimate
goal of the SALT and START processes: a bilateral
reduction in the size and deployment of nuclear weapons."
The Union called upon Orthodox congregations to urge the
U.S. government "to press forward even more vigorously in
the movement to halt the growth of nuclear weapons."[2]

On 25 February 1983, _The New York Times_ published an
article entitled, "Synagogue Council Endorses Nuclear
Freeze" (p. A17). In reaction to this headline, Melanie
Shimoff reported that the Synagogue Council of America,
like the Union of Orthodox Jewish Congregations,
deliberately refrained from using the word "freeze" to
avoid endorsement of specific nuclear freeze proposals
before Congress. In fairness to the _Times_, the Council's
statement, adopted 22 February 1983, does sound like an
endorsement of a nuclear weapons freeze. The Council
declared: "At a time where the superpowers possess
strength enough to wipe humankind off the earth, it is the
height of folly to develop ever deadlier weapons in a

futile search for spurious security."[3]  While the
Council recognizes that "unilateral disarmament" only
invites "nuclear blackmail or outright aggression," it
advocates "mutually agreed upon bilateral disarmament and
reduction programs." Based on these conclusions, the
Council resolves to "call upon President Reagan and the
Congress to press forward more vigorously toward the
achievement of effective non-proliferation treaties; and
to stop the transfer of nuclear arms technology to other
nations." The Council further resolves to:

> Urge President Reagan and Premier Andropov to
> implement a bilateral mutual and verifiable
> total cessation of the production and
> deployment of nuclear weapons while both
> parties reconvene negotiations in an effort
> to achieve significant cutbacks of nuclear
> weapons in an effective phased and verifi-
> able arms control treaty.  (Underline added.)

The Synagogue Council of America is composed of the
six major Jewish religious congregational and Rabbinic
bodies in the United States, and it includes Orthodox,
Conservative, and Reformed Jewish organizations,[4]
representing some 6,000,000 members.
In summary, Jewish bodies have been reluctant to
critize defense policies, including nuclear weapons
policies.  Still they avoid taking sides in the nuclear
arms debate.  Some of the most vigorous supporters of a
strong defense, including nuclear defense, are from the
Jewish community, as the journal Commentary reflects.
Nevertheless, the official statements surveyed above
demonstrate that Jewish bodies have taken a firm, though
somewhat general, position against nuclear war and the
continuing arms race.


A SUMMARY ANALYSIS OF POSITIONS ON NUCLEAR ISSUES

The Just-War Ethicists' Positions

Reinhold Niebuhr identified the basic issues which
are still debated today:  defense by force in the nuclear
age; the possession of nuclear weapons for deterrence; the
"first use" or "retaliatory use" of nuclear weapons; the
devastating capacity of nuclear weapons; and arms control.
He concluded that the United States must maintain a
defense force adequate to resist aggression and to avoid
subjugation.  Military weakness invites attack.  Niebuhr
suggested that individuals may, but nations do not, risk
their existence by adopting a position of defenselessness.
Sufficient security to Niebuhr included the possession of
nuclear weapons to deter their use.  However, he also

recognized the massive destructiveness of these weapons
(strategic only at the time of his writing) and seriously
questioned their actual use. He clearly rejected "first
use" of nuclear weapons and warned against an overreliance
on military strength for security. He urged negotiated
arms control rather than unilateral reductions.

It is unlikely that Niebuhr would substantially alter
the basic principles of his position today. However, the
growth of nuclear arsenals, the development of theater
weapons, and the shifting balance of power away from U.S.
superiority certainly need consideration in assessing his
views, especially concerning ways of relating to the
Soviet Union. Douglass Meeks (UCC) and others have
criticized Niebuhr's arguments for the use of force and
the necessity of power balance ("ethical realism") as
insufficient bases for "peacemaking" and have urged more
constructive attitudes toward the Soviet Union.

Paul Ramsey and Vatican Council II (RC) reached
roughly similar conclusions in the 1960s. Both affirmed
government's responsibility to provide national security
and both insisted that the means of war must be guided by
the principles of discrimination and proportionality.
Ramsey and the Catholic Council proscribed in strong
language the targeting of nuclear weapons (or any weapons)
on noncombatants and population centers. The Council
talked more about the need for peace. Ramsey focused
primarily on technical aspects of the means of war.

Ramsey rejected "first use" of strategic weapons and
"all out" use of nuclear weapons. He sought to establish
strong "firebreaks" between conventional and nuclear
weapons, or, in contemporary terminology, to strengthen
the nuclear "threshold." His discussion of the use of
nuclear weapons is primarily within the framework of
deterrence. He legitimated the "first use" of tactical
nuclear weapons over friendly or border territory against
an invading force, but within the constraints of
discrimination and due proportion. Ramsey also advocated
a strengthening of conventional forces to reduce reliance
on nuclear deterrents.

It may be impossible to use nuclear weapons in Europe
today within the constraints set by Ramsey. The density
of population and the profusion of tactical and
intermediate-range weapons in Europe, combined with the
potential of escalation, may well preclude the possibility
of any discriminate use of theater (including tactical)
weapons. Certainly the potential for indiscriminate and
disproportionate use exists. Therefore, these factors
must be considered when assessing the use of nuclear
weapons in Europe, or elsewhere.

Ramsey's views on conventional forces and the
imbalance of these forces in Europe still apply. It seems
self-evident that if a threat to Western Europe exists,
that if European values should be defended, and if nuclear

means would destroy more values than they preserve, then the only alternatives are to negotiate balanced reductions or increase conventional forces. Forces of NATO and the Warsaw Pact need not be symmetrical, but they must be sufficient to discourage aggressive action.

James Johnson also affirms the need for defense in the nuclear age in accord with the principles of just war. He acknowledges the necessity of possessing nuclear weapons at this time for deterrence. He concludes, however, that our present weapons are probably unusable within the limits of discrimination and proportionality. Therefore, he encourages the development of weapons that can be used morally and an increased reliance on conventional forces. He also advocates a reinstitution of compulsory military service and a nuclear weapons policy of no "all out" response.

Virtually all contributers considered in this study reached the same conclusion: nuclear weapons are horrendous and something must be done to address the "balance of terror." The basic alternatives they proposed include: (1) unilateral disarmament; (2) a multilateral freeze on new weapons and negotiated, balanced, verifiable, reductions of current arsenals, possibly combined with unilateral initiatives and nuclear free zones (especially along the East-West frontier); and (3) a restructuring of defense forces to incorporate more reliance on conventional weapons and less on nuclear.

Very few have advocated unilateral disarmament. The majority have supported the second option or a combination of the second and third alternatives. Johnson is one of the few who has given serious attention to ways of restructuring the force for greater reliance on conventional weapons and developing more moral and usable weapons. Thus, his proposals are potentially more applicable for developing a force that corresponds with moral criteria for "fighting;" and fighting, after all, is the basic mission of military forces.

Because Johnson "speaks" of "fighting" and developing "usable" weapons, however, his proposals run counter to the substance and tone of the church dialogue. Also his ideas conflict with those moralists who ironically favor the more indiscriminate policy of MAD over counterforce strategy, because counterforce weapons are thought to be politically and psychologically more "usable." It is a fair criticism, I believe, that Johnson's recommendations do narrow the distinction between conventional and nuclear weapons, and, thus, potentially weaken the nuclear barrier. A tragic irony of weapons that are characteristically more moral is that they are also more likely to be "used." Recognition of this possibility reinforces the validity of another of Johnson's points: human intentions concerning the use of weapons are morally more significant than the weapons themselves. Even sticks can be used immorally. There is merit, however, in reducing the size and effect of the sticks people use, if we can.

Michael Walzer rejects any "actual use" of nuclear weapons, but supports a stable and balanced nuclear deterrent force. He sees nuclear deterrence as immoral, but a lesser evil than the "actual use" of these weapons. He emphasizes the urgent need for negotiated reductions; however, he cautions against a nuclear weapon freeze because of its potentially destabilizing effects. Also, Walzer strongly affirms the just-war position. Aggression, in his view, is a crime that should be resisted by non-nuclear force, even in the nuclear age.


The Denominational Positions

Though variations exist, there is a striking similarity among the positions held by the Roman Catholic Church and the major Protestant denominations. The commonality of ideas and language evidences extensive cross sharing and common source material. Perhaps the best way to compare the views of the churches is to refer to the chart at Appendix B. I have not included the positions of the "free churches" on this chart because of the lack of official pronouncements by these groups. My impression is that a majority of these churches hold views similar to the positions of the Lutheran Church-Missouri Synod and the Southern Baptist Convention. The position of the historic peace churches is recorded in the chart to facilitate comparison of positions. It is not included in the totals calculated in the last column on the right.

All thirteen denominations represented in this chart have registered significant concern for nuclear arms control and limitation. The combined memberships of these churches is 92,400,000. All but two of the denominations have designated nuclear issues as primary areas of social concern. This suggests that in the years ahead the churches will continue to study and make pronouncements on these issues. It is also likely that their "peacemaking" efforts will become increasingly action oriented. In the past year several have discussed and/or participated in nonviolent protest proposals such as demonstrations, vigils, petitions, and withholding of taxes. Members of many of these churches participated in Ground Zero Week, the massive protest march in New York City in June 1982, and the ongoing nuclear freeze campaign.

None of these denominations, except the historic peace churches, have officially advocated unilateral nuclear disarmament, and all accept some concept of deterrence. The deterrence policies acceptable to the churches, however, are those based on the goals of "sufficiency," "parity," "balance," or "rough

equivalency." No religious body advocated nuclear
superiority. Of the thirteen denominations, ten
(representing 80,000,000 members) urged ratification of
the SALT II agreement and eleven (representing 76,400,000
members) supported a mutual and verifiable "freeze" on
nuclear weapons testing, development, and deployment. Six
of the churches favored "unilateral initiatives" by the
United States in arms reductions, and eight (representing
61,500,000 members) supported a policy of "no first use"
of nuclear weapons. The Catholic Church and the United
Presbyterian Church seriously questioned any "actual use"
of nuclear weapons, and five denominations proscribed
"actual use" of these weapons.

Only the Catholic Church specifically considered the
possibility of increasing conventional forces if necessary
to reduce reliance on nuclear forces. The United Church
of Christ did recognize the need for defense forces
"well-chosen, well-led and well-rewarded." The Southern
Baptist Convention also supported the retention of a
"strong defense."

About half of the churches affirm the validity of the
just-war tradition for addressing issues of war and peace
in the nuclear age. The Catholic Church, the Lutheran
Churches, the Southern Baptist Convention, and the
Presbyterian Church in the U.S. specifically appeal to
this tradition in justifying their statements. Other
churches do not endorse the tradition, but use just-war
criteria for analyzing the morality of nuclear weapons.
Some individuals within the Catholic Church and the
National Council churches employ the criteria while
simultaneously renouncing the theory.

Joseph Fahey's argument exemplifies this last
approach (above, p. 72). In support of his position, he
erroneously claims that the popes no longer employ the
concept of "just war" and that the Catholic Church has
challenged this tradition. Yet, he himself uses the
concepts of this tradition in his argument. He holds that
there is no such thing as a "just" nuclear war. By which
criteria does he make this judgment: discrimination and
proportionality (just-war criteria). Nevertheless, he
concludes that the "just-war principles" are irrelevant
"in a nuclear age." Fahey's logic is clearly
inconsistent. His argument against nuclear weapons,
however, is really an exercise to promote Pax Christi and
to discredit all war, "just" or "unjust." As a pacifist
he rejects any justification for war.

Other denominational representatives, such as Robert
Steffer (Disciples) and Robert Smylie (UPC), have
questioned the just-war tradition because they understand
it as a rationalization used only to "approve" of war and
not as an evaluation procedure for determining justice.
This concept (or misconception, I believe) is not all
together unwarranted. The theory was introduced to the

Christian Church as an argument justifying Christian
participation in war (see Augustine, Chapter 1).
Following the coalition between church and state in the
Middle Ages, churchmen sometimes used just-war terminology
to argue in support of questionable military causes.  In
that age clergymen (including popes) also performed
occasionally as military leaders.  And in contemporary
times, governmental leaders routinely use the language of
justice to marshall public support for martial action.
All this suggests that just-war theory has been abused and
misused.    The complexity of this subject is further
increased when one considers that concepts of justice
vary.  But these same arguments can be addressed to all
moral principles.  If one commits an act of murder and
then argues his innocence, for example, does this
invalidate the moral injunction not to murder?  Does the
moral norm proscribing murder prohibit all action that
might result in the death of another person?  Pacifists
might answer this last question affirmatively; but this
answer is far from universal.  The theory of just war does
approve the use of force, but only within the parameters
of justice.
        To some extent the discussion concerning just war has
been transformed.  Geyer suggests that this tradition may
be a valid theory for limiting war, but the church should
have as a higher priority a theory for waging peace; that
is, a theology of "peacemaking."  Steffer advocated a
similar theme in affirming that the church must stand for
peace, not war.  These affirmations echo the 1929
statement of the PCUS:  " . . . the church should never
again bless a war, or be used as an instrument in the
promotion of war."[5]   Each of these statements reflects
what has become a general theme among most of the
denominations surveyed in this study:  The church's main
business is to work for peace, not justify war.
Consequently, there is less emphasis among the
denominations on just-war theory in the current debate;
and some ecclesiastical representatives, to strengthen
their argument for peacemaking, have firmly rejected the
theory.  This development leaves little rationale for
making decisions when aggression is unavoidable; that is,
when it is impossible to have both peace and justice.  I
would contend that Geyer and Steffer are right concerning
the primary emphasis of the church.  It should strive for
peace.  Nations do need to learn and adopt peaceful ways
of resolving international conflict, especially in the
nuclear age.  Is it not also valid, even in the nuclear
age, to protect life and values and, as a last resort,
with just means, to use force if necessary?
        The most serious deficiency in church positions is
the lack of correlation with the international
political-military context.  Most of the denominations
renounce U.S. nuclear weapons as if they were an

abstraction. The churches refer only briefly, if at all, to Soviet weapons or the balance of forces in Europe. There is little or no discussion of the Soviet "gulag" or of Soviet actions in East Germany, Hungary, Czechoslovakia, Afghanistan, or Poland. Soviet military policy and strategy are scarcely mentioned. On the other hand, many of the churches amply criticize U.S. weapons, strategy, and policy. This criticism is normally preceded by an affirmation that the nuclear peril and the arms race transcend national concerns and, therefore, it is imperative to address at least our contribution to the danger.

To focus only on one side, however, neglects the fact that both sides must be mutually deterred from the use of nuclear weapons. This "monoptic" approach also fails to differentiate qualitatively between the American and Soviet regard for life and freedom. Surely this difference must carry some weight in evaluating policy. If the churches wish to apply moral principles to U.S. policy, as indeed they should, then they must also address the context in which these policies are forged.

## A COMPARISON OF THE ADMINISTRATION AND CHURCH POSITIONS

We began this study with the recognition that the crucial challenge facing humanity is twofold: (1) How to protect and preserve values worth defending?, and (2) How to prevent nuclear war? Most participants in the contemporary debate recognize the validity of both goals. Differences in positions result primarily from the varying degree of importance attributed to each goal. At one end of the spectrum, the weight is placed almost exclusively on preventing nuclear war; at the other end, defense is seen as most crucial. Ironically, positions at both ends pursue the same ultimate objective, peace with justice. Those who stress prevention see nuclear warfare as the greatest destroyer of values. Those who urge strong defense believe that weakness invites aggression, including nuclear war, which destroys values worth defending. So, the essential question remains "how?" not what.

Recent statements by the churches, especially the National Council churches and the Catholic Church, position them toward the "prevention" end of the continuum. Current policy statements and responses to the NCCB pastoral letter place the Administration toward the "defense" end. Following the first two drafts of the Catholic pastoral letter, responses were issued by several members of the Reagan Administration, including William P. Clark, Assistant to the President for National Security Affairs; Lawrence S. Eagleburger, Undersecretary of State

for Political Affairs; Eugene V. Rostow, Director of the
Arms Control and Disarmament Agency (recently discharged);
Casper W. Weinberger, Secretary of Defense; and John P.
Lehman, Jr., Secretary of the Navy.[6] These responses
may be compared with church statements to further
differentiate the positions of the churches and the
Administration. To assist in this comparison I have
employed Ralph Potter's analytical paradigm. Potter
suggests that policy proposals can be analyzed into four
categories: (1) Empirical description of the context,
which consists of selection and interpretation of factual
data; (2) loyalties, including institutions, communities
and values to which commitment is given; (3) philosophical
beliefs concerning elements like human nature,
governmental responsibility, war, and human rights; and
(4) method of moral reasoning, that is, the criteria and
priorities considered in making judgments. In Potter's
view there is a reciprocal interaction between these four
categories in formulating policy proposals. For example,
our view of the context affects and is affected by our
loyalties and beliefs. Potter's observation is also
correct that there is no completely "non-moral view" or
"purely moral view" of policy.[7]

## Empirical Descriptions of the Context

In describing the contemporary international context,
policy makers focus on the Soviet "threat," and therefore
stress the need for defense. Weinberger points to the
"massive Soviet military buildup of the last fifteen
years" and the use of this power to stifle freedom in
Eastern Europe, Afghanistan, and elsewhere. He affirms
that the "threat to peace" posed by the Soviet Union has
not diminished since World War II. Weinberger concludes
that "given the threatening nature of Soviet forces"
modernization of U.S. systems is essential. Maintaining a
balanced, flexible deterrence is crucial for the
prevention of all war, conventional and nuclear.
Eagleburger also focuses on the need to restrain the
Soviet Union. He claims that a freeze on U.S. weapons
will "lock in a Soviet advantage" and imbalance
deterrence. This might tempt the Soviet Union to launch a
first strike with nuclear weapons. He recognizes that
such action "would require momentous depravity by the
Soviet leadership;" but such depravity is recorded
throughout history, particularly among those with
"dictatorial powers." Because the Soviet government is
"not willing to refrain from trying to control or
influence the affairs of other nations and of developing
the military and other means to do so," the United States
must strengthen its own defenses. In the Administration's
view of the world context, maintaining a strong defense is

imperative to deter aggression while simultaneously
seeking to negotiate reductions.  Also, according to
Eagleburger, the Soviets will not negotiate seriously
until "they believe that we can either equal or surpass
them."  Officials consider the effects of nuclear weapons
horrendous, but not as bad as Soviet domination.
    As the churches see the world, nuclear weapons, not
the Soviet Union, pose the greatest threat.  The effects
of nuclear weapons are described in terms of "holocaust,"
"doomsday," and "Armageddon."  Nuclear weapons are
"demonic" instruments that threaten God's creation and the
survival of humanity.  Nuclear war is "unthinkable" and
"unwinnable."  Compared with the devastation of nuclear
weapons, the Soviet threat is not so ominous.  Soviet
behavior may be "monstrous," at times, but Soviet citizens
are humans, not monsters.  Because they too fear the
effects of nuclear weapons, negotiations are possible.
Efforts in trust building, such as unilateral initiatives
in arms reductions, will likely lead to a lowering of the
"balance of terror."  The dangers of nuclear war are so
great that all possible steps to reduce the potential of
such war must be taken, including adopting policies of "no
first  use" and "no use" against non-nuclear forces, a
freeze on nuclear weapons to halt escalation in nuclear
arms, withdrawal of nuclear weapons from combat zones, and
disapproval of new weapons that diminish the distinction
between nuclear and conventional weapons and possibly
invite "first use" of nuclear weapons by the Soviet Union.
The weapons of both the Soviet Union and the United States
threaten the world, so both must be resisted.  Especially
does U.S. policy need redressing because we are the only
nation to have used nuclear weapons and because our
technology has spurred each qualitative advance in the
arms race.  In the view of the peacemakers, nuclear
weapons pose the greatest threat; therefore, prevention of
nuclear war becomes the imperative challenge.
    The churches and the Administration recognize the
need for defense and prevention of nuclear war.  For the
moment, each accepts deterrence as the means required to
achieve both goals.  Given a harsh choice between nuclear
war and appeasement, it would appear that the
Administration would choose war and the churches (at least
those that adopted statements proscribing any "actual use"
of nuclear weapons) would choose peace with _injustice_.  It
would be hazardous to push this conclusion, however,
because one of the features of the "balance of terror" and
deterrence, is uncertainty about future actions.


## Loyalties

    The Administration statements affirm commitment to
the nation and to the values of Western civilization:

peace, individual liberty, freedom of worship, freedom of conscience and expression, respect for the sanctity of human life, and the rule of law through representative institutions (Clark, letter, 16 November 1982, p. 6; Eagleburger, letter, p. 2). Loyalty is also affirmed for Western Europe, NATO, the United Nations Charter, and other democratic states. Our government naturally tends to structure relations at the governmental level and to view other nations in terms of their relationship to U.S. national interests. Perhaps a hierarchy of loyalties for governmental leaders would be the nation, allies, and then, universal humanity.

The loyalties of the churches overlap those of the Administration, but in a different priority. The churches would cite first loyalty to God and individual conscience; then would come universal humanity, the nation and allies. Churches tend to view international relations at the citizen and interchurch level. Loyalty is affirmed to the World Council of Churches and other ecumenical structures, and to the United Nations. Poverty and oppression are stronger factors in international relations for the churches than are political choices regarding U.S. national interests. Churches also affirm the values identified by Administration officials.

The differences of the loyalties and the priority assigned to them by the religious denominations and the Administration have a clear impact on their estimates of the world context and the priority of goals that they establish. The churches see all humanity as fellow members of God's created order and tend to view world crises more from a universal perspective. Governments, including the Reagan Administration (and the Soviet leaders), view crises from the perspective of national interests, which is their chief responsibility as insurers of the public good.


## Philosophical Beliefs

Churches tend to be optimistic in their views of human nature. Because governments are guided by national interests, and recognize that other states are also, they are inclined to be suspicious of human nature. Consistent with this characteristic, the Reagan Administration portrays the Soviet regime as aggressive, untrustworthy, unconscionable, oppressive, and slightly less than human (perhaps depraved is the better word). Soviet ambitions are described in terms of world domination and hegemony, through military conquest or political "Finlandization."

The churches are not much more optimistic in their descriptions of Soviet ambitions. They do affirm, however, that Soviet influence has not constantly expanded and that the Soviet Union may be more genuine in arms negotiations than given credit by the U.S. government. Soviet leaders may display deplorable behavior, but they are not depraved.

The Administration considers war inevitable unless deterred by force. The churches (at least some of them) believe that nations can learn to avoid war and resolve conflict without coercion by force. Ironically, in the nuclear debate the reverse of these beliefs is also expressed. If nothing is done to halt the arms race and reduce nuclear arsenals, many religious leaders affirm that nuclear war is inevitable. The Administration tends to deny this, if sufficient military force can be maintained for deterrence.

## Method of Moral Reasoning

Both the churches and the Administration claim that national policy must be guided by morality. The churches' emphasis on this point is evident. For the Administration Rostow makes the following affirmation in his response to the Catholic letter:

> . . . we share certain fundamental beliefs. I agree totally with your concern that peace must be our objective and that its pursuit should be the central focus of our foreign policy. I also agree that if our government's policies ultimately are to succeed, then these policies must be a moral basis.

Eagleburger describes the prevention of nuclear war as a "moral and political imperative." Clark affirms: "I believe we can agree that the purpose of any moral theory of defense is 'not, in the first place, to legitimize war, but to prevent. . .', and this, of course is what American deterrence policy is designed to achieve." He adds, "our decisions on nuclear armaments, and our defense posture are guided by moral considerations as compelling as any which have faced mankind." Lehman agrees that policy should be moral, but disagrees with the Catholic bishops who suggest that U.S. policy is immoral. He criticizes the bishops as follows:

> One cannot complain about the immorality of nuclear war because of its unlimited impact and then oppose the development of a strategy or a technology that seeks to limit its impact.

Thus, the churches and the Administration affirm that policy should be moral, but disagree on what constitutes a moral policy. No doubt, a part of this conflict is a lack

of understanding of defense policy. We discussed in
previous chapters misconceptions by churches of
counterforce strategy and the intended use of new weapons.
This, however, is not the major factor in the
disagreement. Churches are more inclined to measure
morality by established norms, such as the just-war
criteria, and to view these norms as absolute, or nearly
so. The government gives greater importance to the
context and tends to be guided by pragmatism. Moral norms
are more frequently seen as guidelines, which must be
balanced with considerations of provocation, power, and
necessity. "Ends" tend to count more than "means."

The Administration looks foremost at the need to
prevent Soviet aggression. Nuclear weapons are seen as a
means to this end, especially considering the imbalance of
conventional forces. The churches say that these means
are immoral because nuclear weapons violate the principles
of proportionality and discrimination, which are morally
more binding than the end of constraining Soviet
aggression. Counterforce weapons may be slightly less
indiscriminate, but they are more immoral because they
increase the likelihood of nuclear war. And even limited
nuclear war is morally unthinkable. The churches also
criticize nuclear means because they see consequences
other than deterrence benefits, including the "balance of
terror," a costly and threatening arms race, and the
potential of nuclear annihilation.

Because of the nature and purposes of churches and
governments we should expect differences in perspectives.
These institutions vary in methods of moral reasoning,
philosophical concepts, loyalties, and understanding of
the world context. In assessing policy and policy
proposals like those of the National Council of Churches
and the Catholic letter we should also expect differences.
Religious denominations focus on the ideal. They
rightfully strive for the best possible world. They work
for goals potentially attainable for the betterment of
humanity. They remind us of where we should be going, of
where the finish line is, even while we struggle through
the obstacle course. Certainly our goal should be the
attainment of peace and justice, with pacific means of
resolving conflict and human need. We "ought" to be
peacemakers.

In assessing policy, however, the churches need
reminding that the actual world in which we live is far
from ideal. Once aggression occurs the ideal choices no
longer exist. Then, our choice is between active or
passive resistance, capitulation, or cooperation. If the
churches wish to address policy, in addition to specifying
ideal goals, they must do the hard work of assessing
alternatives in the actual world of international
relations. They must consider the issues of defense as
well as the goal of preventing nuclear war.

Governments are realists as opposed to idealists.
The primary responsibility of government is to provide for
the security and the common good of its citizens. We
expect government to be concerned with defense. Nations
prepare for war to prevent war if possible, but to fight
war if necessary. Both the United States and the Soviet
Union have developed doctrine and weapons for fighting
conventional and nuclear wars which we hope are never
employed. But even the preparations for war are extremely
dangerous. In formulating policy the government needs to
be reminded of these dangers and the need to reduce
international tension and the level of armaments. Arms
negotiations must be undertaken in good faith with the aim
of achieving goals of mutual self-interest. Proposals
should strive for stable deterrence while seeking lower
levels of weaponry. Negotiations on nuclear arms must be
conducted with the goal of preventing nuclear war, not
attaining superior forces for defense.

CONCLUDING PROPOSALS

In this study we have reviewed many opinions
concerning the issues of peace, war, and nuclear weapons.
Hopefully, these views adequately represent the various
arguments in the nuclear debate, both inside the churches
and out. Because the positions of both peacemakers and
policy makers contain elements of truth, it is difficult
to avoid being mesmerized or becoming polarized. Many on
both sides repeat simplistic slogans without questioning
the veracity of their position. It is also clear that
many are more braced for battle than dialogue. When I
walked into the National Council of Churches offices last
year, one greeted me with the question: "Since when is
the Army interested in peace?" I was also offered
extensive assistance there by others. In the defense
establishment there are also those whose views are
polarized. To them a "peacemaker" is a "peacenic." The
issues touch deeply our beliefs, values, and loyalties.
Rather than choosing sides in the debate, I will
conclude by identifying a few morally relevant factors for
both policymakers and policy critics to consider as we
continue the dialogue on national defense policy. As a
general thesis, I contend that we must hold roughly in
balance both aspects of the challenge: How can we protect
and preserve values worth defending while preventing
nuclear war? If we attend only to the prevention of
nuclear war, then we may be unable to protect values. If
we do not have sufficient regard for the danger of nuclear
war, then we may destroy the values we are seeking to
defend.

## Recognition of the Need for Defense

No matter how much we desire a world of peaceful coexistence devoid of armaments, we must recognize that this world does not presently exist. Aggression does exist and it is always immoral; it violates rights and values worth defending. There is no justification for the Warsaw Ghetto, the Gulags of Siberia, Auschwitz, or the Korean invasion. On moral grounds aggresssion ought to be resisted within the limits of proportionality, discrimination, and reasonable prospects for success. The obligation to resist aggression raises the question of how to prevent or deter aggression. This suggests that the means of deterrence, whether negotiating skills or massive military forces, are also critical. Military forces sufficient for resisting or detering aggression must be predicated on the forces of one's adversary. Therefore, recognizing the need for defense mandates a critical evaluation the military capacity available to oneself and one's adversary. U.S. policy formulation, or criticism of this policy, requires a serious look at the balance of forces between the United States and the Soviet Union, between NATO and the Warsaw Pact.

After analyzing the figures for conventional forces in Europe, The International Institute for Strategic Studies (IISS) concludes: "The numerical balance over the last 20 years has slowly but steadily moved in favor of the East. At the same time the West has largely lost the technological edge which allowed NATO to believe that quality could substitute for numbers." The Institute further affirms, however, that the "overall balance continues to be such as to make military aggression a highly risky undertaking. . . . The consequences for an attacker would be unpredictable, and the risks, particularly of nuclear escalation, incalculable."[8] Comparison of forces at the theater nuclear level (TNF) is complicated by the different procedures for calculation used by East and West. If we include in Western figures American submarines allocated to the defense of Europe and the French and British independent nuclear forces, the East still possesses an advantage of 1,410 to 643 in ballistic missile warheads. (The advantage in missiles is slightly less.) Adding available aircraft to the computation leaves the East with a 2:1 superiority. Deployment of SS-20 missiles (each with three warheads) by the Soviet Union is what prompted the NATO decision in December 1979 to deploy 464 cruise and 108 Pershing II missiles, if reductions in Soviet forces could not be negotiated. Presently the Soviets have positioned over 300 of the mobile SS-20 missiles, two-thirds of which are aimed at Western Europe. Based on these TNF figures, the IISS observes: "The major investment that the Soviet Union has made in recent years in modern medium-range

nuclear systems suggests that there are, in the Soviet
perspective, tangible military and political advantages to
be derived from nuclear preponderance in the European
region." The balance "is distinctly unfavorable to NATO
and is becoming more so."[9] When comparing strategic
nuclear figures the IISS concludes that the United States
and the Soviet Union are approximately equal, with the
United States having an advantage in delivery systems
(including aircraft) and the Soviet Union leading in total
equivalent megatonnage. U.S. Department of Defense
analysts also conclude that in ICBM launchers the
superpowers are equal, and in submarine launchers and
long-range bombers the U.S. lead is "diminishing."[10]

Numerical indices of force levels are not sufficient
for thorough analysis; they are significant, however, in
indicating balance and trends, and in shaping perceptions
critical for deterrence. These figures, combined with
other factors, suggest that a conventional attack in
Europe is not probable at this time. If one does occur,
however, it will quite possibly escalate to nuclear
weapons. Presently, the East has some advantage at the
conventional level and a definite and growing advantage in
theater nuclear weapons, one that is not compensated by
including Western strategic weapons. Several implications
may be drawn from the current balance of forces. First,
it appears that both the United States and the Soviet
Union are presently deterred at the strategic level. The
most destabilizing factor is the imbalance of theater
nuclear forces. To maintain a stable deterrence,
restoration of a credible force ratio at this level is
necessary, preferably through negotiations, but if this is
impossible, through deployment. As the TNF battlefield is
Europe, however, and because use of nuclear weapons in
Europe could escalate to strategic levels, thus
threatening U.S. territory (Soviet leaders say that any
attack against Soviet territory is strategic), deployment
of new weapons must be mutually acceptable to Western
Europe and the United States. Also, the conventional
force imbalance needs addressing (see below).

## Recognition of the Need to Prevent Nuclear War

Have increased nuclear arsenals made the United
States and its allies more or less secure? The arsenals
have probably reduced the likelihood of direct
confrontation between the United States and the Soviet
Union because both sides recognize the dangers in such
confrontation. Non-nuclear "proxy" wars, supported but
not fought by the superpowers, will continue to be the
probable point of confrontation. From the standpoint of
the destructive capacity of these arsenals, however, both
the United States and the Soviet Union are less secure.

Certainly more targets can be attacked today than in the
past, and the devastation potential of these weapons is
inconceivable.

The increased levels of strategic and theater
(including tactical) nuclear forces raise serious
questions about the "actual use" and "first use" of
nuclear weapons. In Europe, for example, it does not make
sense morally or militarily to actually use these weapons
first. The number of nuclear forces deployed by
adversaries in Europe far exceeds the amount required to
stop an attack. If a fraction of the available weapons
were used, Europe would be destroyed. When we also
consider the escalation connection between theater and
strategic weapons, it is transparent that the potential
devastation  facing the United States, Europe and the
Soviet Union is morally and politically unacceptable. The
ecological effects of an all-out nuclear war would also be
disastrous for the rest of humanity. Any "first use" of
nuclear weapons, whether tactical, intermediate range, or
strategic, opens the possibility of all-out use. Total,
or all-out, nuclear war cannot be justified by any
criteria, moral, political, or military! Despite rather
nonchalant talk by some about a major nuclear exchange
causing "only" forty million deaths on both sides (if
civil-defense measures were in place), this kind of
warfare is unacceptable. Thus, answers to the "first use"
question must be based on considerations of which
alternative is most likely to deter any war that might
lead to total nuclear war.

The United States is reluctant to publically renounce
a policy of "first use" of strategic weapons because this
could possibly collapse the nuclear umbrella under which
Western Europe and other allies stand. It might well
drive the wedge between Western Europe and the United
States which the Soviet Union desires. We have also
refused to discard a "first use" policy in Europe because
nuclear weapons are seen as essential for deterring both
conventional and nuclear attacks. At present it is
necessary to possess nuclear weapons to deter the use of
these weapons by the Soviet Union. But it would be more
prudent and moral to fight a future war only at the
conventional level. If at this time conventional forces
are insufficient for deterrence, they should be increased.
Surely, the costs of adequate conventional forces are
worth the price of avoiding nuclear war and the reliance
on nuclear weapons to stop conventional aggression. Once
adequate conventional forces are in place, a policy of "no
first use" of nuclear weapons should be announced.

How do we prevent nuclear war? Unilateral
disarmament may reduce the level of destruction, but it
will not necessarily prevent the use of nuclear weapons.
The only time these weapons have ever been used militarily
was when one adversary possessed them unilaterally.

Assuredly, unilateral possession of nuclear weapons qualifies the non-possessors as victims for blackmail, appeasement, and domination. Nuclear superiority is also destabilizing. It will at least perpetuate the arms race and perhaps prompt a first strike if a nation feels seriously threatened. Therefore, a sufficient balance of nuclear and conventional forces is essential.

Deterrence is the only credible alternative in the present context for defending values and preventing nuclear war. Deterrence is believable only if it is based on military capacity to inflict unacceptable damage and the intent and will to use such force. All three aspects of deterrence must be projected to adversaries. Because of the danger of nuclear war, however, we should also communicate that we too are deterred by the adversary from initiating a war that might lead to the use of nuclear weapons. Maintaining the stability of deterrence is the most crucial military issue facing the world today. Conditions and actions which destabilize deterrence should be avoided. These include imbalanced forces, treaty violations, threatening maneuvers, and some technological innovations. Research and development, however, should be suspended only under mutual and verifiable conditions. Factors which strengthen stability should also be pursued, including intergovernmental communications, arms-control treaties, command and control capacities, and intercultural exchanges at the citizen level.

Because of the danger and cost of deterrence, every reasonable effort that is balanced, multilateral, and verifiable should be made to reduce the levels of weaponry. Initiatives that do not destabilize deterrence should also be attempted. It is unrealistic to expect the Soviet Union to enter restrictive arms control agreements if they are inferior in strength. Their massive buildup over the last fifteen years proves that they will not do so. Also, it is unsafe to allow a continuation of unmatched increase in forces by the Soviet Union. At this time, however, rough equality exists between the strategic forces of the East and West. Therefore, now may be the best time since World War II to pursue agreements to control and reduce nuclear weapons. If we build more, it is now evident that they will build more. If they do not stop building, then it is also clear that we too must increase our weaponry. It is at least worth the effort at this time to see how serious the Soviet Union is when it claims it is willing to negotiate. The ultimate elimination of nuclear weaponry is impossible; the technology cannot be disinvented. Yet, cessation of the arms race and reductions in arsenals are imperative. We cannot continue forever the present course. We can test now whether Soviet interests go beyond propoganda and military superiority by offering geniune, balanced proposals for arms reductions.

As we strive for a safer world with fewer nuclear
weapons and a stable, balanced deterrence, the churches
remind us of the urgency of our quest. Their current
crusade against nuclear weapons is not wholly realistic,
and at times it appears that they would sacrifice justice
and security for peace. Surely, however, they are correct
in addressing the moral issues associated with the arms
race, nuclear warfare, and deterrence. While maintaining
forces sufficient for defending human rights and values,
we must also take steps necessary to reduce the dangers of
nuclear war. The churches' universal perspective, their
contacts with Christians in other nations, and their
regard for the sacredness of all human life are
indispensible considerations. The government better
understands the world political context and the
requirements of national security. The churches are more
sensitive to the moral dimensions of the modern world.
Through dialogue and corporate efforts, they can together
forge moral defense policies for the nuclear age.

NOTES

1. Union of American Hebrew Congregations,
Resolution adopted by the General Assembly, 4-8 December
1981, Boston, Massachusetts.

2. Cited from "Resolutions of the Union of Orthodox
Jewish Congregations of America," an unpublished copy of
the resolutions obtained from Union offices at 45 West
36th Street, New York, New York, 10018. Melanie Shimoff
of this office indicated that the Union specifically
refrained from using the term "freeze" to avoid "taking
sides" in the nuclear freeze controversy (telephone
conversation, 10 March 1983).

3. Quotations are from the text of the Council's
statement, published by The Synagogue Council of America
in SCA News, 24 February 1983.

4. Agencies belonging to the Synagogue Council are
the Rabbinical Assembly and the United Synagogue of
America, both Conservative groups; the Rabbinical Council
of America and the Union of Orthodox Jewish Congregations,
Orthodox organizations; and the Central Conference of
American Rabbis and the Union of American Hebrew
Congregations, organizations for Reform Judaism.

5. Langella, ibid., (above, p. 135).

6. The responses by Administration officials were
primarily letters prepared between 30 July-16 November

1982. Some were published in <u>The New York Times</u> and the <u>Washington Post</u>.

7. Potter, <u>War and Moral Discourse</u>, pp. 23-26. For an extensive discussion of Potter's paradigm, see his unpublished dissertation, "The Structure of Certain American Christian Responses to the Nuclear Dilemma, 1958-1963," Harvard Divinity School, 1965.

8. The International Institute for Strategic Studies, <u>The Military Balance, 1982-1983</u> (London: IISS, 1982), p. 131.

9. Ibid., pp. 134, and 135.

10. U.S. Department of Defense, <u>The FY 1982 Department of Defense Program for Research, Development, and Acquisition</u> (1981), pp. II, 10.

# Abbreviations

ABC   –   American Baptist Churches

ALC   –   The American Lutheran Church

EKD   –   Evangelical Church in Germany

EP   –   Episcopal Church

IISS –   International Institute for Strategic Studies

IRD   –   Institute for Religion and Democracy

LCA   –   Lutheran Church in American

LWF   –   Lutheran World Federation

MAD   –   Mutually Assured Destruction

MX   –   Missile Experimental

NATO –   North Atlantic Treaty Alliance

NCC   –   National Council of the Churches of Christ in the U.S.A.

NCCB –   National Conference of Catholic Bishops

PCUS –   Presbyterian Church in the United States

RC   –   Roman Catholic

RCA   –   Reformed Church in America

ROTC –   Reserve Officer Training Corps

SBC   –   Southern Baptist Convention

UCC   –   United Church of Christ

UMC   –   United Methodist Church

UPC   –   United Presbyterian Church in the U.S.A.

# Selected Bibliography

Abbott, Walter M., ed. The Documents of Vatican II. New York: The American Press, 1966.

Arkin, William M. Research Guide to Current Military and Strategic Affairs. Washington, D.C.: Institute for Policy Studies, 1981.

Aron, Raymond. Century of Total War. New York: Doubleday and Company, 1954.

Bainton, Roland H. Christian Attitudes Toward War and Peace: A Historical Survey and Critical Re-evaluation. Nashville: Abingdon Press, 1960.

Barnet, Richard J. Real Security: Restoring American Power in a Dangerous Decade. New York: Touchstone Book, Simon and Schuster, 1981.

Brandt, R[obert] B. "Utilitarianism and the Rules of War." Philosophy and Public Affairs 1 (Winter 1972): 145-65.

Brayton, Abbott A., and Landwear, Stephana J. The Politics of War and Peace: A Survey of Thought. Washington, D.C.: University Press of America, 1981.

Brodie, Bernard. War and Politics. New York: The Macmillan Company, 1973.

Childress, James F. "Just-War Criteria." In War or Peace? The Search for New Answers, pp. 40-58. Edited by Thomas A. Shannon. Maryknoll, New York: Orbis Books, 1980.

Cohen, Marshall. "Morality and the Law of War." In Philosophy, Morality, and International Affairs: Essays Edited for the Society for Philosophy and Public Affairs, pp. 71-88. Edited by Virginia Held, Sidney Morgenbesser, and Thomas Nagel. New York: Oxford University Press, 1974.

Cohen, Marshall; Nagel, Thomas; and Scanlon, Thomas; eds. Wars and Moral Responsibility, A Philosophy and Public Affairs Reader. Princeton, New Jersey: Princeton University Press, 1974.

Dyck, Arthur J. "Ethical Bases of the Military Profession." Parameters 10 (March 1980): 39-46.

Fox, Marvin, ed. Modern Jewish Ethics: Theory and Practice. Columbus: Ohio State University Press, 1975.

Frankena, William K. ETHICS. 2d ed. Englewood Cliffs, New Jersey: Prentice-Hall, Inc., 1973.

Geyer, Alan. The Idea of Disarmament! Rethinking the Unthinkable. Elgin, Illinois: The Brethren Press, 1982.

Ground Zero (Roger C. Molander, Executive Director). Nuclear War: What's in it For You. New York: Pocket Books, Simon and Schuster, 1982.

Heyer, Robert, ed. Nuclear Disarament: Key Statements of Popes, Bishops, Councils and Churches. New York: Paulist Press, 1982.

Isaac, Rael Jean. "Do You Know Where Your Church Offerings Go?" Readers Digest 122 (January 1983): 120-25.

Johnson, James Turner. Ideology, Reason, and the Limitation of War: Religious and Secular Concepts, 1200-1740. Princeton, New Jersey: Princeton University Press, 1975.

_____. "Just War Theory: What's the Use?" Worldview 19 (July-August 1976): 41-47.

_____. Just War Tradition and The Restraint of War: A Moral and Historical Inquiry. Princeton, New Jersey: Princeton University Press, 1981.

_____. "Morally Legitimate Defense." In Warfare in the 1990's, proceedings of a conference sponsored by the Institute for Theological Encounter with Science and Technology. St. Louis: Fordyce House (9-10 October 1981): 30-46.

_____. "Toward Reconstructing the Jus Ad Bellum." The Monist 57 (October 1973): 461-88.

_____. "The Cruise Missile and the Neutron Bomb: Some Moral Reflections." Worldview 20 (December 1977): 20-26.

_____. "What Guidance Can Just-War Tradition Provide for Contemporary Moral Thought About War." New Catholic World 226 (March-April 1982): 81-84.

Johnson, James T. and Smith, David, eds. Love and Society: Essays in the Ethics of Paul Ramsey. Missoula, Montana: Scholars Press, University of Montana, 1974.

Karsten, Peter. Law, Soldiers and Combat. Westport, Connecticut: Greenwood Press, 1978.

Kennedy, Edward M., and Hatfield, Mark O. Freeze! How You Can Help Prevent Nuclear War. New York: Bantam Books, 1982.

Levinson, Sanford. "Responsibility for Crimes of War." Philosophy and Public Affairs 2 (Spring 1973): 244-73.

McDougal, Myres S., and Feliciano, Florentino P. Law and Minimum World Public Order: The Legal Regulations of International Coercion. New Haven: Yale University Press, 1961.

McSorley, Richard S. J. Kill? for Peace? Washington, D.C.: Center for Peace Studies, Georgetown University, 1970.

Michael, Scott G. "Selected Bibliography: The Just-War Theory." Horizons 5 (Fall 1978): 215-25.

Murphy, Jeffrie G. "The Killing of the Innocent." The Monist 57 (October 1973): 527-50.

Nagel, Thomas. "War and Massacre." Philosophy and Public Affairs 1 (Winter 1972): 123-44.

National Conference of Catholic Bishops. "The Challenge of Peace: God's Promise and Our Response." Washington, D.C.: Origins: N C Documentary Service 13 (19 May 1983): 1-32.

Niebuhr, Reinhold. Love and Justice: Selections from the Shorter Writings of Reinhold Niebuhr. Edited by D.B. Robertson. Reprint ed. Glaucester, Massachusetts: Peter Smith, 1976.

O'Brien, William V. Nuclear War, Deterrence and Morality. New York: Newman Press, 1967.

_____. The Conduct of Just and Limited War. New York: Praeger, 1981.

O'Connor, John J. In Defense of Life. Boston: Daughters of St. Paul, 1981.

Oppenheim, L. International Law: A Treatise 3 vols.,
8th ed. London: Longman, Green and Company, 1955.

Paskins, Barrie, and Dockrill, Michael. The Ethics of War.
Minneapolis, Minnesota: University Press, 1979.

Perry, Shawn, ed. Words of Conscience: Religious Statements on Conscientious Objection. 9th ed.
Washington: National Interreligious Service Board
for Conscientious Objectors, 1980.

Potter, Ralph B., Jr. "The Moral Logic of War."
McCormick Quarterly 23 (May 1970): 203-33.

_____. War and Moral Discourse. Richmond, Virginia:
John Knox Press, 1969.

Ramsey, Paul. Basic Christian Ethics. Chicago:
University of Chicago Press, 1950.

_____. Deeds and Rules in Christian Ethics. New York:
Charles Scribner's Sons, 1967.

_____. The Just War: Force and Political Responsibility.
New York: Charles Scribner's Sons, 1968.

_____. War and the Christian Conscience: How Shall
Modern War Be Conducted Justly? Durham, North
Carolina: Duke University Press, 1961.

Rawls, John. A Theory of Justice. Cambridge, Massachusetts:
The Belknap Press of Harvard University Press, 1971.

Rose, John Paul. "United States Army Nuclear Doctrinal
Development: The Nuclear Battlefield, 1945-1977."
Ph.D. dissertation, University of Southern California,
1978.

Rowen, Henry S. "The Evolution of Strategic Doctrine."
In Strategic Thought in the Nuclear Age. Edited by
Lawrence Martin. Baltimore: Johns Hopkins Press,
1980.

Schell, Jonathan. The Fate of the Earth. New York:
Avon Books, The Hearst Cooperation, 1982.

Scherer, John L., ed. U.S.S.R.: Facts and Figures Annual,
Vol. 6, 1982. Gulf Breeze, Florida: Academic
International Press, 1982.

Shannon, Thomas A., ed. War or Peace? The Search for New
Answers. Maryknoll, New York: Orbis Books, 1980.

Russell, Frederick H. _The Just-War in the Middle Ages_.
New York: Cambridge University Press, 1975.

Taylor, Telford. _Nuremberg and Vietnam: An American_
_Tragedy_. Chicago: Quandrangle Books, A New York
Times Book, 1970.

The International Institute for Strategic Studies.
_The Military Balance,1982-1983_. London: IISS, 1982.

Tucker, Robert W. _The Just War: A Study in Contemporary_
_American Doctrine_. Baltimore: The Johns Hopkins
Press, 1960.

U.S., Department of the Army. DA Pamphlet 165-135:
Military Chaplains Review. U.S. Army Chaplain
Board, Fall, 1982.

_____. _Command and Management: Readings on_
_Professionalism_. Carlisle Barracks, Pennsylvania:
U.S. Army War College, Academic Year 1981.

_____. Field Manual 27-10: The Law of Land Warfare.
Washington 25, D.C. July 18, 1956.

_____. Field Manual 100-1: The Army. Washington
25, D.C. 14 August 1981.

_____. _Report of the Department of the Army Review_
_of the Preliminary Investigations into the My Lai_
_Incident (Peers Inquiry), Vol. 1: The Report of the_
_Investigation_. Washington, D.C.: U.S. Government
Printing Office, March 14, 1970.

U.S., Department of Defense. _Report of Secretary of_
_Defense Harold Brown to the Congress on the FY 1981_
_Budget, FY 1982 Authorization Request and FY 1981-_
_1985 Defense Programs_, January 29, 1980.

Wakin, Malham M., ed. _War, Morality, and the Military_
_Profession_. Boulder: Westview Press, 1979.

Walters, LeRoy. "The Just War and the Crusade:
Antithesis or Analogies?" _The Monist_ 57 (October
1973): 584-94.

Walzer, Michael. _Just and Unjust Wars: A Moral Argument_
_with Historical Illustrations_. New York: Basic
Books, Inc., 1977.

_____. "Political Action: The Problem of Dirty Hands."
_Philosophy and Public Affairs_ 2 (Winter 1973): 160-80.

204

Yoder, John H.  The Original Revolution:  Essays on
Christian Pacifism.  Scottdale, Pennsylvania:  Herald
Press, 1977.

_____.  The Politics of Jesus.  Grand Rapids, Michigan:
William B. Eerdman's Publishing Company, 1972.

# APPENDIX A
## Letter to Churches

Dear

Chaplain (Major General) Kermit D. Johnson, U.S. Army
Chief of Chaplains, has asked me to prepare a study which
objectively describes the various positions recently
published by religious ethicists, denominational leaders,
and religious bodies concerning nuclear weapons and
policies.  I am collecting documentation for this
research through my own literature search and by
corresponding with religious leaders.  I consider your
contribution vital because you are familiar with
statements issued individually and collectively by
members of your religious body.  You or another member of
your group can assist in this research by sending (or
identifying) public statements by leaders, study
documents, or official statements that represent the
views of your membership.

The specific topics I am seeking to address include the
following:

1.  The suitability of the principles of Just-War
    Theory for addressing the moral dilemmas of
    nuclear warfare.

2.  The use of strategic nuclear weapons (long-range,
    high-yield weapons such as intercontinental
    ballistic missiles).

3.  The use of limited, tactical nuclear weapons
    (various, shorter-range "theater" weapons such as
    artillery projectiles, neutron bombs, cruise
    missiles, and Pershing II missiles).

4.  The strategic policy of nuclear deterrence.

5.  Other issues of concern related to nuclear
    weapons and policy.

I am attempting to compile the documents and materials
for this research by the end of February, 1982.  Please
send all correspondence to me at the above address.

# APPENDIX B
## Church Positions on Nuclear Weapons Issues

Subject/Position Supported*
Reference Nuclear Weapons

RELIGIOUS DENOMINATION

| Subject/Position Supported* Reference Nuclear Weapons | Roman Catholic[7] | Protestant | | | | | | |
|---|---|---|---|---|---|---|---|---|
| | | United Methodist[8] | American Baptist | Christian (Disciples) | United Presbyterian | Presbyterian U.S. | Episcopal | United Church Of Christ |
| Membership (1=1,000,000) | 51.0 | 9.6 | 1.2 | 1.2 | 2.5 | 0.8 | 2.8 | 1.7 |
| Nuclear Disarmament/Reductions[1] | yes | yes | yes | yes | yes | yes | yes | yes |
| SALT II Ratification | yes | yes | yes | yes | yes | yes | yes | yes |
| Comprehensive Test Ban Treaty | yes | yes | yes | yes | yes | | | yes |
| Freeze Nuclear Weapons & Testing (Mutual, Verifiable)[2] | yes | yes | yes | yes | yes | yes | yes | yes |
| Unilateral Disarmament | no | no | no | no | no | no | no | no |
| Unilateral Initiatives/Cuts | yes | | yes | yes | | | | yes |
| "Counter-Force" Weapons Criticized[3] | yes | yes | yes | yes | yes | | | yes |
| Deterrence[4] | yes | yes | yes | yes | yes | yes | yes | yes |
| First-Strike Policy Renounced | yes | | yes | yes | yes | yes | yes | yes |
| Actual Use Policy Renounced (First or Retaliatory Use)[5] | ? | | yes | | ? | yes | | yes |
| Conventional Forces Increased[5] (If necessary) | yes | | | | | | | |
| "Peacemaking" Adopted as Focus of Central Program[6] | yes | yes | yes | yes | yes | yes | yes | yes |

*In this chart answers are taken from denominational statements. In the past a denomination may have published a statement which I have not found. For example, it is probable that the United Methodist Church supported the SALT II Treaty. A "blank" indicates that I found no statement concerning this subject. A "question mark" means that the denomination raised serious questions on a subject but did not make a conclusive statement. In the case of "deterrence," if a denomination did not advocate unilateral disarmament, I interpreted this to mean at least minimal acceptance of deterrence (See Note 4 below).

Subject/Position Supported
Reference Nuclear Weapons

RELIGIOUS DENOMINATION

TOTAL SUPPORTING POSITIONS

| | Protestant | | | | | Historic Peace Churches | Denominations (except Peace Churches)/Combined Membership |
|---|---|---|---|---|---|---|---|
| | Reformed Church of America | Lutheran in America | American Lutheran | Lutherans Missouri Synod | Southern Baptists | | |
| Membership (1=1,000,000) | 0.3 | 2.9 | 2.4 | 2.6 | 13.4 | 0.5 | 13/92,400,000 |
| Nuclear Disarmament/Reductions[1] | yes | yes | yes | yes | yes | yes | 13/92,400,000 |
| SALT II Ratification | | yes | yes | | yes | yes | 10/79,900,000 |
| Comprehensive Test Ban Treaty | | | | | | yes | 5/57,600,000 |
| Freeze Nuclear Weapons & Testing (Mutual, Verifiable)[2] | yes | yes | yes | | | yes | 11/76,400,000 |
| Unilateral Disarmament | no | no | no | no | | yes | 0/00 |
| Unilateral Initiatives/Cuts | | yes | yes | | | yes | 6/60,400,000 |
| "Counter-Force" Weapons Criticized[3] | yes | ? | | | | yes | 6/65,800,000 |
| Deterrence[4] | yes | yes | yes | yes | yes | no | 13/92,400,000 |
| First-Strike Policy Renounced | yes | ? | yes | | | yes | 8/61,500,000 |
| Actual Use Policy Renounced (First or Retaliatory Use) | yes | | yes | | | yes | 5/ 6,400,000 |
| Conventional Forces Increased[5] (If necessary) | | | | | | no | 1/51,000,000 |
| "Peacemaking" Adopted as Focus of Central Program[6] | yes | yes | yes | | | yes | 11/76,400,000 |

NOTES:

1. Official statements encouraging arms control and reductions to end arms race.

2. Official statements which endorse Congressional Resolution on Nuclear Weapons Freeze or advocate position similar to that called for in the Freeze proposal; that is, a halt on new weapons development, deployment and testing.

3. Official statements opposing deployment of new weapons systems, often identified as "Counterforce," or First-Strike weapons, because of their greater accuracy. The specific weapons systems most frequently drawing negative comment were the MX missile, cruise missile and the neutron bomb.

4. Deterrence as used here includes the strategies based on "minimal," "sufficient," "balanced," "parity," or "roughly equivalent" concepts. No denomination advocated a strategy of "nuclear superiority". Also some churches accept deterrence only "temporarily" and make acceptance contingent on genuine efforts to negotiate nuclear disarmament.

5. The Catholic Church suggests that increases in conventional forces may be necessary to reduce reliance on nuclear weapons for deterrence.

6. "Peacemaking" here includes various concepts (see text). Including it as part of the central program means that continued attention will be given to disarmament, "Freeze" and other nuclear issues.

7. The Roman Catholic position represented in this chart is based on the second draft of the NCCB pastoral letter (forthcoming).

8. The United Methodist position is only partially documented here. It may support other issues not indicated on the chart.

# About the Book and Author

*Nuclear Weapons and the American Churches:*
*Ethical Positions on Modern Warfare*

Donald L. Davidson

This book describes the positions advocated by ethicists and churches in the public debate on nuclear weapons. After tracing the development of just-war theory, the dominant moral position on war in Western thought, Dr. Davidson synthesizes the views of contemporary ethicists on the moral principles associated with the just-war tradition. He then documents the postures of Reinhold Niebuhr, Paul Ramsey, Michael Walzer, and James Turner Johnson with regard to the first use and retaliatory use of nuclear weapons, deterrence policy, the nuclear freeze proposal, the arms race, and disarmament.

The positions endorsed by the Roman Catholic Church and the major Protestant and Jewish denominations in the United States on the issues of nuclear warfare are described in detail, with extensive treatment given to the development of the Catholic Bishops' 1983 pastoral letter on war and peace and the statements of churches affiliated with the National Council of Churches. The views of over 30 denominations, representing more than 110 million members, are considered. The final chapter of the book contrasts the stance of the churches with that of the Reagan Administration.

Proposing guidelines for a moral defense policy in the nuclear age, Dr. Davidson's thesis is that national security requires a recognition of the need to protect and preserve values worth defending while simultaneously taking steps to prevent nuclear war.

DONALD L. DAVIDSON received his Th.M. in ethics, with an emphasis on the ethics of war, from Harvard University, and his Ph.D. in church history from Southwestern Baptist Theological Seminary. Dr. Davidson is on the faculty of the U.S. Army War College, where he is currently an instructor in both ethics and European studies. His professional experience includes service as an Army artillery officer, civilian pastor, clergyman, professor, and Army chaplain.